HOME AND HANDMADE

MELISSA K. NORRIS

TEN PEAKS PRESS®
EUGENE, OR

Unless otherwise indicated, all Scripture verses are taken from the Holy Bible, New International Version®, NIV®. Copyright © 1973, 1978, 1984, 2011 by Biblica, Inc.® Used with permission of Zondervan. All rights reserved worldwide. www.zondervan.com. The "NIV" and "New International Version" are trademarks registered in the United States Patent and Trademark Office by Biblica, Inc.®

Scripture verses taken from the Amplified® Bible (AMPC), Copyright © 1954, 1958, 1962, 1964, 1965, 1987 by The Lockman Foundation. Used with permission. www.lockman.org.

Published in association with the literary agency of WordServe Literary Group, Ltd., www.wordserveliterary.com.

Cover and interior design by Dugan Design Group
Photography by Jay Eads
Stitching and fabric image © afxhome / AdobeStock

TEN PEAKS PRESS is a federally registered trademark of The Hawkins Children's LLC. Harvest House Publishers, Inc., is the exclusive licensee of this trademark.

Some material previously published in *Hand Made* (Harvest House Publishers, 2017) and *Everything Worth Preserving* (Homestead Living, 2023) by Melissa K. Norris. Used by permission.

Neither the author nor publisher is responsible for any outcome from use of this cookbook. The recipes and remedies are intended for informational purposes and those who have the appropriate culinary skills. USDA guidelines should always be followed in food preparation and canning. The author and publisher make no warranty, express or implied, in any recipe.

HOME AND HAND MADE

Published by Ten Peaks Press, an imprint of Harvest House Publishers
Eugene, Oregon 97408

ISBN 978-0-7369-8720-2 (pbk)
ISBN 978-0-7369-8721-9 (eBook)

Library of Congress Control Number: 2024947209

Printed in the United States

25 26 27 28 29 30 31 32 33 / VP / 10 9 8 7 6 5 4 3

To my parents,
for teaching me the old ways and
passing down the traditions of past generations.

To those who share and
preserve their wisdom for future generations.

To my husband,
who lets me know, for better or worse,
how a recipe really tastes.

To Julie and Karen,
for opening your friendship, kitchen,
and soapmaking skills to me.

CONTENTS

Come On In 7

1. Bake 9

2. Simmer 47

3. Culture 79

4. Preserve 111

5. Thrive 133

6. Homespun Holidays 185

Recipe Index 222

About the Author 224

COME ON IN

Today's modern world has many things I'm grateful for, but we're also on the cusp of losing something precious. In our drive-through society and "serve it to me ready to go" way of thinking, we further our hurry-up mindset. We're always in a hurry to do more, but we never seem to reach the place of rest—the respite we're rushing to.

Deep down, we know we're missing something. Our hearts grab onto the promise of a simpler way—a yearning for yesteryear and a reminiscing of a slower-paced time.

In the pages before you, I share the wisdom of people who lived through some of the hardest years the United States ever faced: the Great Depression. While many of the tips I share with you are from that era, others go further back, and you'll see them titled Traditional Living Tips. Like many of our hardships and darkest times, when we reach the other side, with battle scars and healing wounds, we see the snippets of beauty. We discover we learned what is truly important and what we're really capable of. We pare away the unnecessary and the distractions, and we know what is dear to our hearts. Though we'd never have thought it before, we're grateful for the hard times, because without them, we'd never have gained the wisdom.

That is what I'm sharing with you, passed down from my grandparents, my father (whose earliest years and memories are from the Great Depression), and many other dear friends and family members, that their wisdom may bless you and not be forgotten.

By creating things by hand, there is something to be gained beyond just the financial savings and health benefits of cooking and baking real food. It's a kinship with those who have gone before us. A connection with those who passed a special recipe to us, the memories of those we've shared it with, and a promise to those who will share and make it after us. It is my hope that you will find simplicity, new recipes, and old-fashioned wisdom that still apply to our modern lives.

You'll discover old-fashioned, from-scratch cooking, and food so finger-licking good, these will become your new go-to recipes. I firmly believe food should be enjoyed, the best recipes don't have to be complicated, and healthy can still taste good!

You'll find a marriage of the old ways and modern methods—recipes and tutorials for growing your own culinary and medicinal herbs and for making homemade soaps and body care items, and strategies for creating a haven in your home amid our crazily paced lives. The door is flung open, soup is simmering on the stove, a cup of tea is steaming, the rocking chair is ready with Grandma's quilt, and I am waiting. Come on in, friend. Come on in.

CHAPTER 1

BAKE

The kitchen was the hub of our small home. Clad in her apron, my mother could usually be found inside the kitchen nook at the end of the trailer where I grew up. Tall evergreens stood sentinel at the end of our yard; large branches fringed the outside of the kitchen window. During windstorms, the low-hanging branches would sweep across the tin roof. The kitchen faced north into the forest, just feet beyond the thin glass windows, and not much light made its way inside.

Due to necessity and want, my mother cooked all our meals from scratch. Breakfast was oatmeal, homemade pancakes, biscuits slathered with homemade jam or gravy, or eggs with toast. The cookie jar never stood empty, and after trudging in from the hour-long bus ride home from school, some type of home-baked goodie always awaited me.

Food is my mother's love language. And she speaks it fluently.

Dinner was a family affair, often including friends or extended family members. By evening, the kitchen windows were slick with condensation, evidence of the food simmering on the stovetop and baking in the oven. And also evidence of the not-so-well-insulated glass and walls. If you've ever lived in an older trailer, you know exactly what I'm talking about.

My father worked long hours as a log truck driver. He left before dawn and didn't get home until right before dinner. The evening meal was often the only time I would get to see him during the week.

He'd enter the house, the sharp scents of pine and cedar hitching a ride in with him. "Hope you've got enough," he'd say. "I invited so-and-so for dinner."

Mom would survey the saucepan and skillet on the stove. "I'll bring out an extra can of beans and the peaches from last year." She'd turn to me. "Better get the extra leaf for the table."

Soon every burner on the little stovetop would have a pot simmering. Mason jars would offer up their bounty from last year's harvest and then wait empty in the sink to be washed. The only dishwasher to be found was a pair of hands.

The table leaf was stored where we could grab it easily. Dad had a habit of bringing people home for dinner, especially without telling my mother in advance. She learned to cook on her toes. This always made for interesting evenings and supper conversation.

One night the guests arrived, and Dad invited them straight into the kitchen while Mom finished preparing the meal. Our living room didn't get nearly the spotlight the kitchen did when company came.

When a line works, you roll with it. And Dad was always good with teasing.

"Tom invited us over for mazzards," one of the guests said.

My head whipped back and forth from Dad to Mom.

"She's the finest mazzard cook you'll run across." Dad's blue eyes twinkled.

Mom kept her gaze trained straight on the frying pan in front of her. Her grip tightened ever so slightly on the spatula.

I caught another look at Dad. I set the plates with precision, my focus never wavering lest I give something away.

Dad and the couple sat down, and I sat down too. The wood of the worn chair was smooth beneath my hands as I tucked them under my legs.

The gentleman glanced toward Mom as she turned the meat.

"We'd never heard of mazzards before, but we figure it might be something related to a Mallard duck."

I bit the inside of my cheek to keep my lips from twitching upward.

Mom's shoulders stiffened.

"That's a right fine guess." Dad couldn't contain his humor any longer, and a big grin split his face. "Truth be told, I was pulling your leg. There's no such thing as mazzards, but my wife is a fine cook, and you're invited to stay for supper."

I searched the man's face. My fingers curled around the lip of my chair.

Surprise flared in his eyes for a moment. Silence spilled across the empty plates. He glanced at his wife. And then a grin emerged. "You sure had me."

Mom's shoulders relaxed. "You shouldn't tell people that," she said. Her cheeks were flushed, and I knew it wasn't from the heat of the stove.

I caught Dad's gaze. He winked at me. The laughter I'd been holding in burst out. Our mirth filled the cramped kitchen. The couple turned into family friends, and rarely did a supper with them go by without some mention of Dad's famous mazzards.

That wasn't the last time he asked someone over for mazzards. When a line works, you roll with it. And Dad was always good with teasing.

That old singlewide 1974 Fleetwood trailer still stands. My parents purchased a house at the end of the road we all still live on, moving out of the trailer when I entered high school. It later housed my husband and me while we saved up to purchase our property and first home. Even though the tiny kitchen is still there, it no longer has the same warm glow and light I remember from my childhood. The original yellow sink is worn down to the metal in spots from the years of dishrags and water.

But I'm reminded that just like the kitchen of my childhood, even when something is small and dark, God's love fills it, stretching it to hold all who need to enter and find shelter and sustenance. No matter how little we have, when we invite Him into the situation, Jesus multiplies what we have to meet our needs. He takes a tiny kitchen and makes it a place of refreshment for those who walk through the door. He multiplies the single frying pan of meat to feed unexpected guests. He takes our exasperation at having to serve more people than we have resources for and fills us with His strength.

If you drive by the road we live on, you'll dismiss that old white metal-sided trailer with barely a glance. Or maybe you'll think how nice the property would look with a proper home. We're quick to overlook the things that aren't polished or up to the normal standards. But Jesus doesn't look at the outside of things. He looks at the heart. Despite the bleakness on the outside, Jesus enters inside, and when His light spills out, it touches the surrounding walls and beckons others into the warmth. Just like a tiny, cramped kitchen with evergreen branches covering the windows.

LESSONS IN HOSPITALITY

If I were in the middle of preparing supper and my husband waltzed through the door announcing that he'd invited dinner guests who would be here any minute, I don't believe a smile and grace would be my first greeting.

No. My muscles would go into a hyper state and tense together all at the same time. Pulled between trying to tidy up the living room, making sure the bathroom sparkled, coming up with an idea for dessert and more food, and telling him *exactly* how I felt about the situation, I'd look like a dancing chicken. I bet you'd even find a few feathers littering the floor when all was said and done.

While I know my mother wasn't exactly thrilled when my father did this—and he did it on a regular basis—I don't remember ever watching her throw a fit about it. And as a kid, I would not have missed that had it happened.

Our homes reflect who we are. If our first reaction to having someone visit is stress, that's a sure sign something is out of balance. Don't get me wrong—there's nothing wrong with wanting our homes to look nice and tidy. There's also nothing wrong with our houses looking like people live in them. As I write this, there are two stray socks on a chair, crumbs on the counter that need to be wiped up, and we won't even investigate the floor at this point. That's just at first glance in the kitchen.

The out-of-balance part begins in our hearts. If the first thing I'm focused on is the state of my house and what people will think of me when they see it, my pride is shouting. I want my home to be a haven, a place of rest in a frantic world, a place where relationships can be built and where love spills out of the kitchen. And let me tell you, stressing out about the house and becoming irritated about an unexpected guest don't create any of the things I want my home to be.

Martha [overly occupied and too busy] was distracted with much serving; and she came up to Him and said, Lord, is it nothing to You that my sister has left me?...The Lord replied to her by saying, Martha, Martha, you are anxious and troubled about many things; There is need of only one or but a few things. *Mary has chosen the good portion [that which is to her advantage], which shall not be taken away from her (Luke 10:40-42* AMPC*).*

I've always secretly thought old Mary ought to get up and help her poor sister out. Here Martha is trying to feed no fewer than thirteen guests who showed up at her door, without the help of any modern conveniences. Doesn't it make you appreciate your vacuum and dishwasher a tad more?

TRADITIONAL LIVING TIPS

1. Quick breads, such as biscuits and corn bread, were very popular and common during rough times. A biscuit had more versatility than a loaf of bread and didn't require the addition of yeast or the longer rise time. You could make biscuits and cover them with white gravy, spread them with butter and droplets of golden honey, slather them in homemade jam, fill them with sandwich makings for lunch or an egg and cheese for breakfast, or eat them plain for a snack.
2. My father recalls my grandmother making her biscuits right in the flour sack. She'd wash her hands, create a well in the middle of the flour in the sack, and mix everything right there.
3. A traditional pantry consists of whole food items—very basic foods that can be made into a variety of different dishes. Flour (or wheat berries to grind into your own flour) can be used to bread and fry meat; make baked goods, biscuits, and breads; and add as a thickener for gravies and sauces.
4. During those hard years, dried beans were a frugal and easy way to stretch a meal. They could be cooked with a bit of bacon or ham bones and served with corn bread or biscuits. Beans simmered with garden vegetables filled many a tummy.
5. Simple foods were the backbone of meals. Bread and lard sandwiches were a common dish, as was a simple meal of freshly baked bread, sliced tomatoes from the garden, and corn on the cob or fresh-picked greens.
6. Potatoes helped fill in the gap for many families. Diced and fried, you could add a jar of stewed tomatoes or other vegetables when there wasn't any meat available, and cook an entire meal in one big skillet. One of our favorite recipes is breakfast potato cakes made from leftover mashed potatoes. I add an egg and a dash of milk with some onion and garlic powder. I shape them into patties, preheat a cast-iron skillet with a small amount of oil, and then fry the potato patties. When I pull them out, I grate a little bit of cheese on top. It's a great way to shape your breakfast. You don't even have to use an egg, making it even more frugal.
7. The water you use from boiling your potatoes has starch in it, so save the water to use as a replacement for milk in your bread recipes. This is a big carryover from long-past eras where grocery stores didn't stock every food shipped in from every place imaginable, when cows ran dry or there was no money to purchase dairy. You can put the potato water in the fridge for up to a day before using in your recipe. You could freeze it, but it is best used in a recipe immediately. A family friend who is an excellent baker uses only potato water in her cinnamon rolls.

I'm pretty sure no one remembered how clean Martha's home was that day or even what she served, but every single one of those people remembered how he or she felt. Soon after the last bit of bread sopped up the oil on the plates, the taste of the meal was forgotten. But sitting at Jesus's feet and listening to His teaching was an experience they could never forget.

This moment of feeding their souls was interrupted, however, by a frustrated and put-out woman. If Martha was anything like me, she'd probably worked herself into a good state of mad in the kitchen. By the time she made her way to the living room, her sandals slapped the floor in a sharp, wordless retort. Her attitude cut through the air like a January wind. "Don't you care that I'm working, pouring out everything I have left, and my sister hasn't even lifted one finger to help?"

Oh, my friends, how many times have I been there? I've brought the whining pity party not only to my family, but straight to Jesus—just like Martha. *Lord, why haven't You helped me out here? Don't You care about all the hours I've put in and how tired I am? Couldn't You give me a break here? It wouldn't take very much—You are, after all, the God of all creation. I'm not asking for a whole kingdom or anything.*

Hospitality starts in the heart and flows out in our deeds.

I don't think there's anything wrong with asking why, but it's the heart and attitude that accompany those prayers that matter. *Don't You care?* He sent His Son to be nailed on a cross for us. Yes, He cares.

He doesn't want us to be tired or exhausted. Jesus wants us to reach out to Him long before we reach that point.

> *Come to me, all you who are weary and burdened, and I will give you rest. Take my yoke upon you and learn from me, for I am gentle and humble in heart, and you will find rest for your souls (Matthew 11:28-29).*

Just reading those words eases the muscles in my shoulders.

God has already offered me a break, but I'm too stubborn to see it. (I'm not far off from those stiff-necked Israelites sometimes.) God's grace is our break, and it's available to us every day. So often I clamor for His grace but then neglect to extend it to others.

Hospitality starts in the heart and flows out in our deeds.

There are many nights when I'm in the kitchen cleaning up supper and preparing food for the following day. The clock ticks toward 8:30, and I realize I've hardly sat down since the morning. My day starts at 5:30 a.m. with writing and work on my podcast, blog, and website. Then I get the kids up and off to school, have my morning devotions, exercise, take care of the farm animals and garden, make breakfast, and then drive to my day job.

By the time evening rolls around, my feet ache and I long for the comfort of my recliner. The last thing I want to do is finish making lunches for everyone for the next day. Why am I the only one who makes lunches?

And right there Martha and I become best friends again.

Now for starters, I'm not saying that people in your household and family shouldn't help. I'm not saying you have to be superwoman and all of this falls on your shoulders and you'd better be able to bear it, sister. No. Please, don't misunderstand me. If you're truly overwhelmed and believe you don't have any help, I think you should sit down with the members of your family and come up with a plan. Maybe your children aren't so young anymore, and it is time for them to start making lunches or helping with some routine chores. The important part is when you go to speak with them, *you don't do it with a Martha attitude*. Make sure you're approaching them and the situation with grace.

When I'm tired and I still have work to do, I've learned to go to the Lord in prayer. Instead of saying, "I don't know how I can get all of this done, I'm exhausted, and I can't do even one more thing," I remember these words from Scripture:

> *I will refresh the weary and satisfy the faint (Jeremiah 31:25).*
>
> *Whatever you do, work at it with all your heart, as working for the Lord, not for human masters (Colossians 3:23).*

The motive behind the deed is the most important part. When I shift my focus off myself and onto God, reminding myself of His desires, my strength is renewed. This meal I'm making will provide strength and nourishment for the people I love, and preparing it at home saves us money. (Frugality is something that definitely keeps me motivated.) Next, I begin to list all the good things that person does for me. By the time I'm done preparing that meal or whatever task I'm doing, I'm refreshed and ready to go wrap them up in a big hug instead of yelling at them for not helping.

Feed the soul first and there will be enough to fill everything else.

One of the reasons I remember my mother in our kitchen so much growing up is because she was. All our meals were prepared from scratch. We didn't have takeout, drive-throughs, or restaurants. Delis and convenient boxed meals weren't in the budget.

We never went without, but cooking from scratch was a necessity. Knowing there was little money, grocery shopping was done according to what was on sale and what could be stretched the furthest, not by one's desire for a certain dish on a given night. And with three teenage boys in the house during the early part of my parents' marriage, creativity was a must.

I never remember being deprived or feeling like we lived on rice and beans. In fact, my friends loved to have dinner at our house because the food was so good. I still call up Mom and ask for recipes when I recall a dish from my childhood that I don't have written down.

One of the ways she stretched a meal was to find another side dish—especially on the nights when guests showed up unexpectedly. It might have been as simple as a can of corn or a jar of peaches. And of course, some sort of bread item was served at every meal.

In the pages that follow you will find old-fashioned cooking at its finest. There's a reason certain recipes and dishes have been served and passed down for generations. These are the foods I serve my family and my mother served me. They nourish the soul along with the body. May they fill your table, mouth, and hearts . . . just as they have ours.

SPELT FLOUR

Bread is a good filler item, and there's a reason it's been a staple in man's diet for thousands of years. If you're wanting a healthier flour, you may want to go the route I did.

Spelt is an ancient wheat grain mentioned by name in the Bible. It works as a great whole wheat pastry flour. Spelt has a higher protein count and higher water solubility than regular wheat flour, and it also contains all nine amino acids and is much easier to digest. Its gluten content isn't as high as regular all-purpose flour, so when using it in a standard recipe, use 1¼ cups spelt flour for every cup of regular flour as a general guide, or use the same amount of flour but cut the liquid by a quarter: for example, 1 cup of milk would be ¾ cup of milk if using spelt flour.

I grind my own spelt flour, but you can usually find it preground in the health food sections of grocery stores, specialty baking areas, or online.

FLAKY BUTTERMILK BISCUITS

- 2 cups all-purpose flour
- 1½ tsp. baking powder
- ½ tsp. baking soda
- ½ tsp. salt
- ½ cup cold butter, cut into small pieces
- 2 tsp. honey
- ¾ to 1 cup buttermilk

One of the most versatile bread items—and one of the tastiest—is the humble biscuit. This little darling can be ready to go, from start to finish, in 20 minutes. If you've ever had biscuits in the can from the store, once you try this recipe, you'll never want to use store-bought again. This biscuit recipe makes the best, flakiest, melt-in-your-mouth biscuits you'll ever eat. I'm serious—you may well want to double the recipe. This recipe is courtesy of my mother, considered one of the best bakers in our valley, as my older brother proclaims and I concur.

If you don't have buttermilk, do *not* substitute regular milk. Instead, add 1 tablespoon lemon juice to the milk and let sit for a few minutes until it's curdled. You can also learn how to make real buttermilk at home on page 104. As to the flour, you can try a mixture of part whole wheat and all-purpose flour, but you get the most flakiness from straight all-purpose. (Shhh, don't tell my grain mill!)

Preheat oven to 400°. In a large bowl, mix together the dry ingredients. Using a pastry cutter (or two forks, but you'll be making these enough to get yourself a pastry cutter), cut in the butter until it turns the flour into little pea-size clumps. Add the honey and buttermilk and stir until just combined. Start with ¾ cup of buttermilk and only add the last ¼ cup if needed to hold the dough together.

Dump the dough out onto a lightly floured surface and fold it together a few times with your hands. Pat out into a 1-inch-thick circle. The key to flaky biscuits is to not overhandle the dough. You want the butter to melt as it bakes (this is where the wonderful flaky layers come from) and not from the heat of our hands by overkneading or overmixing.

This is important: I used to cut out my biscuits with an upside-down glass. Don't do it. If you want a mile-high biscuit (and you do), use a metal biscuit cutter. This cuts through the dough cleanly, allowing it to rise easily. A glass cup pinches the sides of the dough closed, making a short, squat biscuit.

Place your biscuits in a cast-iron skillet or on a baking sheet and bake for 15 to 18 minutes, until the tops turn a luscious golden brown.

Biscuit dough freezes really well. I often make a double batch and freeze the second sheet of unbaked biscuits. After an hour or so (or whenever you remember), transfer the biscuits to a sealable freezer container and store in the freezer for up to six months. Take out and bake as normal whenever the urge (or unexpected company) hits you. You may need to increase baking time by 2 minutes.

CRACKERS

One of the areas I struggle with in my from-scratch journey is snack foods. The packages in the store are so tempting, for both their ease of use and the taste, but the price tag and ingredients make me cringe.

Relax. I've got a cracker recipe for you that not only tastes great, but is quick. The dough whips up in five minutes, and the crackers are baked in ten minutes, meaning homemade crackers are ready for you to eat in just fifteen minutes. Can we say faster than a trip to the store?

- 1¼ cups flour (whole wheat, fresh ground, or all-purpose)
- ¼ tsp. onion powder
- ¼ tsp. garlic powder
- ¼ tsp. chili powder
- ¼ tsp. smoked paprika (regular paprika works fine too)
- 4 T. butter
- ¼ cup water
- 1 T. honey
- Sea salt to sprinkle on top

Preheat oven to 400°. Measure out dry ingredients into large mixing bowl. Cut in the butter until the mixture looks like pea-size clumps. Add in water and honey and stir until just combined.

Turn out dough onto lightly floured baking sheet or stone and pat into a rough circle. Roll out dough into a ⅛-inch-thin circle. (If you don't roll the cracker dough thin enough, the crackers won't be crunchy . . . but they'll still be delectable.) Use a pizza cutter to cut crackers into desired shapes. Sprinkle with sea salt and bake for 10 minutes. Leave crackers on baking sheet to cool.

CHOCOLATE CHIP COOKIES

Is there any more beloved cookie than chocolate chip? I always bake half the cookies the day I make this dough, and the rest gets formed into a log for the freezer to become the perfect slice-and-bake cookie. This recipe has been adapted from my mom's original recipe because we don't use shortening at our house.

- 1⅓ cups butter, softened
- ¾ cup brown sugar
- ¾ cup white sugar
- 2 tsp. vanilla
- 2 eggs
- 3 cups flour, sifted (for chewier flat cookies, use 2½ cups flour)
- 1 tsp. baking soda
- 1 tsp. salt (if using salted butter, make it closer to ½ tsp.)
- 2 cups semisweet chocolate chips

Preheat oven to 375°. Cream together the butter and sugars for 3 to 5 minutes. (I've tried using coconut oil, but if you use coconut oil only do 1 cup, as it tends to spread out and make flat cookies.) Mix in the vanilla and eggs. In another bowl, stir together the flour, soda, and salt. Combine the dry ingredients with the wet and stir in the chocolate chips.

Drop by the rounded tablespoonful onto a cookie sheet. (A small ice cream scoop helps keep cookies uniform.) Bake for 8 to 10 minutes, until the cookies are barely browned on the top, and then remove from the oven. Let the cookies sit on the sheet for 5 minutes before transferring to a cool rack. This helps create soft, melt-in-your-mouth cookies.

FLAKY PIE CRUST

If you've read my book *The Made-from-Scratch Life*, then you're familiar with this pie crust recipe. It belonged to my great-grandmother, and when I tell you it's the best pie crust ever, I'm not kidding. Not only is it melt-in-your-mouth flaky, but it's super easy to work with. I've gotten emails and texts the day before Thanksgiving from people telling me they've never had a pie crust recipe turn out before and they're amazed at how easy this one is to prepare, and the taste, oh, the taste—they were talking about it for weeks afterward. No joke.

4 cups all-purpose flour (or 5 cups spelt flour)
1 T. sugar
2 tsp. salt
1¾ cups cold butter, lard, or coconut oil
1 egg, beaten
1 T. apple cider vinegar
½ cup very cold or ice water

Our favorite combination of fats is half butter, half lard. Whichever fat you use, it's important that it be very cold (but not frozen; frozen butter doesn't work as well as straight from the fridge). Flaky pastry happens when the fat melts as it's baking, not when you're mixing. If you're using fresh ground flour, chill it before attempting to make the crust. You can also freeze the dough. It thaws well in the fridge and is nicely chilled for rolling out.

This makes 4 individual pie crusts for an 8- or 9-inch pie plate.

Combine dry ingredients. Cut in butter, lard, or coconut oil. You can even use a mixture of the different fats. Add the egg and liquids, stirring until the dough just holds together. Do not overwork the dough.

Chill for at least 15 minutes.

Divide dough into four equal parts. Turn out onto a lightly floured surface or waxed paper. Roll to ⅛-inch thickness. Bake with your favorite pie filling.

To create a baked pie shell for cream pies, roll out one crust and fill an 8- or 9-inch pie plate, fluting up your edges. Pie crusts will puff up if baked without anything in them, so you have two options. First, you can use a fork to prick the sides and bottom of the pie crust (don't worry, the filling covers all that up) fairly generously. Second, you can fill the crust with pie weights. You can either purchase pie weights or line your crust with parchment paper and fill the crust with uncooked dried beans or rice. The liner of parchment paper helps keep the rice or beans from sticking to the dough and makes removal a breeze.

Preheat oven to 475° and bake for 8 to 10 minutes. For hot pies (cooked fillings), use the pie crust when it's hot. For chilled pies, let it cool before filling.

BUTTERMILK PIE

You can't get much more old-fashioned and simple than a buttermilk pie. Back when almost every home had chickens and a milk cow, the ladies would look for a way to use what they had on hand to fill out their meals. Some buttermilk pie recipes call for lemon, but many homes of old, especially those in colder climates, would not have had easy access to citrus fruits, so I chose not to include it in this recipe.

A buttermilk pie is especially common and traditional to serve during the holidays. For the crust, use the Flaky Pie Crust recipe on page 18 or the Sourdough Pie Crust recipe on page 89. This makes one 9-inch pie.

1 unbaked pie crust
3 eggs
½ cup butter, softened
¾ cup brown sugar
¾ cup white sugar
3 T. flour
1 cup buttermilk
2 tsp. vanilla
¼ tsp. salt
½ tsp. ground nutmeg

Preheat oven to 425°. Roll out pie crust and place into a 9-inch pie plate. Crimp the edges and set aside.

Beat eggs in a large bowl until foamy. Beat in butter and both sugars with the eggs. Next, stir in the flour, buttermilk, vanilla, and salt. Pour into the prepared pie plate. Sprinkle the nutmeg evenly over the top of the buttermilk pie.

Bake for 15 minutes. Reduce heat to 350° and finish baking for 10 to 15 more minutes. The top of the pie will turn dark, but it will be a delicious creamy custard inside. Make sure to remove the pie from the oven when a knife inserted 1 inch from the side comes out clean. The center will be slightly wiggly when you remove it, but it will set up as the pie cools. Overbaking makes custard pies weepy and watery.

CHOCOLATE MERINGUE PIE

This is *the* chocolate pie recipe—as in dark chocolate, smooth, and hard not to devour by yourself. You may want to bake two: one for you and one for everyone else.

I've adapted this recipe from the classic *Better Homes and Gardens* cookbook. This uses cocoa powder instead of chocolate squares, and I call for quite a bit less sugar than many other recipes. This way the sweetness doesn't detract from the wonderful chocolate flavor.

One of the secrets to a good meringue pie is to put the meringue on hot pie filling. Make your meringue right before the filling.

Meringue:

3 egg whites (save the yolks for the pie filling)

½ tsp. vanilla

¼ tsp. cream of tartar

6 T. sugar

Pie Filling:

1 cup sugar

⅓ cup flour or 3 T. cornstarch

6 T. cocoa powder

¼ tsp. sea salt

2 cups milk

3 egg yolks, slightly beaten

4 T. butter

1 tsp. vanilla

1 prebaked pie crust for 9-inch pie

Topping:

1 cup heavy whipping cream, chilled

¼ cup powdered sugar

½ tsp. vanilla

Meringue

In a mixer,* beat the egg whites, vanillla, and cream of tartar until soft peaks begin to form. Slowly add in the sugar, a tablespoon at a time, and keep beating until it turns shiny and stiff peaks form.

**Note:* Trust me. I've tried doing it by hand; it never formed stiff peaks, and the next day my arm would barely work.

Chocolate Pie Filling

Preheat oven to 350°. In a large saucepan combine sugar, flour or cornstarch, cocoa powder, and salt. Mix with milk and cook on medium heat until mixture begins to simmer with little bubbles; continue to cook, stirring constantly, for 2 minutes. Remove from heat (leave your burner on) and whip in the slightly beaten egg yolks. Return to heat and, stirring constantly, cook for 2 more minutes. Remove from heat (turn off your burner now) and stir in the butter and vanilla.

Pour into prebaked pie shell and spread meringue over hot pie filling, making sure the meringue touches the crust. This will help seal it and prevent the meringue from shrinking up during baking.

Bake for 12 to 15 minutes, until the meringue is golden on the peaks. Remove from oven and allow to cool completely before cutting into a little bit of chocolate heaven.

Variation: Instead of making the meringue, simply make the chocolate pie as indicated, pour filling into baked and cooled pie shell, and chill in fridge for 2 hours. Top with the whipped cream topping.

Whipped Cream Topping

Place whipping cream in a mixing bowl and whip until stiff. Stir in the sugar and vanilla until dissolved. Spread over top of pie and serve.

To make powdered sugar at home, simply place regular sugar in a high-powered blender or food processor and pulse until powdered. If you pulse too long, it will clump a little bit due to heat, but it will still whip up just fine when added to the cream.

CARROT CAKE WITH BUTTERMILK SYRUP

Of course, carrots make one of the best cakes there is. You can whip up a 9 × 13-inch cake for a crowd in no time with a carrot cake. Most of you are familiar with cream cheese frosting on a carrot cake, but that's only because you've never had it topped correctly before. You'll never miss it now that you have this recipe. Trust me, it makes the best carrot cake you will ever have. You may never go back to cream cheese frosting again.

Cake:

- 3 eggs
- ½ cup melted butter, melted coconut oil, or avocado oil
- ¾ cup buttermilk
- 1½ cups sugar
- 2 tsp. vanilla
- 2 cups flour
- 2 tsp. baking soda
- 1 tsp. cinnamon
- 1 tsp. nutmeg
- ½ tsp. salt
- 2 cups grated carrots
- 1 can (8½ oz.) crushed pineapple, drained

Buttermilk Syrup:

- ⅓ cup sugar
- ⅛ tsp. baking soda
- ¼ cup buttermilk
- ¼ cup butter
- ½ tsp. vanilla extract

Carrot Cake

(If you don't have any crushed pineapple, increase grated carrots to 3 cups, add ¼ cup brown sugar, and increase oil amount to 1 cup total.)

Preheat oven to 350°.

In a large bowl beat together eggs, oil, buttermilk, sugar, and vanilla. Mix together the dry ingredients and stir into wet ingredients. Then add the carrots and pineapple and mix until combined.

Pour into a greased 9 × 13-inch pan and bake for 45 minutes.

When it comes out of the oven, begin preparing the Buttermilk Syrup.

Buttermilk Syrup

Combine the sugar, baking soda, buttermilk, and butter in a small saucepan. Bring to a boil over medium heat and boil for 5 minutes. Stir often and keep a close eye on it—once it boils it will boil over very easily. I turn my heat down to medium low and allow to simmer.

Remove from heat and add vanilla extract. Poke holes in top of cake with a toothpick and pour glaze over still-warm cake. Allow cake to soak up the glaze a bit before cutting and serving.

PUMPKIN APPLESAUCE CAKE

Growing up, I learned to use what we had. Butter and oil can get expensive, but during the height of apple season, you can get second apples (some blemishes and bruises) very cheap, if not often free. While they might not be a crisp eating apple, they make great applesauce.

Mom always made applesauce in the fall. It's truly best warm right off the stove. We love it over biscuits, on pancakes, and of course, just for plain eating. The other reason I love applesauce is because I can use it in my baking as a substitute for oil. This is one of our favorite fall cakes. Pumpkins and apples should play together more often.

- 4 eggs
- 1½ cups sugar
- ¾ cup applesauce
- ¼ cup melted coconut oil or butter
- 2 cups cooked pumpkin or 1 can (15 oz.) pumpkin
- 2 cups flour
- 2 tsp. baking powder
- 1 tsp. baking soda
- 2 tsp. cinnamon
- 1 tsp. salt

Preheat oven to 350°. In a large bowl, mix the eggs, sugar, applesauce, oil or butter, and pumpkin. Beat by hand until light and fluffy (or use an electric mixer).

In another bowl, mix together the flour, baking powder, baking soda, cinnamon, and salt. Stir into pumpkin mixture until thoroughly combined. Spread evenly in a 9 × 13-inch pan. Bake 25 to 30 minutes. Top with Buttermilk Syrup (page 22).

PEACH PUDDING CAKE

If you've never had an old-fashioned pudding cake before, you, my friend, are in for a treat. They don't require any frosting nor do they require making actual pudding or using those little boxes filled with powdered stuff.

A pudding cake is a cross between a cake, pie, and cobbler, but oh-so-simple to make and just about the best thing that will cross your lips all day. This recipe was inspired by my friend Laurie at Common Sense Home.

- 2 cups diced peaches
- Dash of nutmeg (optional)
- Dash of cinnamon (optional)
- 1¼ cups sugar, divided
- 1 tsp. baking powder
- ¼ tsp. salt
- ½ cup milk
- 3 T. melted butter
- 1 tsp. vanilla extract
- 1 cup flour
- ½ cup sugar
- 1 T. cornstarch
- ¾ cup boiling water

Preheat oven to 350°. Scatter peaches in an 8 inch cast-iron skillet (a square pan will work too) and sprinkle with a dash of nutmeg and cinnamon if you like.

Mix together ¾ cup of the sugar, baking powder, salt, milk, melted butter, vanilla, and flour. Spread batter over top of fruit.

Stir together the remaining ½ cup sugar and cornstarch in a bowl until combined. Sprinkle over the top of the batter.

Pour the boiling water over the top of the batter and pop in the preheated oven. Bake for 45 minutes or until a toothpick comes out clean. The beauty of this cake is that the boiling water and cornstarch create a thick, delectable pudding that melts in your mouth.

Variations: You can use any fruit in this pudding cake, making this a true old-fashioned recipe that lends itself to whatever fruit is in season or you have in the freezer. Use two cups of whatever fruit you choose. Here are some of our family's favorite recipes.

- Apple: Thinly slice apples and sprinkle with ½ teaspoon cinnamon.
- Blackberry: Sprinkle berries with a dash of cinnamon and nutmeg.
- Blueberry: Sprinkle berries with ½ teaspoon cinnamon and 1 teaspoon lemon juice.
- Cherry: Sprinkle fruit with ½ teaspoon almond extract and ½ teaspoon vanilla.

CUSTARD RICE PUDDING

You'll find many puddings in older cookbooks. It was a way to use up odds and ends of food that weren't enough on their own to feed an entire family, but when transformed into a pudding, could serve a family. Many of these baked pudding dishes made sure food didn't go to waste. As a bonus, they allow you to pop the dish in the oven instead of standing over a stove flipping or cooking items individually.

This first pudding recipe comes from my mother's kitchen. While I did eat it cold growing up, one can only wait so long before diving in, and because baking the pudding seems to take forever when you're little, it's best served warm. Patience and I had a tough time becoming friends when I was little, and we occasionally still squabble.

- 2 eggs
- ½ cup sugar
- ¼ tsp. salt
- 2 cups milk
- ½ tsp. vanilla
- 2 cups cooked rice
- ½ cup raisins or other dried fruit of choice (optional)
- Dash of nutmeg

Preheat oven to 350°. In a mixing bowl beat eggs, sugar, and salt slightly to mix. Add in milk, vanilla, rice, and raisins if using; stir until well combined. Pour into a 1-quart baking dish. Sprinkle with nutmeg.

Fill a larger pan with 1 inch of water. Place prepared rice pudding dish inside of the pan of water. Bake for 50 to 60 minutes or until a knife inserted 1 inch from the edge comes out clean. This can be served as dessert or breakfast.

TRADITIONAL LIVING TIP

Rice pudding was a frugal dish for breakfast or dessert. Dried fruits could be added for variety and flavor, but it was often made with the items on hand. Rice can also be used to help a pot of soup or stew stretch further.

CUSTARD BREAD PUDDING

4 eggs
1 cup sugar
2 tsp. vanilla
1 scant tsp. salt
4 cups milk
2 cups cubed raisin bread

This recipe originated from the River House Restaurant, a small restaurant that operated on the banks of the river near our home when I was growing up. They were only open on weekends, but they were well known for their bread pudding, one of the only options on their menu for dessert. It's been slightly altered, as the original recipe called for a whole lot of sugar, and as much as I love my sweet tooth, the addition of the raisin bread adds its own sweetness, so we had to nix some of the sugar. Both the restaurant and the sweet couple who ran it are gone now. Good recipes live on, acting as a memory and tying us back to times and people we love.

Bread puddings go way back in the kitchens of old. Many times, cooks used pudding as a way to make stale bread palatable. However, if you use stale bread, it's going to taste stale, so I prefer to not go that route.

One of the ways you can make this recipe versatile is to use whatever bread you happen to have. The restaurant always used raisin bread, which adds to the flavor profile, but you can use any type of bread you like.

Preheat oven to 350°. Mix all ingredients, except the bread, with a mixer or blender until smooth. Cover the bottom of a 1½-quart casserole dish (or a dish that is small enough to fit inside another pan with water) with the cubed raisin bread. Pour the egg mixture over the bread.

Fill a larger pan with 1 inch of water. Place the casserole dish inside the pan of water. Bake for 1 hour. Test if custard is done by dipping a knife in water and inserting it into the pudding 1 inch from the edge. If it comes out clean, the custard is done.

Variations:

- If not using raisin bread, add ½ cup raisins and sprinkle the top of the pudding with nutmeg.
- Add ½ cup dried blueberries and 1 teaspoon lemon extract. Sprinkle with a dash of cinnamon and nutmeg.
- Add ½ cup dried cranberries to the bread and add the juice of a fresh-squeezed orange and zest to the rest of the ingredients, cutting back the milk to 3¾ cups to allow for the juice.

CHOCOLATE CUSTARD BREAD PUDDING

Preheat oven to 350°. Grease the bottom of a 1½-quart casserole dish. Place cubed bread in the bottom and sprinkle with chocolate chips.

In a blender, blend the rest of the ingredients until thoroughly combined and pour over top of the bread cubes and chocolate chips. Place casserole dish inside a larger pan filled with 1 inch of water. Bake for 55 to 60 minutes or until a knife inserted one inch from the edge comes out clean.

Serve warm or cold. A splash of whipping cream on top is splendid.

- 2 cups cubed French bread
- ½ cup semisweet chocolate chips
- 4 cups milk
- 4 eggs
- 1 cup sugar
- 2 tsp. vanilla
- ¼ cup melted butter
- 6 T. cocoa powder

PUMPKIN CUSTARD BREAD PUDDING

Preheat oven to 350°. Mix all ingredients except the bread and optional nutmeg and cinnamon with a mixer or blender until smooth. Cover the bottom of a 1½-quart casserole dish with the bread. Pour the pumpkin mixture over the bread.

Fill a larger pan with one inch of water. Place the casserole dish inside the pan of water. Bake for 1 hour. Test if custard is done by dipping a knife in water and inserting it 1 inch from the edge. If it comes out clean, the custard is done.

Sprinkle the top with a dash of nutmeg and cinnamon for a pop of color. You can serve this by itself or with whipping cream or vanilla ice cream.

- 3 eggs
- 1 cup pumpkin puree
- ¾ cup sugar
- 6 T. real maple syrup
- 2 tsp. vanilla
- 1 scant tsp. salt
- 2 tsp. cinnamon
- ½ tsp. ground nutmeg
- ½ tsp. ground ginger
- 3 cups milk
- 2 cups cubed bread
- Nutmeg (optional)
- Cinnamon (optional)

DOUGHNUTS

Every evening during the fall and winter months, I helped my dad feed our herd of cattle. During particularly cold spells, we'd have to drive down to the bottom pasture where the watering ponds were. Dad kept a big ax in the back and he'd hack through the ice, sometimes almost a foot thick. One year the cold was so deep, we drove the full-size pickup truck out onto the ice so Dad could chop through the very center of the pond with the ax. He inched the tires off the bank and onto the frozen pond. My ears strained for any pop or crack, fingers curled around the door handle.

Dad exited the truck. The headlights reflected off the dark ice. Ice chunks flew beneath the blade of the ax. Water sloshed and my pulse thudded, my gaze sweeping the ice for any signs of weakening beneath our weight.

After a good-size drinking hole was cut, Dad backed the truck off the pond. Once on solid ground, I decided the event was much more exciting than scary. *Just wait until Mom hears. We get to do all the exciting stuff with Dad.*

Doughnuts:
- 2 eggs
- 1 cup sugar
- ¼ cup melted butter
- 1 cup milk
- 4½ cups flour, divided
- 1 T. salt
- 1 T. baking powder
- 1 tsp. vanilla
- Oil for frying (coconut oil and lard are my favorites)

Glaze:
- ¼ cup butter
- 2 cups powdered sugar
- 1 tsp. vanilla
- 2 T. milk

When we got home, I flung open the door of the trailer. Warm air bathed my nose and lungs. A tantalizing scent greeted me. My boots clunked down the hallway floor. There, spread out on the kitchen table was one of the most beautiful sights I could imagine. Homemade doughnuts, still hot from the oil, drizzled with glaze.

Let me tell you, homemade doughnuts are a treat worth writing home about, and definitely worth making, even if you haven't just come in from the ice or feeding cows.

Slightly beat the eggs in a large mixing bowl. Add sugar and mix. Add the melted butter and mix again. Add the milk and mix.

In another bowl, mix together 3 cups of the flour, salt, and baking powder. Add to wet ingredients and combine. Mix in the vanilla and the additional 1½ cups flour.

Roll out dough on a lightly floured surface to ½-inch thick. Using a doughnut cutter, cut out doughnuts. Save those doughnut holes—we'll use them first to test the oil, plus they're a bite-size delight.

In a deep saucepan (a Dutch oven works best), heat enough oil so the doughnuts can move freely without touching the bottom of the pan when they are frying. Old-fashioned oil temperature test: stick the end of a wooden spoon into the oil; if it sputters and bubbles, the oil is ready to cook. The modern and most reliable method is to use a thermometer and heat the oil to 375°. Once you add the doughnuts, the temperature will drop down a bit, putting it at the perfect place to transform the white dough into delicious bites of golden brown.

Drop a few doughnut holes into the hot oil. They should turn golden brown after approximately 2 minutes on each side. With the first batch, place them in the oil and at 2 minutes, check the side facing down into the oil—if it's golden brown, go ahead and flip all of the doughnuts in the saucepan and cook for the same amount of time on the other side. If it's not golden brown yet, let it cook another minute and check again. Adjust the temperature if the oil is too hot (starts smoking) or takes too long to cook. Fry all the doughnuts and doughnut holes, a few at a time.

Using tongs or a slotted spoon, remove doughnuts from oil to either paper towels (for ease of cleanup) or onto a baking rack and let cool just enough to not burn your mouth.

Glaze

Melt butter in a saucepan over low heat. Remove from the heat and then add the powdered sugar, vanilla, and milk. Beat until smooth, then drizzle the glaze over the doughnuts. Don't have powdered sugar? No need to run to the store. Put your regular white sugar or evaporated cane juice in a high-powered blender or food processor and run until sugar is powdered.

Variations:

- For chocolate glaze, add ¼ cup cocoa powder with the powdered sugar.
- For maple-flavored glaze, add 1 teaspoon maple extract or substitute ½ cup maple syrup for 1 cup powdered sugar.

Yield: approximately 2 dozen, when rolling back in the scraps and doughnut holes

CINNAMON SUGAR DOUGHNUT HOLES

Prepare the doughnut holes as directed above. Melt the butter. Mix together the sugar and cinnamon. Dip doughnut holes in the melted butter, then roll in the sugar mixture. Store doughnuts in an airtight container to keep them fresh—if you have any left over, that is.

Fried doughnut holes
¼ cup butter
⅔ cup sugar
1 T. cinnamon

FRENCH BREAD

When it comes to bread, there's little as versatile as a nice crusty loaf of French bread. It's delicious hot out of the oven and slathered with a bit of butter all by its lonesome or served with a hot homemade soup.

The other beauty of a loaf of French bread is the things we can turn it into. From bread puddings to stuffing or just plain, delicious breadcrumbs. But first, let us bake French bread.

French bread takes a bit longer to make than other breads due to an increased rise time. This longer rise time actually helps create the texture of the French bread. This recipe is adapted from *Betty Crocker's Picture Cook Book*, published in 1956.

Bread:

2¼ tsp. active dry yeast

1¼ cups warm water (yeast activates at 105° to 115°)

1½ tsp. sea salt

3 T. softened butter

4 cups sifted all-purpose flour (if you don't have a sifter, use a spoon to measure flour into measuring cups and level off)

Egg White Glaze:

1 egg white combined with 2 T. water

Mix yeast and water in a large mixing bowl or the bowl for your stand mixer. Let the mixture stand for about 5 minutes or until foamy. Stir in the rest of the bread ingredients until combined. If using a stand mixer, knead for 8 to 10 minutes with kneading attachment or dough hook. If mixing by hand, lightly flour your countertop and knead dough for 8 to 10 minutes. It should feel smooth and elastic, without sticking to your fingers or the countertop.

Grease a bowl and place dough in it, turning it to bring the bottom side that touched the grease first, upright. Cover with a tea towel and let rise for an hour and a half in a warm area. The top of the fridge or in the oven with the light on work great.

Punch dough down. Lightly flour your countertop and roll dough out into a large rectangle about 15 × 10 inches. Take the long side of the rectangle and roll it up tightly; place it on a parchment paper–lined cookie sheet. If you don't have any parchment paper or a silicone baking mat, grease the cookie sheet and lightly flour it.

With one hand on each end of the roll, gently roll it back and forth to make the loaf longer and tapered at the ends.

Take a sharp knife and cut slashes along the top of the dough at 2-inch intervals approximately ¼-inch deep. Brush the top of the dough with cold water and let rise for another hour and a half.

Preheat oven to 375°. Brush the top of the doubled loaf with cold water again right before baking and place in preheated oven. Bake for 20 minutes, then remove from oven and brush with the egg white glaze. Bake 25 minutes longer.

Remove from oven and immediately slather the loaf with some butter. Allow to cool. Serve and keep remaining loaf on the counter, covered with a tea or flour sack towel.

This bread makes excellent bread pudding and stuffing once it's aged for a day or two on the counter.

Yield: 1 large loaf, approximately 16 inches long

OLD-FASHIONED WHITE BREAD

My mother received her great-grandmother's cookbook, a 1938 edition of *Watkins Cook Book*. Tucked among its almost eighty-year-old pages are many wonderful from-scratch recipes and notes. Some of my favorite recipes have instructions saying, "Bake in a moderate oven," with no temperature given. This is some old-fashioned cooking!

One of my favorite bread recipes comes from this cookbook, and I've adapted it below.

Another interesting note is the lengthy triple-rise for this bread. Most modern recipes only use two rises, but I'm finding more traditional and older recipes used three rises. This produces some of the best sandwich bread we've ever had. It holds up nicely without being too soft or scattering lots of crumbs everywhere.

- 4½ tsp. active dry yeast
- 2 cups warm milk (you can use warm water, but milk produces a richer bread)
- 2 tsp. sea salt
- 2 T. sugar
- 6 cups sifted all-purpose flour
- 4 T. soft butter
- 1 T. melted butter

Instead of all-purpose flour, you may also use sifted fresh ground hard white wheat, whole wheat pastry flour, or a mixture of half whole wheat and half all-purpose. I've tried both fresh ground hard white wheat and all-purpose flour with this recipe. Both turn out wonderfully. This recipe makes two standard-size loaves.

Dissolve yeast in warm milk with salt and sugar and let sit until foamy, about 5 minutes. Add in flour, 1 cup at a time. Mix in the butter and knead dough by hand on a lightly floured surface for 8 to 10 minutes or in your stand mixer with the dough attachment for 10 minutes or until dough passes the windowpane test. (A test to see if dough has been kneaded long enough is to take a small piece and stretch it. The dough should stretch thin enough, you can almost see through it before it breaks. This is called the windowpane test.)

Cover with a towel and allow to rise in a warm area for 2 hours, until doubled in size. Punch down and let rise again for 1 hour.

Grease two loaf pans well. Lightly flour hands and counter. Divide dough in two and pat one piece into a rectangle on the counter; measure the narrow end of each rectangle to the long side of your loaf pan (this will ensure it fits perfectly into your loaf pan).

Roll it up from the narrow end; take the two ends of the roll and lightly tuck them under the roll and place it in the bread pan. Repeat with the other dough ball.

Melt 1 tablespoon butter and brush the top of both loaves with butter. Allow loaves to rise until doubled in size, about 1 hour.

Preheat oven to 400° and bake for 20 minutes. Then lower the temperature to 350° and bake for 40 minutes until the top is well browned and the sides have started to shrink away from the pan.

Take the bread out of the oven and then remove loaves from the pans. Slather again with butter and place loaves on a wire rack to cool.

MASTER BREAD DOUGH

3 cups lukewarm water
1½ T. active dry yeast
1½ T. apple cider vinegar
1½ T. salt (both sea salt and pink Himalayan work fine)
6½ cups flour

About eight years ago, I stood staring at the mile-long list of ingredients in teeny tiny print on the loaves of bread on the grocery store shelf. High-fructose corn syrup, monoglycerides, azodicarbonamide, food coloring, and soybean oil . . . just to name a few. I don't even know what half of those things are. We should not have to carry a dictionary with us to know what we're eating. Our food should be simple, with simple ingredients. But the only bread that had normal ingredients in it was more than five dollars a loaf. This wasn't a price I could afford on a weekly basis. My family wasn't ready to give up bread, and I wasn't ready to feed them questionable ingredients. Anyone else have that battle?

After sharing my woes with a friend, she told me her dad had found this new bread recipe that took just five minutes a day, and he'd been baking all their bread for more than two years.

Say what? This mamma could totally carve out five minutes for homemade bread.

The recipe came from the book *Artisan Bread in Five Minutes a Day* by Jeff Hertzberg and Zoë François, and it's changed my life. Yes, changed my life. I've used this basic recipe for close to a decade. Not only have I tweaked it to make it even more reliable, but I've also used it as the base for many different recipes, creating a master dough and turning my kitchen into a bakery. Imagine this: one dough, always in your fridge and ready to go for bread, rolls, pretzels, cinnamon rolls, pizza dough, and more. All homemade! You'll never pop a can again.

And the best part? Not only does it take five minutes of active time to whip up the dough, it only uses five ingredients. You'll find my basic recipe is slightly different from the one in the book. A friend started making the dough and mentioned to me she'd added vinegar. I started doing some research on vinegar and acid products in bread dough, and I quickly followed suit. Vinegar acts as a natural preservative and helps the texture of the dough. My great-grandmother used vinegar in her pie crust for the same reason. Acid in baked goods creates a better end product, when used in correct proportion. It's why so many recipes use buttermilk.

A few notes: This bread does only take about five minutes of active time, but when you mix up a batch, you do need about two hours of rise time. Plan to be home after an hour or so to keep an eye on the rise of the dough. For the flour, you can use whole wheat, all-purpose, or a mixture. If you're just starting baking and eating whole wheat flour, use 4 cups whole wheat and 2½ cups all-purpose flour.

Grab a big bowl, preferably one with a lid. Mix the warm water and yeast together. Allow yeast to activate, about 6 minutes, until it turns foamy. Stir in vinegar, salt, and 3 cups of flour. Continue adding flour 1 cup at a time until it's all incorporated. This is meant to be a wet dough. It's pretty shaggy in texture, so don't worry if it doesn't feel like regular bread dough you'd be kneading. No kneading here!

Cover dough with a clean tea or kitchen towel and allow it to rise in a warm area. You want the dough to double or triple in size. After the dough has risen, cover it with a breathable lid. I have a large bowl with a lid that latches down on both sides, but I latch only one. Or you may use plastic wrap, but don't seal it tightly on the sides. Airtight is not the goal here. Now pop that baby in your fridge. Wet dough is much easier to handle chilled, and the time in the fridge actually helps develop the dough. Best part—this dough sits in your fridge for up to two weeks, allowing you to bake when you want or need to. Yes, sometimes the need to bake is strong.

Ready to bake? Pull out your bowl of dough. Dust your hands and the countertop with a little bit of flour. Or feel free to use a piece of parchment paper to keep the counter clean and line your bread pan or baking sheet. If you have a bench knife, it makes removing a section of the dough and forming the dough ball extremely easy.

Remove approximately a third to half of the dough from the bowl. It will stretch, and you'll have to kind of rip it apart or use a serrated knife to separate it. It will also stick to your hands a bit if they aren't well floured.

Yield: 1 large loaf when using one-third to half the dough

RUSTIC ROUND LOAF

½ batch Master Bread Dough (⅓ batch for a smaller loaf)

For a rustic round free-form loaf of bread, form the dough into a ball on a piece of parchment paper.

Allow the ball of dough to rise for 30 to 40 minutes on the parchment paper. Don't worry if it doesn't double in size or spreads outward. You can also place it in a Dutch oven to encourage it to rise upward instead of out. Taking a sharp knife, dust the top of the ball with flour, and create three slashes across the top of the dough (flouring the knife blade will help it not to stick). This gives the bread a more even rise (as opposed to it cracking where it wants to on top) and gives that true artisan feel.

Preheat your oven to 450°, with a large cast-iron skillet or baking stone set on a rack in the middle of the oven to preheat also (you could use a cookie sheet in a pinch, but the stones or cast iron radiate the heat better) and a broiler pan on the lower rack.

When the oven is preheated, carefully (use your oven mitts please) slide out the middle rack and lower the parchment paper with your loaf onto the heated cast-iron skillet or stone.

Take a cup of hot water, pour into the broiler pan, and shut that oven door quick. The hot water creates a steamy environment in the oven as the bread bakes, giving you that crunchy outer texture and soft interior. If you prefer a softer crust, omit this step. Bake for 30 to 35 minutes.

CHEESE BREAD

½ batch Master Bread Dough

¼ to ½ cup all-purpose or whole wheat flour

1¼ cups grated cheese

I like to use cheddar in this recipe, but use your favorite. Optional add-ins for this bread include minced herbs, diced olives, diced jalapenos, and 2 cloves finely minced garlic.

Take the master dough (you're seeing a pattern here, right?) and knead in another ¼ to ½ cup of flour, or enough flour until you can form a dough ball and roll it out. Roll dough out into a rectangle about the same length as your bread pan and six inches wide. Evenly sprinkle with 1 cup of cheese and add in toppings of your choice, or be a purist and just let that cheese shine through, your choice. Generously grease a standard-size bread pan.

Roll up the dough and place inside prepared bread pan. Sprinkle reserved ¼ cup cheese on top of bread. Let rise for an hour or until doubled in size. Preheat the oven to 375° and bake for 40 minutes.

REGULAR BREAD PAN LOAF

½ batch Master Bread Dough

Grease a regular bread pan or line it with parchment paper.

Flour or grease your hands and take the dough from the bowl. Form the dough into a rectangle, the short side being the approximate length of your bread pan. Roll it up into a log and place into your bread pan. Let it rise for an hour.

Preheat oven to 400°. Bake for 30 minutes or until the top is golden brown. Pull out of the oven and slather the top with some butter. Let cool for at least 30 minutes before slicing.

CINNAMON RAISIN BREAD

Don't get me wrong, there is nothing as wonderful as a hot-out-of-the-oven cinnamon roll, all that ooey-gooey goodness literally dripping onto your taste buds. And that recipe is coming up soon, but first we must talk about the quicker and less sweet—but equally as yummy—cousin to cinnamon rolls. That would be cinnamon raisin bread, or cranberry orange bread, or blueberry bread. You can make all of these rolled bread delights with your master dough. (And we won't even talk about the exquisite French toast they make.)

- ½ batch Master Bread Dough
- 1 cup raisins, divided
- 1 cup all-purpose flour (or whole wheat, your choice)
- 3 T. melted butter, cooled slightly
- 2 T. cinnamon
- 2 T. brown sugar
- 2 T. white sugar
- 1 beaten egg
- Softened butter or coconut oil for greasing your bread pan

Take your master dough and knead in ½ cup of the raisins and the flour on a well-floured surface. Roll dough out into a rectangle about the same width as your bread pan and approximately 20 inches long. Smear the melted butter over the surface of the dough. Generously grease a standard-size bread pan—don't be afraid of the fat!

Sprinkle, as evenly as possible, the cinnamon, brown sugar, and white sugar over the dough, followed by the remaining raisins. Roll up the dough and place inside the prepared bread pan. Let rise for an hour or until doubled in size.

Preheat oven to 350°. Brush beaten egg over the top of the dough with a pastry brush, and bake for 40 minutes.

Variations: Use dried blueberries, cherries, or cranberries in place of raisins. Add the zest of one orange if desired.

CINNAMON ROLLS

Made-in-Pan Glaze:

½ cup butter

½ cup brown sugar

Bread:

½ batch Master Bread Dough

½ to 1 cup all-purpose flour

Filling:

¼ cup melted butter

Cinnamon

½ cup brown sugar

Raisins, chocolate chips, nuts, or other dried fruit (optional)

Grab an 8-inch and a 6-inch cast-iron skillet. (A 9 × 13-inch pan will work too, but cast iron is so versatile and truly does wonderful things for yeast breads.) Place butter and brown sugar in the bottom of the cast-iron skillets—about two-thirds in the larger skillet and one-third in the smaller skillet, but I just eyeball it. Turn your oven to preheat and place skillets inside until butter is melted. Pull the skillets out (remember, the handles are hot!) and set them on top of your stove. Turn off the oven for now.

Liberally dust your counter with flour. Take the master dough and place on top of the flour. Work up to 1 cup of all-purpose flour into the dough, until you can pat it out into a ¼-inch rectangle.

Slather the top of the dough with melted butter and dust or dump (however heavy- or light-handed you want to be) with cinnamon to preference. Sprinkle brown sugar on top and add your toppings of choice. Roll the dough up like you would a sleeping bag. Slice ½-inch-thick rounds and place evenly, filling-side up, inside the cast-iron skillets. You'll get 11 to 12 cinnamon rolls. Let rise in the warm oven for about 25 to 30 minutes, or until the cinnamon rolls are all touching and doubled in size.

Remove rolls and preheat oven to 375°. Bake rolls for 20 to 25 minutes, or until they're golden brown on top.

Have a large plate ready and immediately invert the cinnamon rolls on it when they come out of the oven. Let all that lovely glazy syrup in the bottom of the pan drizzle down over the cinnamon rolls. As soon as you can avoid burning your tongue, dig in!

Variation: Chocolate Cinnamon Rolls. In my husband's opinion, it's not dessert unless it's chocolate. I often make chocolate cinnamon rolls. Add ¼ cup cocoa powder to the pan with the other glaze ingredients, and ¼ cup cocoa powder sprinkled with the filling ingredients. You can omit the cinnamon if you wish, but chocolate and cinnamon do go well together. Instead of raisins, sprinkle with semi-sweet chocolate chips.

SOFT PRETZELS

½ batch Master Bread Dough
1 cup all-purpose or whole wheat flour
Option 1:
5 cups water
¼ cup baking soda
1 egg, beaten
Coarse salt
Option 2:
1 egg, beaten
Salt

Preheat oven to 425°. Line a baking sheet with parchment paper.

Flour your countertop and plop the master dough onto it. Lightly knead in 1 cup of flour. Tear or cut off approximately ⅓ cup of dough (I just set a ⅓ cup measuring cup on the counter and eyeball it).

On your floured surface, roll the ball out into a long, skinny rope. Roll it a bit skinnier than you think it should be—remember, it's going to rise. It should be about 21 inches long. Once you have your long rope of dough, take both ends and draw them back to the center of the dough, twist once in the middle, and press them down onto the bottom half of the circle, creating a classic pretzel shape. Don't worry if they're not perfect—you'll be making these again and again, and soon you'll be an old pro. Repeat this process until all the dough has been rolled and shaped.

We have two options for how we're going to "finish" our pretzels before baking. Option 1 is considered traditional, while Option 2 is probably a wee bit less work. Option 2 is a variation I discovered at www.SallysBakingAddiction.com, and I highly recommend you try both to see which you prefer.

Option 1

In a good-size saucepan, whisk together the water and baking soda. Bring it to a boil. Get a large slotted spatula (mine was a tad bit smaller than the pretzel, but it still did the trick). One at a time, dip each pretzel into the boiling water for 30 seconds. Lift the pretzel out and let the water drip off.

Place pretzel onto prepared baking sheet. Beat egg and brush on top of pretzels (a pastry brush works great). Coat with coarse salt. The bigger the better in my opinion.

Option 2

Beat egg in a shallow bowl. Coat both sides of the pretzel in the egg wash (just like making French toast) and place on baking sheet. Sprinkle with salt.

Bake for 10 to 12 minutes or until golden on top. If you did Option 2, turn the oven to broil and bake for another 5 minutes to get them nice and brown. I set the timer at 4 minutes because no one wants black-topped pretzels, and the broiler and I have a testy relationship.

Variations:

- *Cinnamon-Sugar Pretzels:* Mix together ¾ cup sugar and 1 tablespoon cinnamon in another bowl. When pretzels come out of the oven, slather them with butter, and then dip the top of the pretzel into the melted butter and roll it around in the sugar cinnamon mixture.
- *Honey Mustard Sauce:* Mix ½ cup mustard, ½ cup honey, 2 tablespoons plain yogurt, a dash of salt, and a pinch of pepper. Dip pretzels in to your heart's content.

PIZZA DOUGH

- 1 cup flour
- ½ batch Master Bread Dough

Preheat oven to 425°. Knead the flour and master dough together. Roll out dough on a well-floured surface and place on pizza pan or stone, or make a deep-dish pizza with an 8-inch cast-iron skillet. Pile high with your choice of toppings—my family's favorites follow—and bake for 15 to 20 minutes, until the cheese is nice and bubbly with bits of gold on top.

NO-RISE PIZZA DOUGH

- 2¼ tsp. active dry yeast
- 1 cup warm water
- 2 cups flour
- ½ tsp. salt
- 2 T. olive oil
- Dried herbs (about 1 tsp. total)
- ¼ tsp. garlic and onion powder (optional)

If you're pressed for time and don't have the master dough ready to go, try this quick method for pizza dough. All-purpose flour provides a lighter crust, but you can use whole wheat or a mixture of both.

Preheat oven to 425°. Mix together yeast and water in a large bowl and let activate for 5 minutes (it will turn bubbly and foamy). Mix the flour, salt, and olive oil into the dough until combined. Next, add in the dried herbs, and garlic and onion powder if using. Once all ingredients are combined, lightly flour your counter and dump the dough onto it. Knead by hand for about 3 minutes until dough holds together nicely. If dough is too sticky, add a bit more flour until you're able to handle it. It should be fairly smooth and just a little bit tacky, but not shaggy wet. Let the dough rest while you prepare the rest of your toppings.

TOMATO BASIL CHICKEN PIZZA

Our favorite summer pizza is when the tomatoes are fresh on the vine and basil is growing right next to it in the herb garden.

- 1 pizza crust
- Olive oil
- Sliced tomatoes
- Diced cooked chicken
- Mozzarella cheese
- Fresh basil leaves
- Parmesan cheese (optional)

Preheat oven to 425°.

Smear a light layer of olive oil on the crust and place sliced tomatoes and cooked chicken on top. Place the mozzarella cheese over all of it. Add basil leaves. You can add a light grating of Parmesan on top for a second cheese option and more flavor, because really, can you have too much cheese on a pizza?

Pop pizza in the oven and bake until golden brown, approximately 12 to 15 minutes.

For an extra kick, add a light layer of pesto to the dough along with the olive oil.

EASY PIZZA SAUCE

I never purchase pizza sauce, and neither will you when you see how easy it is to make at home. Simply use one 16-ounce jar of tomato sauce. I actually can all of our tomato sauce, so if you're a fellow canner (or soon to be, because in my book you're either a canner or soon to be one), just grab a pint from your pantry.

- 1 pint (16 oz.) tomato sauce
- 1 tsp. garlic powder
- 1 tsp. onion powder
- ½ tsp. dried oregano

Empty tomato sauce into a small saucepan. Bring to a boil and then turn to medium heat and allow to boil gently for about 10 minutes to allow sauce to thicken up slightly. Stir in spices. Spread over pizza dough.

Variation: Don't have any tomato sauce? Use a pint jar or 14.5-oz. can of whole, halved, or diced tomatoes. Drain off excess liquid and puree in a blender or food processor, then follow above instructions.

WHITE SAUCE CHICKEN PIZZA

Grilled chicken is delicious on this pizza.

Preheat oven to 425°.

Mix together the cream cheese, onion, garlic, dill, chives, and yogurt or mayonnaise. Smear the white sauce mixture evenly over the crust. Toss the chicken, zucchini, onion, and mushrooms over the white sauce. If you have the type of mozzarella that's soft and in a long log, just slice it and place the slices on top (that's our favorite), but if you've got the kind in a brick, go ahead and grate it. If you have Parmesan, grate a small amount on the very top, like a light dusting of snow. You can really use any cheese you want. Put pizza in the oven and bake until golden brown, about 15 to 20 minutes.

- 8 oz. cream cheese, softened
- ¼ cup minced onion
- 1 clove garlic, minced
- ¼ tsp. dried dill
- ¼ tsp. dried chives
- ½ cup yogurt or mayonnaise
- 1 pizza crust
- 2 cups cooked chicken
- 1 cup thinly sliced zucchini
- Thinly sliced onion to taste
- Sliced mushrooms
- Mozzarella
- Parmesan (optional)

FAKE-IT SAUSAGE PIZZA

This next pizza is one my mom made growing up. We never had delivery or frozen pizzas, but sometimes Mom would make a big pan of this for a treat. Sausage was expensive, and since we had our own hamburger, Mom would make a "sausage" pizza by using ground hamburger and adding a teaspoon of allspice to the meat when browning. You can use whatever cheese you like, but colby jack and mozzarella work well together on this one.

Preheat oven to 425°.

Smear the top of the crust with pizza sauce. Layer on toppings, ending with the grated cheese. Bake for 15 to 20 minutes, or until cheese is melted and golden.

- 1 pizza crust
- Easy Pizza Sauce (recipe at left)
- 1 lb. hamburger
- 1 tsp. allspice
- Onion, diced or thinly sliced (optional)
- Olives (optional)
- Green bell peppers, diced (optional)
- Cheese of choice, grated

CHAPTER 2

SIMMER

Buried deep within all of us is a secret longing. A dream not yet fully unfolded, but formed and tucked into the corners of our minds. It fills the nooks and crannies of our thoughts. When we read or hear about someone accomplishing or doing something close to our dream, it rises up inside of us, pushing to break free from the longing into reality.

We may share our dream with those close to us, or we may clutch it tightly, afraid if we speak of it or shed light on it, the dream will shrink.

Every night before bed, my mother would read to me. We had a strict one-chapter rule—no more and no less, even when our heroine had to dangle over the cliff until we could pick up again the next night.

My favorite book was *Little House in the Big Woods*. Our little trailer would morph into the cabin and I would play under the sheltered branches of our evergreens just like Laura and Mary did under their big oak tree. I loved the way words on a page could string together and come to life. Those words transported me across time and plunked me down with friends. Having a little bit of spunk, I always felt Laura was my kindred spirit, especially when she got into trouble.

After we'd finished the Little House series, we began other books. One of those books was called *A Gold Star for Eric* by Colleen L. Reece. My mom told me that Colleen grew up in Darrington, the neighboring town where my mother had been raised, and she was an author.

"You mean people write books for their job?"

"Yes, she's an author. That's what she does."

The seed tucked down deep into the soil of my heart. "That's what I'm going to be when I grow up," I pronounced. We never know which words will become prophetic in our life.

Years went by. I got married and went to pharmacy technician school and started my job at our local pharmacy. Once a week I attended a local writer's group. The yearning was there, and my dream of being published pushed at me.

I attended conferences, wrote faithfully, and submitted my work to agents and editors. Rejection letters came back. This was back when email was in its infancy and I went through many a book of stamps. Our postmaster commented, "You must be quite the prolific writer."

Yes, prolific I was. Making headway toward my dream of anyone else reading my work, not so much. I had the stack of rejection letters to prove it.

As months slid into years, the dream of becoming a real writer simmered in my heart. I kept writing, stealing time in the evenings after work and after my husband went to bed. After I had my first child, I'd slip in a few sentences during naptime or on my lunch break at work.

Ten years after I'd first started writing for publication, I attended yet another writer's conference, but this time—this time!—a literary agent liked my sample chapters enough to ask for the entire manuscript. I mailed it off to her, all my hopes and dreams from more than a decade tied into that thick envelope and ink on paper.

I didn't fret over checking the mailbox each day like before. It would take longer; she had the entire book to read.

Late August rolled around, when the grasses in the pastures reach tall, holding their heads of seed high with pride toward the setting sun. Golden sunlight bathes the valley and seems to catch on the mountain ridge, holding on for just a few more moments before letting twilight take the stage.

It was in this moment, when the sun was suspended, that I opened our mailbox. There was my self-addressed stamped envelope from the literary agent. Like the sun holding onto daylight right before dusk, I held the envelope for a just a few more moments before opening it.

As I entered our driveway, my tennis shoes slowed on the gravel. The letter crinkled in my hands.

Your writing isn't good enough for publication.

Tears blurred the green of the trees, and hope bolted into the approaching twilight. The words were spelled out before me, in literal black and white. What I'd always feared deep down was true: my writing wasn't good enough. *I wasn't good enough.*

Without words, I fell into my husband's arms and cried. My dreams of being a real writer fled in my tears. As I dried my face, he said, "You know, if this is upsetting you so much, maybe you shouldn't do it anymore."

And I agreed. The roller coaster of hoping and being let down was too much. The dream I'd held onto since I was eight years old sank.

My fingers didn't type a single story for more than two years. I quit our writing group.

But you see, God isn't confined to our feelings. He doesn't work like we'd expect and often, not even when we want Him to. He allows us to see His plan when He knows we're ready, and not a minute before.

Even though I'd turned off the heat on my dream of being a writer, thought the dream was dead and over, God had different plans. In the corner of the living room—the lamplight stretched over my

Bible—He chose to show me His plan. Despite the loss of my first pregnancy and the struggle to conceive, two children slumbered peacefully in my home. Both my husband and I had jobs.

God had blessed us, and I knew it. So why did I have this restless feeling deep down in my soul? Why wasn't I content with the gifts I'd been given?

Like that first bubble when water begins to boil, my long-sleeping dream rose. A writer. "God, You gave me this desire to be a writer, but if it's not Your plan for my life, please take it away. Show me what You would have me do, not what I want to do, and let me be content with that."

When we surrender to God, He can do things beyond our current wants or expectations.

I used to think I'd wasted those two years by not writing. *How much further along I'd be if I'd just kept writing in faith of God's calling.*

There are two things I know to be true. First, if you're walking in God's plan for your life, the devil will fight you. Second, no matter what the enemy tosses at you, if you give it to God, He'll turn it into a blessing.

I no longer see those years I stopped writing as a failure or a setback to where I should be. Instead, I see them as a time God was using to evaporate all the things in me that weren't needed, a refining period.

> *These have come so that the proven genuineness of your faith—of greater worth than gold, which perishes even though refined by fire—may result in praise, glory and honor when Jesus Christ is revealed (1 Peter 1:7).*

I had tied up my worth and value in my writing. The rejection letter wasn't just about my writing; it went straight to my heart as a rejection of me. I was looking to outside sources to validate me, to reassure me I was enough. When we look to anything other than Jesus to show us we're enough, we'll never measure up.

There are so many things we look to as measuring devices instead of where our eyes should be. We turn to the number on a scale, the amount of money in our bank account, the kind of car we drive, the type of foods we eat, our kids' grades or accomplishments, the cleanliness of our home.

I don't know about you, but the number on the scale never stays where I want it. The money in my bank account doesn't grow fast enough. Though I try to eat healthy, I don't always reach for the healthiest thing in the kitchen and I've been known to still munch away on a candy bar or two . . . or three. (Hey, the mini ones aren't very big.) My house will look amazing for a day—why can't all the unannounced guests come right then?

No matter what, eventually the things we place value on—those things we're looking at to tell us deep down we're a good person, we're doing something right, and we matter—will fail us. There's only one thing that won't.

> *The Lord is my rock, my fortress and my deliverer; my God is my rock, in whom I take refuge, my shield and the horn of my salvation. He is my stronghold, my refuge and my savior—from violent people you save me (2 Samuel 22:2-3).*

It took me two years to learn the only way I could be whole was to seek Jesus and His will. Chasing the things of this world and what we want are a sure recipe for heartache.

After praying that prayer and truly giving up my wants, God began opening doors for my writing.

He knew I needed those two years to learn that I was enough simply because His Son had died to save me, and because He loved me. Not because I could string words together or at times my prose was eloquent. You and I, we're enough because He knit us each of us together in our mother's womb, He called us to Him, and He shows us His love anew every morning.

God cares about our heart, and once it's in the right place, He will open the doors. They're usually not the doors I'd pick, and often, they're not even doors I knew existed, but they're always the right ones. Though I confess—sometimes I still require a bit of hindsight to realize this.

I don't always enjoy the simmering period, but it results in the most beautiful of things. It takes longer than I'd like most of the time, but in both our food and our hearts, it's only through this process that we get the desired end result.

> *Consider it pure joy, my brothers and sisters, whenever you face trials of many kinds, because you know that the testing of your faith produces perseverance. Let perseverance finish its work so that you may be mature and complete, not lacking anything (James 1:2-4).*

Fads come and go, but I've found the things that have stood the test of time are the best. A recipe handed down from generation to generation. Kindness and grace when least expected or deserved. Cookware and methods stretching back to the pioneer days and beyond.

Cast iron is by far my favorite in the kitchen, from my skillets to Dutch ovens and loaf pans. You'll discover why in the words below. And if you're skeptical or haven't had the best of luck with it in the past, keep reading, my friend. It's worth the effort to try again.

CAST IRON

The cast-iron skillet and Dutch oven are two of my favorite pieces of cookware. Cast iron is superior in so many ways to today's newer cooking pans. Once heated, cast iron retains its heat, making it a more even cooking surface. I get higher and fluffier rolls when I bake them in a cast-iron pan.

Unlike pans treated with questionable nonstick coatings that flake off over time and may release chemicals, cast iron will last a lifetime and can be handed down to the next generation. Plus, the 8-inch cast-iron skillet works perfectly for brownies and corn bread, while a 9-inch cast-iron skillet works great for pies and even deep-dish pizzas. Having fewer dishes in my cupboards is a plus. I especially love that I can take my cast iron from the stovetop to the oven to the wood stove, and even use it outside over an open fire to cook our food.

Don't believe the fallacy that food sticks to cast iron either. If properly seasoned, it becomes nonstick, turning out perfect eggs over easy and pancakes like a pro. It takes very little to care for cast iron, but it is a tad different than regular dishes and cookware. Here's how to keep your cast iron in good condition and lasting for a lifetime.

Seasoning: After purchasing a new pan or one at a garage sale that needs to be reseasoned, wash it out with hot water and a rag. Use coarse salt to scrub off cooked-on food. If it's in really bad shape, you may need to use steel wool to scrub it clean. For pans we've rescued that had layers of cooked-on food and rust, we have used a Dremel tool attachment; just be careful you don't grind too far, you need the pores to remain to be able to hold the oil to create a seasoning.

One of the biggest mistakes people make with seasoning is choosing the wrong oil and using too much. If you've ever had a cast-iron pan feel sticky, tacky, or gummy, it's because too much oil was used. I've tried lots of different oils over the years and have found the best results for a long-term seasoning that doesn't flake or turn brittle is grapeseed or avocado oil. If your pan is being used daily, or almost daily, then lard or bacon grease is fine, but do NOT use lard if you store the pan without use for periods of time, as it will turn rancid.

Once the pan is clean and dry, pour a small amount of oil into the warm pan and, using a lint free rag, rub it in all over, both inside and out. Wipe off any excess oil. Place it in a preheated 400° to 500° oven until it starts to smoke (this can vary based on oil choice) or on a stovetop over high heat. As the oil cooks, it fills the pores of the pan, forming a nice black finish (this is where stick-free comes in). Once the pan has started to smoke, carefully (all parts of the pan will be HOT) apply a very thin amount of oil to the surface. Turn off the heat and allow it to cool.

Even if a pan says *preseasoned*, I still season it myself before use—usually twice, especially if it's rusty or was in rough shape when I got it.

The older cast-iron pans do have a smoother surface due to the casts. Newer casts are a bit bumpier, but you can still achieve a good seasoning on them and make them nonstick. The only new cast-iron brand I've found that has a smooth finish is from the company Smithey. If you happen to be fortunate enough to run across some old cast iron at a thrift store or garage sale, grab those treasures and give them a fresh seasoning and new life in your kitchen.

Cooking: When cooking eggs or pancakes, make sure to melt butter or oil in the pan first. This will help you achieve a nonstick cooking surface and further season your pan.

Cleaning: Let your pan cool down slowly. Never pour cold water into a hot pan, or it could crack. There's lots of controversary on using soap in a cast-iron pan. Historically, soap with a lot of lye in it would damage the finish of cast iron, ruining your lovely nonstick surface. Today's liquid soaps are actually detergents. The key is cleaning the pan while it's still warm with hot water. I've had people balk at not using soap, but friends, heat kills bacteria just fine. If you want to use dish soap and find it doesn't harm your pan, then go on ahead and use it. I rarely find I need it on my cast iron. I simply rinse mine with hot water and wipe it out with a nonabrasive cloth. If you have baked-on food, scrub off the sticky parts with table salt. You can also find specialized chain mail scrubbers for cast-iron pans or a wooden scraper. Wipe the pan dry and recoat it with a thin layer of oil before storing.

Storage: Your cast-iron pans will store best in the open. If you must stack them, always store cast-iron Dutch ovens with the lid slightly ajar to allow airflow.

DUTCH OVEN RECIPES

Everyone should have a few good comfort food recipes, and that includes soups. Soups and stews can be cooked in a Dutch oven (you saw that coming, right?), and they also stretch the budget to feed more mouths. You can make a complete meal out of a few vegetables and a small amount of meat.

Let's get our soup on!

BONE BROTH

If using chicken, save the bones from a roast or whole bird. This stock can easily be done with turkey, beef, or pork as well. Don't worry if there's a bit of meat still on there; it just adds to the flavor.

When trimming off the ends of carrots, celery, onions (save the skins too), squash, or any other vegetable, toss them in a freezer container. You'll be surprised how quickly you'll get a few cups from the parts you'd normally discard. You can also use any wilting or needs-to-be-used-up-fast veggies from the fridge.

- Bones
- Vegetable ends
- Garlic
- Apple cider vinegar
- Water
- Fresh or dried herbs

In a large stock pot or slow cooker, place your bones, vegetable odds and ends, and about four to six cloves of smashed garlic (again, leave the skins on—less work for you and more nutrition for the broth). Pour ¼ cup apple cider vinegar over the bones and let sit for about 15 to 20 minutes. The vinegar will help break down the bones faster and pull out all of the good gelatin and collagen.

Cover with water until all the vegetables and bones are submerged. Toss in whatever herbs you have. Rosemary is a favorite of mine to add in, as well as oregano, thyme, and a bit of sage.

Let simmer on low for 12 to 24 hours. Pour contents (careful, it's hot) through a strainer. I use a fine-mesh strainer or a colander lined with cheesecloth. Place in the fridge or freezer.

I have come to adore my Instant Pot for making broth. Follow the steps above but use the soup setting or the pressure setting on high for one hour. You will get an amazing gel with only one hour of cooking compared to the 12 to 24 a slow cooker or stove top requires.

TRADITIONAL LIVING TIP

Cooking a whole bird, ham, or roast with the bone was a way to make more meals from one item. The bones and skin were saved to make bone broth or soup the following day.

CHILI

There are all kinds of theories when it comes to chili, and many swear true chili doesn't include beans—just the meat, peppers, and spices. Staunch supporters of a no-bean chili won't be happy with my version. For many homes, beans are a frugal way to stretch a meal even further. Use any beans you'd like for this chili—pinto, black, white, or whatever you have on hand. Soak your beans for at least 12 hours, but no more than 24 hours, in cold water.

Some people like to use a tablespoon of vinegar in the water when soaking, but I find it causes the beans to be tough. The thought is the acid in the vinegar helps break down and reduce the phytic acid in the beans. However, we noticed the beans didn't seem to ever get all the way done (aka tough!), so we still soak our beans for 24 hours (which helps reduce the phytic acid) but don't use vinegar any longer.

- 1 cup dried beans
- 3 to 4 cups water, plus more for soaking beans
- 1 lb. ground beef (or meat of choice)
- 1 onion, diced
- 5 cloves garlic, diced
- 1 to 2 jalapeños, to taste
- 1 red bell pepper
- 1 qt. drained stewed tomatoes *or* 2 cups tomato sauce
- 1 T. honey
- 3 to 4 T. chili seasoning mix (page 150)

Soak dried beans for 24 hours, then drain and rinse the beans thoroughly in clean water. Place about 3 cups of the soaked beans in a slow cooker and add enough water to cover by an inch. Add the meat, onion, garlic, peppers, and tomatoes. Cook on low for 6 to 8 hours. If needed, add more water. Right before serving, add the honey and seasonings. Start with 3 tablespoons seasoning and taste. I've found with herbs and seasonings, the flavors are diluted when cooked for a long time, so you'll save on the amount of spices and herbs needed while getting the most flavor by adding right before serving. Add more if needed. Serve with fry bread (recipe follows).

Yield: 8 servings

FRY BREAD

This is my favorite dish to serve with chili. Many accounts credit Native Americans with inventing fry bread. It became a common dish in the latter part of the 1800s, when they were forced to depend on government staples instead of their historical foraging, hunting, and gathering way of life and diet. The government gave out flour and lard for provisions, and the humble fry bread was born.

Unfortunately, deep frying foods has gotten a bad rap, and many people shy away from preparing meals this way. Though cooking food in hot oil does add some calories, we consider these meals a treat and not a regular occurrence at our table. I'm more concerned with the type of oil being used. I prefer to use unrefined coconut oil mixed with lard for our deep frying. The mixture of the two together works well for me in keeping a delicate flavor for breads.

I've tried several different versions, and my two favorites are presented here. The first version uses both flour and cornmeal and is great for making tacos. The second version uses all flour and is also delicious for tacos, but it really shines when you prepare it as dessert.

For fry bread, start by measuring out about half a cup of coconut oil and half a cup of lard. Use an 8-inch cast-iron skillet, if you have one. Melt the oil over medium-low heat. Once it's melted, you should have about an inch of oil in your pan. After two minutes, check the oil with a wooden spoon. If a little bubble forms around the stick, the oil is ready to use. If not, heat it for another couple of minutes and check again, adjusting the heat if needed. Add your dough of choice from the recipes at right!

Remember to keep a watch on your oil, especially if it reaches the smoking point. And if you have an oil fire, never, ever try to put it out with water—this will just cause the fire to spread. An oil fire should be put out by smothering or using a fire extinguisher.

FRY BREAD WITH CORNMEAL

- 2 cups flour
- 1 cup cornmeal
- 2 heaping tsp. baking powder
- ½ tsp. salt
- 1 cup water
- Coconut oil or lard for frying (approximately 1 cup)

Mix dry ingredients together. Add water and stir just until it comes together; don't overstir or knead it. If needed, add a few more tablespoons of water. Let sit for at least 30 minutes, but you can let it go longer and it won't hurt a bit. I once forgot it for more than 5 hours, and it then became dinner instead of lunch. Don't you just love a dough that works with you like that?

Heat the oil. When oil is ready to fry, separate the dough into 6 balls. Flatten dough on a lightly floured counter and, using your fingers, push, pull, and mold it into a lumpy circle. I love this, because it looks old-fashioned and doesn't matter if I get it to a perfect thinness. Hear that, pie crust and tortillas? Rustic is the new home baker's best friend.

Being careful of grease splatters, add your dough to the oil. It should bubble when the dough hits the oil. Allow to fry for about 1 minute, until it starts to turn golden brown. Flip and finish cooking for 1 minute longer. If your dough isn't browning in the minute time frame, increase the heat slightly.

Place on a plate with an absorbent towel and continue adding layers of freshly cooked fry bread.

Yield: 6 servings

DESSERT FRY BREAD

- 3 cups flour
- 2 heaping tsp. baking powder
- ½ tsp. sea salt
- ¾ cup buttermilk
- ½ cup water
- Coconut oil or lard for frying (approximately 1 cup)

Mix dry ingredients together. Add in buttermilk and stir until just combined. Add water if needed. Let sit for up to 6 hours, but at least 30 minutes. Form into 6 balls of dough. On a lightly floured surface, flatten the dough ball with the palm of your hand. Form into a rustic circle. Fry in hot oil for about 1 minute each side until golden brown. Dry on a plate lined with an absorbent towel.

Variations:

- Sprinkle with cinnamon, a touch of sugar if you want, and drizzle liberally with honey.
- Brush with butter when it first comes out of the oil, and then roll in a shallow dish of mixed cinnamon and sugar.
- Smear your favorite jam or jelly on top, and then dust with powdered sugar or whipped cream.

Yield: 6 servings

HAM AND BROCCOLI CHOWDER

2 T. butter
½ cup minced onion
3 cloves garlic, minced
3 T. flour
2 cups chicken broth (you may use water or some bouillon, but the flavor is in the broth)
2 cups chopped broccoli (fresh or frozen)
1 to 2 cups milk
1 cup grated cheese
2 cups diced, cooked ham
½ tsp. salt (or to taste, depending upon your ham)
Dash of pepper

Place a soup pot or Dutch oven on the stove and turn to medium heat. Melt the butter, and then add the onion and garlic. Sauté for about 3 minutes or until onions are translucent. Stir in flour until it creates a thick paste.

Pour in the broth, stirring until fully combined. Add the broccoli and let simmer for about 5 minutes, or until broccoli is cooked, stirring often.

Stir in 1 cup of milk and the cheese. You can alter the flavor by using your favorite cheese. We really like fresh grated Romano and cheddar together, but Gouda, Swiss, and mozzarella will also taste fantastic! And if you add in some smoked cheese, oh my, invite me over for dinner, okay?

Add ham, salt, and pepper. Let simmer on low, stirring occasionally, for 15 minutes. If chowder becomes too thick, simply thin with a little bit of extra milk.

For a dairy- and gluten-free option, use coconut oil in place of butter, extra chicken broth in place of milk, and organic cornstarch or arrowroot as your thickener.

Yield: 8 to 10 servings

SON OF A GUN STEW

The stew recipe below was named when it was first tasted and someone exclaimed, "Son of a gun, this stew is good." It has been called such ever since. Whenever we lost power, my mother would prepare this on top of our woodstove. It's long been a family favorite. You may use fresh, frozen, or canned vegetables. I use home-grown and canned pints of most of the vegetables, but however you roll is fine.

The secret ingredient is the chili powder. There's not enough to make the stew spicy—just enough to give it the perfect flavor.

- 1 T. butter
- 1 lb. stew meat
- 1 cup minced onion
- 2 to 3 cloves garlic, minced
- ¼ to ½ cup minced celery (optional)
- 1 cup diced carrots
- 2 to 3 medium-size potatoes, cubed
- 2 cups corn or green beans
- 2 cups peas
- 2 cups tomato sauce
- 2 cups water or broth
- ½ tsp. chili powder
- Salt and pepper to taste

In a large pot over medium heat, melt the butter; brown the stew meat, onion, garlic, and celery if using. When meat is browned and vegetables are partially cooked, add in the remaining ingredients. Allow to simmer on low for an hour or two, until the potatoes are cooked all the way through.

Serve with biscuits or bread slathered with butter.

Yield: 12 servings

CRAB BISQUE

I'm going to confess, I'm not much of a seafood lover, but this soup has made me a convert. My husband is happiest out on the ocean, and our summers are planned around the opening of crabbing season. This is his recipe and creation.

- 5 T. butter, divided
- ½ cup minced onion
- ½ cup diced carrots
- ½ cup cooking sherry or wine
- 3 cloves garlic, minced (about a tablespoon)
- ¼ cup flour
- 2 to 3 cups chicken broth
- 1 cup heavy cream
- 1 to 2 cups cooked crab meat
- 1 T. lemon juice
- 1 tsp. Worcestershire sauce
- Salt and pepper to taste
- Dash of sriracha (optional)

In a large stock pot or Dutch oven, melt 1 tablespoon of the butter over medium heat and add in onion, carrots, sherry, and garlic. Sauté 3 to 4 minutes, until vegetables are turning soft. Dump this onto a plate or small bowl and return pot to the heat.

Melt remaining butter over medium heat. Stir in flour until it creates a thick paste. Slowly whisk in chicken broth and allow to simmer until thick, about 3 to 4 minutes, stirring constantly.

Dump in precooked onion, carrots, and garlic. Allow to simmer for 15 to 20 minutes. Use an immersion blender to puree the vegetables into the roux.

Stir in the cream, crab meat, lemon juice, Worcestershire sauce, salt, and pepper. Cook for another 5 minutes, until everything is heated through. If you're like my husband and like some heat, add a dash or two of sriracha to your bowl only, just to be nice to those of us who don't have stomachs or taste buds made of iron.

Yield: 6 servings

SPAGHETTI AND MEATBALLS

A homemade marinara sauce is something of beauty, mainly due to its simplicity, giving a true delight to the taste buds. This is an easy way to stretch a few ingredients into a full meal if needed.

I use a quart of home canned stewed tomatoes or tomato sauce. If you're using dried herbs instead of fresh, decrease the amounts of basil or oregano to teaspoons.

Spaghetti Sauce:

- ¼ cup olive oil
- ½ cup minced onion
- 3 cloves garlic, minced
- 4 cups stewed or canned tomatoes or tomato sauce
- ¼ to ½ tsp. salt
- ¼ tsp. ground black pepper
- 2 to 3 T. finely chopped fresh basil or oregano

In a saucepan over medium heat, heat the olive oil and sauté the onion and garlic until tender. Add the tomatoes, salt, and pepper. Either smash tomatoes with a potato masher or use an immersion blender. The potato masher gives a chunkier sauce, whereas the immersion blender gives a smoother texture. Stir in herbs and simmer on low for 30 minutes to an hour, until sauce has thickened.

Yield: 2 to 3 cups

MEATBALLS

The beauty of meatballs is they are so incredibly versatile. Really, any ground meat will make a meatball—you can use beef, sausage, turkey, ground venison, or a mixture.

One of the bases of meatballs besides the meat is breadcrumbs. Of course, the store shelves have those little cylinder cardboard cans or boxes of breadcrumbs, but they come at a pretty penny when you can easily make them at home yourself. See the next recipe for my method.

- 1 egg, beaten
- ¼ cup water or milk
- 1 cup breadcrumbs (see page 61)
- ¼ cup minced onion
- 3 cloves garlic, minced
- ½ tsp. dried oregano (optional)
- ½ tsp. dried sage (optional)
- ½ tsp. dried basil (optional)
- ½ tsp. salt
- Dash of ground black pepper
- 1 lb. hamburger

Preheat oven to 375°. In a large mixing bowl, beat the egg with a fork until foamy and then incorporate the water or milk. Add the breadcrumbs, onion, garlic, herbs if using, and salt and pepper and stir until thoroughly mixed. Last, stir in the hamburger until everything is combined.

With a tablespoon, scoop up a heaping spoonful and roll into a ball; repeat until all of the mixture is made into meatballs. Place them in a 9 × 13-inch baking dish. Bake for 25 minutes.

Remove meatballs from oven. Add to pot of spaghetti sauce and serve.

Variation: Instead of serving these meatballs with spaghetti, spoon or brush on barbecue sauce or your favorite spicy jelly or jam. Return to oven for 3 to 5 minutes (be careful to watch so your glaze doesn't burn). Remove from oven and serve.

Yield: approximately 25 meatballs

Double or triple the recipe to have premade meatballs on hand in the freezer. Form meatballs and place on a baking sheet and freeze until firm. Then transfer meatballs to a freezer bag or container. Thaw overnight in fridge and bake as if fresh. To use frozen, place in sauce or soup frozen and allow to simmer in sauce with the lid on for 20 minutes, or until cooked through.

BREADCRUMBS

Women in an old-fashioned kitchen and home used up every bit of what they had. They didn't run to the store for this and that. Instead, they figured out how to use everything in their home and off their land without letting food go to waste.

One of those things is something the average American doesn't think twice about tossing out: the heels of the bread loaf. But now that I'm about to share how easy it is to make breadcrumbs, you'll be like a pioneer cook of old and will never toss those again because you'll be turning them into something fabulous.

The best thing about homemade breadcrumbs is the flavor. They add much more depth to the recipe than store-bought ones. Think of mixing together sourdough, whole wheat for nuttiness, French bread, regular white, and any of your other favorites.

There are two ways to dry your bread—because we need it really dry in order to make the crumbs. But remember, we don't want stale, as in really old bread, as that flavor does transfer into the crumbs.

The first is as old-fashioned as it gets: leave the bread out on the counter unsealed (you could lay a tea towel or breathable towel over it) for a couple of days. The second option is to break up the bread into small chunks and put them on a rimmed baking sheet. Bake in a 300° oven for 15 minutes, flipping the pieces over halfway through, until they're dried out. Remove from the oven and allow them to cool.

TRADITIONAL LIVING TIP

Many foods were prepared with the thought of how they could be turned into another meal. Served fresh, bread is a great addition to supper, but then you're able to take the ends of the loaf and create breadcrumbs or bread pudding that takes the food into a second meal.

Once you have your dry bread, you'll need either a blender or a food processor. I prefer my food processor for this one. Blend the bread until it forms into crumbs. The longer you blend it, the finer the crumbs. You can also add dried herbs to make savory breadcrumbs.

Use immediately in your recipe of choice and store remaining breadcrumbs in the freezer for future use. I pour mine into a quart-size Mason jar for freezer storage. This allows me to know at a glance exactly how many cups I have left for a recipe.

BARBECUE SAUCE

If you don't want to use a ketchup base for this sauce, you can use tomato paste and dilute it with water, or boil down stewed tomatoes and add a splash of vinegar and mustard.

2 cups ketchup
1 cup brown sugar
½ cup finely minced onion
5 cloves garlic, minced
¼ cup apple cider vinegar
3 T. Worcestershire sauce
½ tsp. ground black pepper

Combine all ingredients in a saucepan and bring to a boil. Stir and reduce to a simmer. Allow to simmer for an hour, until sauce has thickened and turned a pretty dark red. Use immediately, or store in the fridge or freezer.

Variations:

- Want a little heat? Add ¼ teaspoon of red pepper flakes or cayenne pepper.
- Add a fruit flavor. For glazes on meat, try a cup of your favorite jam or jelly in place of the brown sugar. Grape, apple, peach, and plum are all favorites at our house. Cut back the ketchup to one cup and reduce the cooking time to about 20 minutes.

MEATBALL MINESTRONE SOUP

I don't know about you, but I love a good mix-and-match recipe for whatever ingredients or fresh vegetables I have on hand. This soup can taste different all year long simply by swapping out the vegetables and types of beans you have growing or on hand. That is a win! While I love it with meatballs, you can also omit the meat, as the beans are quite filling on their own.

- 2 T. extra virgin olive oil
- 1 cup diced yellow onion
- 1 cup chopped carrots
- 1 cup chopped celery
- 1 cup chopped zucchini
- 4 garlic cloves, minced
- 1 T. Italian seasoning
- 1 tsp. salt
- ½ tsp. fresh ground pepper
- 4 cups broth (chicken, beef, or vegetable)
- 1 pint (14.5 to 16 oz.) canned tomatoes (don't drain)
- 1 pint jar (or 15.5 oz. can) green beans or 1½ cups fresh
- 2 (15.5 oz.) cans kidney beans, drained and rinsed or 3 cups cooked beans
- 1⅓ cups uncooked rice or 7 oz. uncooked pasta
- 24 meatballs (frozen or fresh; see recipe page 60)
- 3 cups fresh spinach, chopped
- Grated Parmesan

In a large stock pot or Dutch oven, heat the olive oil over medium heat. Sauté the onion, carrots, celery, and zucchini for 5 minutes, until they start to soften and release their juices, stirring occasionally.

Add the garlic, Italian seasoning, salt, and pepper and sauté for another 2 minutes.

Add the broth, tomatoes, green beans, and kidney beans and bring to a boil.

Add uncooked rice or pasta, reduce to a simmer, cover, and cook for 25 minutes (or until rice or pasta is done).

Add meatballs as directed below.

Add fresh spinach and cook for an additional 5 minutes, until wilted.

Serve with freshly grated Parmesan.

Variations:

- *Frozen meatballs:* Do not thaw; just add in with rice or pasta.
- *Fresh meatballs:* Place meatballs in a single layer into hot oil and brown for 3 to 4 minutes. Use a slotted spoon to remove and brown the other half of the meatballs; remove all meatballs to another dish. You may have to add another dash of olive oil to sauté the vegetables. Add in with spinach.
- *Vegetables:* You can mix and match any vegetables you have on hand. Swap out mushrooms or cubed winter squash for the zucchini. Use any variety of dried beans you have on hand such as pinto, great northern, butter, or lima. Substitute kale or stinging nettle for spinach.

BLACK BEAN SOUP

As a teenager, I worked as a barista at our local coffee and deli shop. We served a soup of the day and this was my favorite. It was one I was determined to create at home. This soup is delicious for lunch or dinner and can be served as is or with tortilla chips, on baked potatoes, or over lettuce for a mock taco salad. You could use any bean you like, but I've always used black beans.

- 1 T. olive oil
- 1 cup diced onion
- 4 cloves minced garlic
- 3 (15.5 oz.) cans black beans, undrained *or* 4½ cups cooked black beans + reserve cooking liquid
- 1½ cups chicken or beef broth
- 1 pint (2 cups) thick and chunky salsa
- 2 T. lime juice
- 1 T. ground cumin
- Salt and pepper to taste
- ½ tsp. crushed red pepper (optional)
- ½ cup plain yogurt or sour cream

Heat oil in a large stock pot or Dutch oven over medium heat. Sauté onion and garlic for 2 minutes.

Blend beans with liquid and broth until smooth in a food processor or high-powered blender (add more broth or bean liquid if needed to produce desired texture; it should be thick but not as thick as a puree).

Add bean mixture, salsa, lime juice, cumin, salt, pepper, and crushed red pepper if using. Bring to a boil, then reduce heat on low and cook with lid on for 25 to 30 minutes. Stir occasionally.

Serve with a dollop of yogurt or sour cream on top.

CREAM OF ASPARAGUS SOUP

There is nothing as lovely in early spring as cream of asparagus soup. Rather than toss the ends from the asparagus when making other dishes, I frequently save those that aren't too woody and use all end pieces in this soup. Whether using ends or whole stalks, this soup turns out delicious.

- 2 T. butter or olive oil
- ½ cup diced onion
- 4 cloves garlic, minced
- 2 lbs. asparagus, cut into 1-inch pieces
- Kosher salt
- Freshly ground black pepper
- 4 cups chicken broth
- ½ cup heavy cream
- 1 cup grated white cheddar

In a heavy pot or Dutch oven over medium heat, melt butter or olive oil and add onion, cooking for 5 minutes. Add garlic and sauté 1 to 2 minutes. Add asparagus, season with salt and pepper, and stir in broth. Bring to a simmer and cook covered until asparagus is very tender, approximately 15 to 20 minutes.

Use an immersion or regular blender and puree soup. For regular blenders, pause a few times and remove the lid to avoid overheating the soup. When finished, return the soup to the pot on low heat. Add the cream and cheese; cook until cheese is fully melted and incorporated. Serve and enjoy!

CHICKEN NOODLE SOUP

When we think of food as medicine, I can't think of any other recipe more associated as a remedy to take if you have a cold or are feeling under the weather than chicken soup. Especially this version, which features bone broth and the addition of herbs, making this a feel-good and taste-good meal. I prefer to roast a chicken on Sunday and then make this with the leftovers during the week. All cuts taste delicious, though my husband prefers thigh meat, as he likes the flavor depth the darker meat provides.

- 1 T. butter
- 3 to 4 celery ribs, diced
- 1 cup diced onion
- 1½ cups chopped carrot (or 1 pint canned carrots)
- Salt and pepper to taste
- 4 cloves garlic, diced
- 8 cups (2 quarts) chicken broth
- 3 cups cooked, chopped chicken
- ½ tsp. dried sage
- ½ tsp. dried oregano
- 4 to 5 cups dried egg noodles or 1 batch homemade egg noodles (page 68)

In a large stock pot or Dutch oven, melt butter over medium heat. Sauté celery, onion, carrots, salt, and pepper for 5 minutes. Add garlic and cook for 1 minute.

Add broth and bring to a simmer.

Add chicken, herbs, and noodles. Simmer with lid on for 8 minutes if using homemade fresh egg noodles. If using dried noodles, cook to time indicated on package.

Variations:

- Instead of noodles, substitute 1 cup uncooked rice; increase simmer time to 18 minutes.
- Use 1 T. fresh herbs in place of dried.
- Substitute rosemary, thyme, and/or basil.
- Substitute turkey for chicken.

HOMEMADE EGG NOODLES

- 2 cups flour (all-purpose, bread, semolina, or durum wheat)
- 2 to 3 room temperature eggs (start with two and add the third if needed)

There is truly little else as simple to make as pasta. It's eggs and flour (sometimes a wee bit of water), and if you've never had fresh pasta before, oh my friend, you're going to love it! Homemade pasta is a great way to use an overabundance of eggs when your chickens are laying like crazy in the spring and early summer months or you have extra from the store. You can make a double and triple batch to dry or freeze to preserve the noodles for use in the fall and winter months. You'll notice I don't use any oil or salt in the dough. Oil can affect the way the dough rolls out, and because we're not using any additional liquid, the salt may not get dissolved or evenly distributed (that's why we salt the cooking water, not the dough).

Egg noodles have a general ratio of 1 cup flour to 1 egg, so you can make up as much or little as you want. For our family of four I prefer to use the listed ratio/recipe size.

Place the flour in a shallow bowl or large dinner plate, creating a well in the center.

Break two eggs into the center of the well. Use a fork to lightly beat eggs, and add in a little bit of flour to the eggs. Continue pulling in the flour into the egg mixture until the dough begins to form.

Once a dough forms and holds together into a ball, remove dough ball from plate/bowl and begin to knead on the countertop. If dough sticks, sprinkle some flour; if it's too dry, sprinkle a small amount of water on it. I do half a tablespoonful or so at a time. Knead the dough until it's smooth, about 8 minutes.

Cover dough with plastic wrap, beeswax wrap, or a damp cloth, and allow it to rest for 20 to 30 minutes (don't let it dry out or leave it uncovered).

Divide the dough into quarters; leave the remaining dough you're not rolling out covered up. Either using a rolling pin or your pasta roller, begin to roll dough out. If it sticks to the machine or the roller, sprinkle lightly with flour. (If dough shrinks back when rolling by hand, let rest for another 10 minutes.)

When dough has reached desired thinness (it will puff up slightly when cooking), cut into preferred noodle size and shape.

Allow pasta to hang for 10 to 20 minutes before cooking fresh. You can use a drying rack or place a yard stick over the back of two chairs (get creative!).

Repeat this process with remaining dough, working with one-fourth of the dough at a time.

To cook, bring water to a boil and toss in a bit of salt. Add noodles; stir lightly to prevent sticking. Allow to simmer for 6 to 8 minutes. (I prefer 8 minutes myself, but I like a noodle that's more cooked than some, so test it at 5 to 6 minutes the first time to see where you like it.) If using a pasta rolling machine, I prefer to roll my dough about 5 to 6 times starting from the largest number on the machine and then working down to desired thinness. Remember, if dough feels like it's sticking, lightly flour your sheet of pasta before rolling out and cutting.

Serve warm with your favorite sauce or in your favorite soup, pasta salad, or casserole.

Yield: 4 to 5 servings

Fresh Pasta Storage Options

Ideally, you'll cook up some of that pasta fresh right after making it. Because it's just that good! But if you have company coming or want fresh pasta in a few days and know you won't have time to make it, you have a few options for storing the pasta without drying it. If you want to have fresh pasta for several days, allow it to dry for about 10 minutes on the drying rack, then lightly flour a glass dish. Nestle the pasta in bird nests, about one-fourth of the pasta in one nest (just like we sectioned it off when rolling out). I stack my nests on top of each other with a light dusting of flour between them. Seal tight and store in the fridge for up to 3 days. Do the same bird nests on a lined cookie sheet and flash freeze. Once frozen, take nests of pasta and place in sealed container and store in the freezer. Cook from frozen state, increasing cooking time by about 2 minutes.

CHICKEN DUMPLINGS

There is nothing more comforting than a big bowl of homemade chicken dumplings. Not only is this old-timey dish a comfort food, but it's actually packed with nourishing things to feed your body during those cold winter months.

One of the beautiful things about cooking from scratch is the ability to adapt a recipe to what you happen to have on hand and the time you have available. If you have an afternoon at home and a whole chicken, then you'll want to take this route. But hey, we don't always have the luxury of a few hours, so I've included variations at the end of the recipe when you need to whip this up quick style, because we should still be able to create wonderful home-cooked meals when we're pressed for time.

If you don't have a whole chicken for this dish, you can also use cuts of chicken with the bone in, about 4 pounds' worth. The garlic isn't traditional in this dish, but it adds wonderful flavor. The herbs are also optional, and you can use any combination you'd like—all of them, if you're feeling daring!

Chicken Mixture:

- 1 whole chicken (or small turkey)
- Salt and pepper
- 1 large onion, diced
- 2 celery ribs, diced
- 4 cloves garlic, minced (optional)
- 4 medium carrots, diced
- 1 bay leaf (optional)
- ¼ cup fresh thyme (optional)
- 4 fresh sage leaves (optional)
- ¼ cup fresh chopped rosemary (optional)
- ½ cup cream (optional)

Dumplings:

- 1 cup flour
- 2 tsp. baking powder
- ½ tsp. salt
- 2 T. melted butter or coconut oil
- ½ cup buttermilk (regular milk works if needed)

Place the whole chicken or turkey seasoned with salt and pepper in a large cast-iron Dutch oven (or a large stock pot if that's what you have) and fill it with water until the water is about three-fourths of the way up the chicken. Bring to a boil and allow to gently simmer with the lid on for about 1 hour.

After an hour, add the vegetables and herbs and cook for another 30 minutes, or until all vegetables are tender. After vegetables are done, using tongs or a big slotted spoon, remove chicken from the pot onto a big plate or platter to cool. Once cool enough to handle, shred chicken and return to pot. Keep remaining carcass to make a batch of homemade bone broth (I toss mine in the freezer if I'm not going to make broth right away).

To make this really rich and decadent, add the cream.

For the dumplings—my absolute favorite part—measure and mix together the dry ingredients. Pour in the melted butter and buttermilk or milk and mix until just combined. Don't overmix—dough will be a bit wet and sticky. Drop by the tablespoonful (I just use my mixing spoon) into the stock. Keep chicken stock at a simmer and cook for 10 minutes with the lid on; remove the lid and simmer for 10 minutes more.

For a more traditional dumpling, flour a countertop and roll the dough out to ¼-inch thick. Using a pizza cutter or sharp knife, cut the dough into 1-inch strips and then into 2-inch-long pieces. Drop into chicken stock that is just at a simmer and cook for 10 minutes with the lid on, and then 10 minutes more with the lid off.

Variations:

- *30-Minute Chicken and Dumplings:* Need to make this fast? Use 4 cups (1 quart) of chicken broth, 2 to 3 cups of shredded or diced cooked chicken, and 2 tablespoons butter. Dice fresh vegetables very small, or use frozen or canned vegetables (drained) instead to speed up cooking time. Follow instructions for dumplings.
- *Chicken and Biscuit Bake:* Don't like dumplings? (I'll pretend I didn't know that about you; my mother is the same way.) You can do an oven variation and top this with biscuits. You'll need to prepare the mixture in a cast-iron Dutch oven so you can transfer it to the oven, or you can pour the mixture into a 9 × 13-inch baking pan, but be very careful as it's hot! Using the biscuit recipe on page 16, place biscuits on the surface of the chicken soup. Place in a preheated 350° oven, uncovered, and bake for 30 minutes or until biscuits are golden on top.

SHEPHERD'S PIE

Whenever my mother made Shepherd's Pie, I was ready for seconds before I'd even taken the first bite. After we phased out store-bought condensed soups, I had to come up with a version that was still delicious and fit the bill for my beloved casserole.

This is my childhood favorite from the 1980 *Better Homes and Gardens All-Time Favorite Hamburger Recipes* . . . revamped real-food style.

- 1 lb. hamburger
- ½ cup diced onion
- 3 cloves garlic, minced
- 1 jar (16 oz.) tomato sauce or 2 cups home-canned tomato sauce
- 16 oz. canned green beans or canned corn, drained
- ¾ tsp. sea salt
- Dash of fresh ground pepper
- 1 beaten egg
- 2 to 3 cups mashed potatoes
- ½ to ¾ cup shredded cheddar cheese

Preheat oven to 350°. In a large skillet, brown the hamburger, onion, and garlic. Drain off fat. Place hamburger mixture in a 1½-quart casserole dish. Stir in tomato sauce, green beans or corn, salt, and pepper.

Beat an egg and blend in with the mashed potatoes. If needed, add a small amount of milk to create creamy potatoes, but not runny.

Spread, or drop by the spoonful, the mashed potatoes on top of the meat mixture. Sprinkle cheese on top. Bake for 25 to 30 minutes, until cheese is melted and everything is hot.

Yield: 4 to 6 servings

BERRY DUMPLINGS

I have yet to find the berry that isn't delicious in this dish. Our two favorites are blueberry and blackberry, but experiment with whatever combination of fruits you have on hand.

Berry Mixture:

4 cups fresh or frozen berries

1⅔ cups water

¾ cup sugar

½ tsp. cinnamon

2 tsp. lemon extract or 1 tsp. bottled lemon juice

Dough:

1 cup flour

1½ tsp. baking powder

1 T. sugar

⅛ tsp. salt

½ cup softened butter or coconut oil

¼ cup milk

Place berries, water, sugar, cinnamon, and lemon extract or juice in a large pot and stir until sugar is dissolved. Bring to a boil over medium-high heat, stirring often.

Mix together all the dry ingredients for the dough, and then cut in the softened butter or coconut oil with a pastry cutter. Add in the milk until just combined into a slightly wet dough.

Drop the dough by the spoonful onto the top of the boiling berries, until most of the surface of the berries is covered. Cover the pot with a tight-fighting lid, turn the heat down to medium-low, and allow to simmer with the lid on for a full 20 minutes (no peeking). After 20 minutes, remove the lid and serve.

While this would be wonderful with whipped cream or vanilla ice cream, we usually just eat ours as-is. If you happen to have any leftovers, simply heat it back up before serving again. There's just something about warm berries that's the best.

OLD-FASHIONED OATMEAL

- 1 cup water
- ½ cup rolled or steel-cut oats
- Pinch of salt
- 2 T. butter
- 2 tsp. brown sugar
- Dash of cream or milk
- ½ banana, sliced, or ¼ cup berries (optional)
- ¼ tsp. ground cinnamon or nutmeg (optional)

Having been raised through the end of the Great Depression, my father knows a thing or two about lean times. I love hearing his stories and the way it has shaped his thinking and practices. Tough times give us a new appreciation for the simple things around us. Hard times create a thankfulness for what we have, instead of a pining for what we don't.

My father likes his food like he likes his life—simple. One thing I've always been a bit astounded by is his breakfast. Every morning since I can remember and up until today, he has a bowl of oatmeal for breakfast.

If my mom fixes pancakes, waffles, biscuits and gravy, eggs, and bacon, it doesn't matter—he still has a small bowl of oatmeal with it. If she doesn't fix anything else, he still makes his pot of oatmeal. And he's quite content and happy with just his pot of oatmeal. I prefer a little more variety in my breakfast. While I'd like to think I'd be happy with oatmeal every morning, I'd probably complain a bit after the first week.

Bring water to a boil in a small saucepan. Stir in oats and a pinch of salt. Place a lid on the saucepan, reduce the heat to low, and allow to cook for 7 to 8 minutes (10 to 20 minutes for steel-cut oats). Remove lid and take off heat.

Stir in butter, brown sugar, and a dash of cream or milk until combined. Add fruit and cinnamon or nutmeg if desired.

Yield: 1 to 2 servings

TRADITIONAL LIVING TIP

Oatmeal was a filling and frugal way to fill bellies. It can be cooked all by its lonesome for breakfast, used in pancakes, muffins, or bread, and can also be ground into flour. Steel-cut oats are a chewier and heartier, less processed option. I only use organic oats to avoid possible glyphosate contamination, known to be found on oat products.

HOW TO COOK OUTDOORS WITH A DUTCH OVEN

Many older recipes will take advantage of simmering and Dutch ovens instead of using a regular oven. The pioneers could still prepare many of their favorite dishes using their open campfires, coals, and Dutch ovens, even though they weren't in their regular kitchens with a wood stove and oven. When the power goes out today, there is nothing as lovely as being equipped with skillet or stovetop recipes, and, of course, a wood stove or an outdoor burner. This is also true if your oven goes out or is otherwise occupied with another dish.

One of our favorite family activities when we're camping is to have a Saturday night Dutch oven cook-off potluck. So, if you're walking through a campground and see 4 or 5 Dutch ovens lined up, you'll know it's us. We go cooking-show style and judge which dish is the best for the night, which means we get to eat everyone else's food—and when there's a competition involved, everyone brings their best recipes. Score!

When cooking on an open fire, keep a few things in mind. First, you're not actually cooking over the flames. Flames give off very uneven heat. You're after the coals.

You may use wood coals, as this would be traditional, but it's easier to use charcoal, especially when you're first learning. Make sure you use charcoal that has not been treated with lighter fluid. Even though your food is enclosed inside the cast-iron Dutch oven, you still don't want those fumes if you can help it.

You'll want to get a spider Dutch oven if you plan on doing outdoor cooking. A spider Dutch oven has three legs on it. This helps you to set your pot over the coals and it won't tip as easily. If you happen to have a Dutch oven without the legs, you can still use it outdoors by finding three rocks and creating a tripod for it to sit on.

Make sure you pick a fire pit, gravel surface, or sandy area where your hot coals won't be a fire hazard, and avoid tall, dry grass or brush in your area.

When cooking outdoors, you need to plan ahead in order to preheat your oven. It's not like turning on a knob or pushing a button inside the house. You need to light your coals about 15 to 20 minutes before you plan on using them to cook with. You can buy a metal chimney with a handle on it that you pour coals into. Set the filled chimney on top of a paper bag or other tinder material. Light the tinder material from underneath—the fire will burn up into the chimney and ignite the coals.

When the coals begin to turn gray, you're ready to start cooking. Put a small layer of coals down on the ground to heat and cook the bottom of your food. The Dutch oven will sit on top of these. You'll actually put the majority of the coals on top of the oven. A Dutch oven meant for outdoor cooking has a flat top with a lip on the rim to keep the coals from rolling off. Generally, put a third of your coals underneath the oven and two-thirds on the lid. You'll want to place the coals around the outer edge of the lid for best heat distribution.

Place your Dutch oven, with the food inside and the lid on, on top of the hot coals. It will take 15 to 20 minutes for the Dutch oven to fully heat. If it's really cold outside or there's a lot of wind, it will take longer and often require more coals. Placing your Dutch oven inside a campfire ring will help block the wind.

To avoid any hot spots over the coals, you'll want to rotate your Dutch oven lid counterclockwise a quarter turn and the Dutch oven pot clockwise a quarter turn every 30 minutes or so. But if you get involved in camping fun and forget to turn the lid and pot, it still turns out fine. There's a lot of forgiveness in this cooking technique!

If you're cooking a dish that requires more than an hour of cooking time, you'll need to start a second batch of coals and add new ones for heat. You'll see the old coals burn down to ash.

Remember, it's easier to add more heat than it is to cool down, especially when we're talking cast iron, which is more efficient at retaining heat than regular metal pots and pans. Start with a smaller number of coals and add more if necessary to reach the desired temperature.

To determine how many coals you need, the general rule is to take the diameter of your Dutch oven and double it. We never figure it out by math anymore or look up the chart, but you may find this handy until you've gained more experience. I recommend using about 5 more coals than you think you'll need so you have extra you can add, if need be, that are already heated.

Below is a chart to use for the size of Dutch oven and the desired temperature range. These are approximate because cooking outdoors is an adventure, and temperatures fluctuate. If it's cold and windy, you'll need more coals to reach the same temperature. If it's in the middle of August on a scorching afternoon, you'll probably need fewer. Don't worry, there's room for experimentation. If your food isn't cooking fast enough, add more coals. Cooking too fast, pull off some of the coals. You've got this.

Number of Coals per Dutch Oven Size

	325°	350°	375°	400°	425°	450°
TOTAL NUMBER OF COALS FOR 8-INCH OVEN	15	16	17	18	19	20
COALS ON TOP/BOTTOM FOR 8-INCH OVEN	10/5	11/5	11/6	12/6	13/6	14/6
TOTAL NUMBER OF COALS FOR 10-INCH OVEN	19	21	23	25	27	29
COALS ON TOP/BOTTOM FOR 10-INCH OVEN	13/6	14/7	16/7	17/8	18/9	19/10
TOTAL NUMBER OF COALS FOR 12-INCH OVEN	23	25	27	29	31	33
COALS ON TOP/BOTTOM FOR 12-INCH OVEN	16/7	17/8	18/9	19/10	21/10	22/11
TOTAL NUMBER OF COALS FOR 14-INCH OVEN	30	32	34	36	38	40
COALS ON TOP/BOTTOM FOR 14-INCH OVEN	20/10	21/11	22/12	24/12	25/13	26/14

The suggested coal amount and ratio above is more along the lines for baking and mimicking your oven at home. For simmering and stewing like a regular stovetop, you'll put almost all your coals on the bottom and just a few on the lid. For browning meat (tacos are a favorite outdoor food in the heat of summer with fresh garden veggies) or general frying, put all of your coals on the bottom to concentrate the heat.

DUTCH OVEN PIZZA

Want to bake pizza in a Dutch oven? Of course—especially on those hot summer nights when you don't want to turn on the oven.

Start your coals before you begin assembling your toppings and rolling out your dough (see recipes on pages 43 to 45) so they have time to get hot and sizzling (and your kitchen is staying nice and chill). I recommend using a 10-inch oven if you have it for this at the 425° mark, but the smaller 8-inch or larger 12-inch ovens will work too.

I bake deep-dish pizzas in the house in my 9-inch cast-iron skillet and don't use parchment paper, but I recommend lining your Dutch oven with it for cooking pizza outdoors. Parchment makes it easier to pull the pizza up and cut it when done.

Roll out the dough and transfer it to the Dutch oven, pushing it down in the center and letting the dough come up the sides to create a good deep bed for all the fixings. Top with your favorite sauce and toppings. Put on the lid.

Place coals (take into account your outside temperature and weather and adjust accordingly) on the ground or in your designated cooking area. Put your Dutch oven on top of the coals and place the remaining coals on the top of the lid.

Check the pizza after 20 to 25 minutes (remember, it takes about 15 minutes for it to preheat). If the bottom seems too hot (burning crust on the bottom), remove some of the bottom coals. If the cheese isn't beginning to melt, add more coals to the top and continue baking. Check in another 10 minutes or so. When cheese is melted and bubbly, remove the lid and use your pot lifter or a good set of potholders to remove the Dutch oven from the coals. Remember, the entire oven will be hot. Place in a safe area, allow to cool, and enjoy your pizza!

CULTURE

June sun bathed the pasture and yard surrounding our homestead. Plants stretched toward the light, leaves unfurling to the warmth, and roots burying deep in the rich soil. Insects buzzed about the blossoms.

My gaze fell on the weeds competing with the vegetables. Inside, a load of laundry waited to be hung on the line and another to be folded. Breakfast dishes needed to be washed and supper needed to be prepped. Two blog posts and a magazine article were due.

Meanwhile, a cacophony of squawking and flapping of white feathers reminded me that the meat chickens needed to be fed, watered, and moved to fresh grass before I left for work. I needed to check the pigs' and cattle's water, too, and I couldn't ignore the blocks of weeds and buttercups encroaching on the flower beds. The raspberries would need to be picked this weekend.

Exhaustion rolled over me, like the hot air from the oven on baking day. The urge to lie down in the middle of the patio and sleep almost won. How could I be this tired when I'd just gotten out of bed?

I'm normally energized by the new crops and promise of harvest. But this season the new growth mocked me. Weariness snaked through every fiber of my body, and I forced myself to gather the kids up and drop them off at my mom's before heading off to work. Over my lunch break I sat in my car at the local library, hoping to make a dent in my writing projects during the 30 minutes I had to myself.

A friend pulled up and I rolled down the window. After exchanging greetings, she paused and looked at me. "Are you okay? You look really tired."

Tears threatened. That isn't something a woman normally likes to hear, but relief welled up in me. "I *am* tired," I said. "I've been tired for months." My sleep and diet were as they should be, but this tiredness was different. It was an exhaustion without reason. It settled deep in my bones and seemed to mount every day. Growing like the weeds in my garden.

By the grace of God and sheer force of will, I waded through the day. That weekend I got to connect with a dear friend I hadn't seen in more than six months. Upon seeing me, she said, "What happened to your hair?"

I fingered the edges of my hair. It had once been almost waist-length, but now the wispy strands barely brushed the tops of my shoulders. "It's really thin now, isn't it?"

Sometimes God uses other people to help us realize we need to take a new direction. At my friend's urging, I made an appointment to see the doctor. Through lab work, we discovered my thyroid wasn't functioning normally.

I was tired due to the low function of my thyroid and adrenal glands, but there were other factors at play. If you've ever thought, *If one more thing is added to my plate, I'll break*, or, *I can't go on like this*, something has to give, my friend.

We need to take a closer look at the culture we're living in. Today's society is very different from the culture of even our mothers' time, let alone our grandparents' and great-grandparents'. With the advent of the internet and social media, we have more information being thrown at us than ever before—than ever before in the history of mankind. Of course, this has huge benefits (how often have you needed to google something and found the information in seconds?), but there are other results as well. One of them is the pressure to keep up with everything we see other people doing. The picture-perfect meals, the beautifully designed homes, the carefully put together outfits, the latest achievements of so-and-so. Many times this leaves us feeling like we're not measuring up. We feel like we're lacking.

With social media and smartphones, we also have the addition of decision fatigue. When you hear a ping on your phone to read a post or an email—even if you don't realize it (even if you don't pick up your phone)—your brain is still making the unconscious decision whether you're going to pick up the phone.

Interestingly enough, our brains respond the same way to clutter in our homes. Even though we don't realize it, when things are out of place, our brain is cataloging what that item is, if it belongs there, and if it should be moved or not, all without our realizing it.

Add this up, and our brains are making more decisions today than ever before. It's no wonder we're more anxious and tired.

So what do we do? We put more on our to-do list and demand more of ourselves, never realizing we're setting ourselves up for failure.

Case in point: I have one day off during the workweek. On this day, the kids are at school and my husband is at work. This is the day I plan to deep-clean the house, film videos or shoot photos for my website, complete large chunks of writing, and cook a big enough meal that we'll have leftovers for the next night. I bake snacks and fix lunches I wasn't able to do over the weekend, plus—depending on the season—grow, harvest, and preserve our own food.

On one particular day, I started out with a long to-do list. It included laundry, cooking supper, baking bread for the week, picking berries and canning a batch of jam (along with having all the dishes and kitchen cleaned afterward), writing an article and editing photos for a recipe tutorial, and cleaning both bathrooms. Did I mention I also have Tuesday night Bible study on this day?

I don't need to tell you I didn't manage all of that. I lamented to my mom that I hadn't accomplished everything I wanted to that day. She asked what items I had on my list I hadn't been able to get to. After reading it off, she said, "No one could get all of that done in a day."

We live in a culture that tells us to hurry up and do more. But that is not what God intended for us. Part of my exhaustion was due to my thyroid issue, yes, but I was expecting more of myself than was humanly possible. I needed to give myself a break.

The more frazzled and exhausted we feel, the less time we have for listening to the still, small voice of the Lord, and the quicker we are to snap at our loved ones. We create a culture of stress and defeat, of impatience and shortness—manifested not only in our minds, but in our attitudes and responses toward those we love. When I'm running around on empty and in a hurry, I'm not usually fond of anything that upsets the already precarious balance I'm foolishly trying to carry.

To *culture* something means to *maintain it in conditions suitable for growth*. In order to grow and maintain good health, we need adequate sleep, balanced nutrition, interaction with the world around us, and love. But that doesn't account for the health and well-being of our mind and soul. We're often so entrenched in our daily lives, with more on our to-do lists than there are hours in the day, that we're left feeling frazzled and unsettled. We forget to culture our mind, attitudes, and soul for growth. We've got to make the decision to cultivate a culture that maintains conditions suitable for growth.

Well, that sounds all fine and dandy, but how does one actually do it?

> *Do not conform to the pattern of this world, but be transformed by the renewing of your mind. Then you will be able to test and approve what God's will is—his good, pleasing and perfect will (Romans 12:2).*

We need to renew our minds from the things that cloud our vision of what is truly important. When we're bogged down with everything we need to get done in a day, we lose the ability to test and approve what God's will is for our life. The world will tell us to do more, to make sure we're measuring up to impossible standards, but God will tell us to rest in Him.

When I was in the midst of my exhaustion and helplessness, I actually wept when I read this verse one morning:

> *Come to me, all you who are weary and burdened, and I will give you rest. Take my yoke upon you and learn from me, for I am gentle and humble in heart, and you will find rest for your souls. For my yoke is easy and my burden is light (Matthew 11:28-30).*

I yearned for rest. Physically and mentally.

Jesus promised it to His children. And He never makes a promise He doesn't keep.

When I wake up now, no matter how I'm feeling, but especially if I'm feeling tired, I offer a simple prayer: "Lord, help me to get done what I need to today and nothing more. Let me seek You first, and give me the wisdom and strength to do what You would have me to do, and to be able to see what that is."

Not only does God answer the prayers of His children, but He grants each of us enough strength to get everything accomplished we need to in a day if we're truly doing His will.

Instead of carrying the heavy banner of *I can't do one more thing*, I can lift up the truth of God's Word. I can do what the Lord has set forth for me today in His strength, and so can you.

But when looking at what we're going to do for the day, we've got to do some pruning. We're getting out those shears and getting this tree into shape. Decide what things truly must be done for the day and prune off the rest.

I break down my priorities like this:

I know if I don't feed my body nourishing food that I make at home, my health is at risk due to the cellular damage to my esophagus and upper stomach from years of acid reflux. Not only is my health at risk, but so is my budget. There is a definite cost to sacrificing my time for other activities and not planning out my meals and preparing them at home from real food ingredients.

If I don't get our crops planted, harvested, and preserved, my grocery budget goes up. My family and my health need to come before the website, blog, and articles.

Next, I look at the items I need to get done in order to meet my obligations to readers, publishers, and other partners in regard to my writing and podcast. These need to come before any other online work or writing.

While your list might not include the writing and home business aspect, prioritizing things definitely helps me focus on what has to get done, instead of a long list of everything that overwhelms. Take the time to go over everything you're doing in a day and week. Pray over it and then get to work pruning.

The way people lived before we had supermarkets on every corner and drive-through convenience beckons to me like a lazy river on a hot August day. We make it a goal to practice as many old-fashioned or traditional ways of life as possible on our homestead. One of those traditional practices is making cultured foods.

Cultured foods have been around for thousands of years. It's only in more recent years that modern homes have lost this old-fashioned way of cooking and preparing foods.

What is a cultured food? Cultured foods go through some type of fermentation process, which allows the good and beneficial bacteria to grow and sustain life, while preserving the shelf life of the food and making it healthier for us.

Cultured foods include raw apple cider vinegar, milk and water kefir, yogurt, sour cream, buttermilk, cream cheese, sauerkraut, fermented pickled vegetables, and sourdough. Not all sour cream, buttermilk, and cream cheese still contain the live beneficial bacteria. If you're buying store bought, you'll need to look for live cultures on the labeling, and even then, they can still have additives.

You can't get much more homemade or old-fashioned than cultured foods. You'll even see accounts in the Bible of fermented foods!

Most of us today think of yeast as the dried grains or flakes found in the little packets or jars on store shelves. But yeast in that form is relatively new. Did you know that the shelf-stable yeast purchased in the store was first developed during World War II? How quickly we as a society forsake a time-honored tradition for something fast and easy! It's a shame, because fermented and cultured foods contain good bacteria that our bodies can be lacking. Many of us are lacking a proper balance of gut flora, and the consumption of good lactobacilli can help support intestinal health. Fermented foods also help break down the enzymes in food, making it easier for us to digest and allowing our bodies to absorb more of the nutrients from the food we eat.

Sourdough, often referred to as wild or natural yeast, is one of the oldest forms of baking there is. Many pioneers would take their jar or crock of sourdough with them on the long trek across the prairies or through the mountain passes to go north to Alaska during the gold rush years. In fact, some accounts tell of miners who would sleep with their sourdough to keep it from freezing. While I do love my sourdough, I'm certainly glad I don't have to take it to bed with me.

Sourdough's effectiveness depends on the combination of yeast and lactobacilli. The yeast feeds and creates carbon dioxide and ethanol. The lactobacilli feed on ethanol, and this creates lactic acid. The bubbles of the carbon dioxide create the pockets in the dough that cause it to rise, while the lactic acid keeps other unwanted organisms at bay and acts as a preservative. Pretty cool, huh?

This is also why when you're using your sourdough to bake products that need to rise, like bread, you need to do it in its active time, after it's recently been fed and is creating lots of bubbles. We'll go into more detail within specific recipes.

Grains and wheat contain phytic acid. It's thought by many that phytic acid prevents us from absorbing phosphorus and also binds to other minerals like calcium, zinc, iron, and magnesium. However, by soaking the flour when you make sourdough, the phytic acid level is lowered, allowing your body to better absorb the needed minerals in the food you're making. When we fast-track the production of our food, we miss critical steps that affect our health. Can you tell why I love sourdough?

You'll find many recipes for beginning a sourdough starter, but I didn't want to use any recipes that called for added sugar or store-bought yeast. I was determined to start my sourdough starter the way the pioneers did.

It's amazingly simple to do. All you need is a glass jar, water, and flour. Wild yeast lives in the air around us, and we're simply going to capture it for our sourdough. You can also purchase sourdough starters online. Each area has different yeasts that naturally grow and live there, so you'll see sourdough starters listed by names such as San Francisco or Alaskan Starter. One of the benefits of purchasing a starter is you know you're getting a live culture and you may pick the exact "flavor," so to speak. Either way you decide to go is just fine, but you'll find the instructions below for starting your own sourdough starter from scratch.

You can use any flour of your choice, but I believe you'll have the most luck with a whole wheat flour or rye. I grind my own flour at home and have used organic hard white wheat, hard red wheat, and spelt flour for my starter. If you don't grind your own, I'd recommend a local stone-ground whole wheat flour if possible; at the very least use an unbleached flour.

When you first begin your starter, it will require twice-daily feedings for the first few weeks (see optional feeding alternatives if twice a day seems overwhelming). After that it will depend on how much you're using your starter in regard to how often you feed it.

If you find you're not using it often, you can store it in the fridge and feed it once a week.

SOURDOUGH STARTER

4 T. (30 grams) flour
2 T. (30 grams) lukewarm water

If you read earlier versions of my sourdough starter recipe, you'll notice the amounts have changed slightly. I now use less flour and slightly less water. After having had thousands of students go through my sourdough course and testing, I found less flour with less water provided consistent results, and anytime we can use less flour, the better (aka cheaper). Rest assured, sourdough starters are quite resilient, and if you use slightly less or more flour/water, it really will be fine. After a decade and thousands of kitchens later, I've found this method to be the best.

You do not have to use a scale for successful sourdough or baking. For centuries people have baked and done sourdough without one; however, weighing ingredients does make things consistent, and many home bakers find the addition of weight extremely helpful.

I've found a four-cup capacity glass jar (aka a quart) works the best for housing my sourdough starter. I prefer to use a Fido jar that has the wire bail and clasp, without the rubber gasket, or a wide-mouth quart-size Mason jar with a plastic lid (these aren't airtight) or some cheesecloth or coffee filter with a metal band.

Note: At each feeding you'll be using 4 tablespoons of flour and 2 tablespoons water.

Day 1

To begin with, place 2 tablespoons lukewarm water and 4 tablespoons of flour in a clean glass jar. Stir until well combined. Close the lid or the jar without the rubber gasket, or place a double piece of cheesecloth or coffee filter over the top and secure into place with the metal band.

Place the jar in a warm area where you can keep an eye on it. When first activating your starter, you may find you want to keep it between 68° and 74°. Twelve hours later, check the starter for signs of any bubbles. Bubbles mean your starter is active, but you'll only see one or two at this point. If you don't see any bubbles, don't panic; just go ahead and add 2 tablespoons lukewarm water and 4 tablespoons of flour. Stir until combined, scraping the side of the jar. Cover and let rest.

Day 2

Morning: You should see some signs of activity in your starter—either little bubbles on the sides of the jar or on the top of the sourdough starter. Feed the starter. Remember to scrape the sides of the jar to incorporate all the starter when stirring.

Twelve hours later, feed the starter.

Day 3

Morning: Remove half of the starter from the jar and either put it in your compost pile or in the garbage (it will smell sour and attract fruit flies if you have any, so take care if it's the garbage inside the house). You don't want your starter to outgrow your jar, and it's not strong enough to use yet. Feed the starter.

Twelve hours later, feed the starter.

Days 4 through 7

Stir and feed your starter morning and evening or every 12 hours.

Continue to feed the starter in this pattern for a week, removing some when there isn't enough room in the jar for the starter to rise after feedings. By the end of the week, you should see lots of bubbles and the starter should be rising a few hours after it is fed.

If you don't see any bubbles after three days, you'll need to throw it out and start over.

It's best to store your starter where you'll see it to help you remember to feed it. I leave mine on the kitchen counter next to the sink.

Alternative Feeding Schedule

Think there's no way you can do the twice-daily feeding? Many people have had success with once-daily feedings with a larger quantity of flour and water. If feeding once a day, use ¼ cup warm water and ½ cup of flour.

You can try this method, but if you don't see much activity, you may want to switch back to the twice-a-day feeding schedule.

Troubleshooting

- If you see a clear or light brown liquid on top of your starter, pour it off the top and feed your starter. This is called hooch, and it's a sign your starter has run out of food and either needs to be fed more often or a larger amount.
- Your starter isn't rising very much. Try feeding it a little bit more at each feeding and make sure it's in a warm area if your home is cold.
- You forgot to feed your starter and there's a grayish layer of liquid on top. As long as there's not mold growing on it, drain off the liquid and scrape off the top layer of the sourdough starter. Feed it twice a day for a few days, and it should be right as rain.

Let's get ready to put that sourdough to use!

When the starter is a week old, you can begin baking items that don't require doubling as bread does. Pancakes, waffles, and tortillas are three of our favorite sourdough recipes.

The general rule of thumb is that your sourdough starter should be strong enough to bake bread between two and three weeks of life. However, I sometimes find that it takes about two months before my sourdough starter really has full power.

Two of the easiest recipes to start with are sourdough pancakes and waffles. Because I keep my sourdough starter on the thick side, you'll see we don't add any flour to the batter. Just remember to always leave ¼ cup of the sourdough starter in your container so you have enough to build your starter back up with.

SOURDOUGH WAFFLES

I like to make up a big batch of waffles and then freeze some of them for mornings when we're pushed for time. I place waffles on a cookie sheet in a single layer and flash freeze them for an hour. Transfer waffles to a freezer container. When ready to eat, place frozen waffle in a toaster to reheat.

Mix all of the ingredients together and pour onto a preheated waffle griddle. This is delightful with maple syrup or applesauce. Homemade sweetened whipped cream would also be nice, or maybe pumpkin or apple butter as well.

Yield: 8 to 10 full waffles (with 8 × 9-inch waffle maker)

- 2 cups sourdough starter
- 1 T. melted coconut oil, butter, or avocado oil
- ¼ cup yogurt, applesauce, or cooked pumpkin (this gives it a fun, seasonal variety as well)
- 3 T. brown sugar
- 2 eggs
- 1 tsp. baking soda
- ½ tsp. salt
- 1 tsp. vanilla
- ½ tsp. cinnamon

SOURDOUGH PANCAKES

This recipe was adapted from *Simply Sourdough: The Alaska Way*.

Mix all of the ingredients together.

Heat a cast-iron skillet on medium-low heat and pour batter into desired shape and size for pancakes.

Yield: approximately 9 (6-inch) pancakes

- 2 cups sourdough starter
- 2 T. melted butter, coconut oil, or avocado oil
- 3 T. yogurt or kefir
- 3 T. brown sugar
- 1 egg
- 1 tsp. baking soda
- ½ tsp. salt
- 1 tsp. vanilla
- ½ tsp. cinnamon or nutmeg

SOURDOUGH PIE CRUST

- 1¾ cups all-purpose flour or whole wheat pastry (or 2¼ cups spelt flour)
- 1½ tsp. sugar
- 1 tsp. salt
- ¾ cup + 2 T. cold butter
- 1 cup sourdough starter

In a large bowl mix together the flour, sugar, and salt. The secret to flaky pie crusts is having the butter melt as it's baking, not when you're handling it. Take the cold butter and cut the stick lengthwise and then into smaller chunks, handling it as little as possible. I've tried grating frozen butter in, but I prefer larger chunks of butter, both in flavor and texture.

Using a pastry cutter or two forks, cut the cold butter into the flour mixture until it resembles little peas.

Add the sourdough starter and stir just until the dough holds together. You may add a teeny bit of cold water if needed (if using whole wheat, you generally need to add more water), but remember, just until it holds together. This will depend on the hydration, or wetness, of your sourdough starter.

Cover the bowl and let the dough rest for 5 to 7 hours. An hour before using, chill in the fridge for at least an hour.

Divide dough in half. If only using one crust, wrap the other half tightly in plastic wrap and freeze until ready to use.

To use, lightly flour your work surface and rolling pin. Roll to ¼-inch thick and place in pie plate. Crimp edges and use in your favorite quiche or pie recipes.

Yield: 2 single-crust pie shells

SOURDOUGH TORTILLAS

- 2 cups flour (more if needed)
- 2 heaping tsp. baking powder
- ½ tsp. sea salt
- ⅔ cup sourdough starter
- ¼ cup water

Measure out dry ingredients into a mixing bowl. Add the sourdough starter (it does not need to be in an active state) and water. Depending upon the thickness of your sourdough starter (its level of hydration) you may need to add a few more tablespoons of water or flour to get the dough to come together. Don't overmix; stir just until it's combined.

Cover the bowl with a towel and let sit on the counter for 5 to 8 hours. Letting the mixture sit for a longer time allows the sourdough to break down more of the phytic acid in the flour, but it also creates a more sour flavor. My children aren't overly fond of the sour part (I happen to love a good sourdough bread), so when I'm making this for the whole family, I generally go with the shorter souring time.

Form into 6 balls of dough. On a lightly floured surface, flatten the dough ball with the palm of your hand. Form into a rustic circle. Cook in a preheated cast iron skillet until golden brown.

Yield: 6 (8-inch) tortillas

BAKING BREAD AND ROLLS WITH SOURDOUGH

A few things you need to know when baking bread with sourdough as your main leavening agent: Store-bought yeast works very fast—one of the reasons that specific strain of yeast was chosen. But the natural yeast in the sourdough has different strains and takes longer to rise. Plan for at least 4 to 8 hours of rise time on your sourdough products.

One of the benefits of this longer rise time is that the additional flour you add to the dough ingredients with the starter will have time for the bacteria to begin to break down the phytic acid and aid in digestion. Most traditional food experts recommend 7 to 12 hours for the phytic acid to be broken down, or longer. However, if you or your family are not particularly fond of a really tangy (nice way of saying "sour") flavor, you'll want to use the shorter rise and souring time.

With natural sourdough yeast, you can either do a single rise or a double rise. I've found the single rise works best when your starter is younger and not as strong and you don't want the stronger taste. It generally takes about 4 to 6 hours, so you don't have the full souring time and therefore not as much of the phytic acid is broken down.

The double rise is like working with store-bought yeast in that you will punch it down, form your rolls or bread, and allow the dough to double in size again, except your time between rises is much longer, about 4 to 6 hours for each rise, and the result will have a stronger sour taste. Either option is fine. I usually go with the single rise, as I get a higher rise and my kids don't like the stronger flavor of a double rise. Personally, I love a good tang on the bread, but the goal is for my entire family to eat and enjoy it.

Remember, your sourdough starter will need to be at least several weeks old, about 21 to 30 days old, before you rely on it as the sole leavening agent in your bread. Oftentimes a young starter, one only a week old, will have a false period where it may double in size and be extremely active, but this quickly tapers off and isn't reliable enough yet for bread. When the starter is mature and reliably doubling in size after feeding, you can bake bread with the starter in its active state. Sourdough starter is in its active state a few hours after feeding when there are bubbles and it's beginning to rise or double in size. The starter should be almost doubling in size about four hours after feeding. You can mark the level on the outside of your jar, feed it, and then see how much it rises above it. This will let you know how strong and active it is and approximately how much time passed from feeding until it became active.

CARE OF YOUR SOURDOUGH STARTER

Once your new sourdough starter is established, there are two methods to keeping it alive. One is to leave it out on your counter, feeding it twice a day in the same routine you used when creating it. This is great if you're using it almost daily or at least every two days. If you find yourself only using it once a week or wanting to take a break from it for vacation or other reasons (ain't no shame in that), then you'll want to use method two.

The second method is to feed the starter and then immediately after feeding put it in the fridge. The cold greatly slows down the activity of the bacteria and allows you to leave it in the fridge for at least a week before feeding it again. I confess, sometimes I've forgotten mine in the way back corner of the fridge. In fact, I've left it for six months, scraped an inch of dark gray/black sludge off the top, took the part underneath the hooch layer, and revived it. Sourdough starters, once established, are extremely hard to kill.

If you forget for a long period of time, you will find a very dark, almost black layer of liquid on the top. Drain it off, scrape off the top layer of your sourdough, and feed it. Leave it out on the counter for a few days and feed it every 12 hours. Sourdough is amazingly adaptive.

I usually bounce between both methods, depending upon the season I'm in. The summer months are filled with canning, gardening, and harvesting, so I don't bake nearly as much. This is when I use the refrigeration method primarily. Come fall I'll leave it out for a few weeks during baking sprees and then put it back in hibernation for a bit. Choose whatever works best for you at the time.

When using the refrigerator method, bring your sourdough starter out of the cold 2 to 3 days before you want to bake bread, and feed your starter every 12 hours. On the day of baking, feed the starter, and when you see it begin to rise (usually 2 to 3 hours after feeding), begin making your recipe.

For many people, the goal of having a sourdough starter is to not rely on store-bought yeast and for the health benefits. However, I've come to learn that my desire for my family to be healthier and more self-sufficient (and cutting out an ingredient is saving money) doesn't do any of us any good if they don't like the food and don't want to eat it.

If you're just switching from regular store-bought bread, I suggest starting with the following bread recipe first. Our goal is for you to have success right off the bat, with both the bread and your family's taste buds, so you'll be more likely to keep with it.

This recipe uses some store-bought yeast with the sourdough starter, which means you can technically try this one out even if your starter isn't quite mature enough yet to work fully on its own. Best part, it's so delicious they'll think they're still eating regular old white bread, but you and I will keep the secret—it's actually sourdough.

I first got this recipe from a dear gentleman. His sourdough starter had died, and he heard I had an active one. I shared a cup of my starter with him and he brought me a loaf of this bread. My family may have almost swooned when they ate it.

Of course, I asked for his recipe and he shared it with me. It was a copy of the Sourdough White Bread recipe from Patrick McManus's *Whatchagot Stew: A Memoir of an Idaho Childhood with Recipes and Commentaries*, but he'd altered the recipe to the loaf he'd given me. Is it just me, or does anyone else love seeing handwritten notes on a recipe?

I altered it slightly from the original recipe he'd given me (making this recipe twice altered and once removed), as it called for powdered milk and I generally don't have that on hand. This is the beauty of recipes—we get to tweak them to make them our own. I've also included notes on how to check if the dough is ready and forming loaves if you're newer to bread making or need a brushup.

SOURDOUGH WHITE BREAD

3 tsp. sugar
2¼ tsp. active dry yeast
1⅔ cups warm water (around 110°)
⅓ cup milk
1 tsp. salt
2 T. melted butter
2 cups sourdough starter
6 cups all-purpose flour

In a large mixing bowl combine sugar, yeast, and warm water (not hot, as that will kill the yeast, but lukewarm); stir and let sit for about 5 minutes until it turns foamy. Add milk, salt, melted butter, sourdough starter, and 2 cups of the flour. If you have a mixer, mix dough and continue adding ½ cup flour at a time until it's kneadable. Knead for 8 minutes.

If you're doing this by hand the old-fashioned way, continue stirring and adding in the flour until it's smooth enough to handle. Turn out onto a floured surface and knead by hand until dough is smooth, about 8 to 10 minutes.

Place dough in a greased bowl, cover with a towel, and place in a warm area. Allow dough to double in size, about an hour or so usually.

Punch dough down.

Take out two standard-size bread pans and either grease them well (we seem to be a society that is afraid of fat—but don't skimp on the greasing or your loaf will stick to the pan) or line them with parchment paper. I reuse the same piece of parchment paper multiple times with bread.

Lightly flour hands and counter. Divide dough in two and pat one piece into a rectangle on the counter—measure the narrow end of your rectangle to the long side of your loaf pan (this will ensure it fits perfectly into your loaf pan). Roll it up from the narrow end, take the two ends of the roll, lightly tuck them up under the roll, and place the loaf in the bread pan. Repeat with the other dough ball.

Cover with a towel and allow to double in size. This usually takes anywhere from an hour to an hour and a half.

Preheat oven to 400°. Bake loaves 25 to 30 minutes. You can test if a loaf is done by thumping the top of the bread—it should have a hollow sound when finished.

Remove loaves from oven and immediately slather the top with some butter. Don't be afraid of too much butter—there is no such thing. Allow to cool for about 15 minutes in the pan, then remove to a cooling rack. Wait at least another 15 minutes before slicing.

SOURDOUGH WHOLE WHEAT SANDWICH BREAD

2 cups sourdough starter
1½ cups water
¼ cup honey
1 T. sea salt
1 egg
6 T. melted butter
5 to 6 cups spelt (spelt requires more flour than regular wheat) or whole wheat flour

This is a true sourdough bread recipe, meaning there is no store-bought yeast and it takes close to eight hours of rising time for the natural yeast to do its work. I adapted my regular whole wheat honey buttermilk sandwich loaf to this one. We don't need the buttermilk in this recipe, however, because the sourdough itself will act as our acidic ingredient.

Remember, working with sourdough is an art form, and you'll get it down. Depending upon the hydration level of your sourdough and the warmth of your room, you may need to adjust both the amount of liquid and the time frame.

When making a risen bread product like rolls and bread, you'll want your sourdough to be in its active state. Feed it morning and night a few days before using. Feed it a few hours before making the dough.

If you're using all-purpose flour you may need to increase the measurement to 7 cups, but start with 6. This recipe makes two standard loaves.

In a large mixing bowl or your stand mixer bowl, stir together everything but the flour. If grinding your own flour at home, you'll get a lighter bread if you sift it, so sift your flour. Mix in 1 cup flour at a time on low speed, or stir by hand.

When all the flour is added, knead with attachment or by hand for 5 minutes. The trick to keeping whole wheat bread soft is to not add too much flour. The dough should be sticky and climb up the dough hook.

If using fresh-ground flour, let the dough sit for 10 minutes to continue soaking up the moisture. Knead for 4 more minutes, adding slightly more flour if needed in order to handle the dough.

Cover with a towel and let dough rise in a warm spot (the oven with the light on works great) for 3 to 4 hours.

Lightly oil the counter and grease your loaf pans. Divide dough in half and roll out one dough ball into a rectangle. Form into a loaf and place inside prepared bread pans; repeat with the other half of the dough. Allow to rise until doubled, which can take anywhere from 3 to 5 hours. To encourage a last bit of burst in height, preheat the oven to 400° with the bread in the oven. This extra heat will make it shoot upward.

Bake for 10 minutes then turn the oven down to 375° for another 10 to 15 minutes. Take the bread out of the oven and remove the loaves from the bread pans to a wire rack. Slather with butter and let cool.

Alternative rise: If you'd rather not have the longer rising time but still want to use all traditional sourdough, form the loaves from the get-go and let them rise until doubled in the bread pans and then bake. This works well for a shorter rise time and if your sourdough starter isn't very strong yet.

LONG FERMENTED SOURDOUGH SANDWICH BREAD

¾ cup (175 grams) water
1 cup (200 grams) active starter
1 T. (15 grams) melted salted butter
1½ tsp. (7 grams) sugar
1½ tsp. (7 grams) salt
2¾ cups (400 grams) all-purpose or bread flour

Place water in a large mixing bowl and add in starter with melted butter; stir to combine. Add in remaining ingredients and stir until well combined. Dough should clean the sides of the bowl.

Knead for 8 minutes and do the windowpane test (page 33). Knead for 2 more minutes if the dough is not yet at the windowpane stage, and check again. The dough shouldn't stick to your fingers.

Lightly grease a bowl and place bread dough in the bowl, rotating the bottom of the dough upright to cover all surfaces of the bread with oil. Cover with plastic wrap or beeswax to keep dough from drying out. Allow to bulk ferment at room temperature for 8 to 24 hours (a colder room temperature leads to a longer time).

Lightly flour the work surface and roll out dough into a rectangle. Roll up into a loaf, tucking edges under to create tension on top. Place in parchment-lined or greased loaf pan.

Allow to rise, covered, approximately 2 to 4 hours until doubled and even with the edges of the loaf pan. Right before baking, brush the top with melted butter.

Bake in a preheated 400°oven for 30 to 32 minutes.

Remove from loaf pan onto cooling rack, slather with more butter, and allow to cool for at least 15 to 20 minutes (longer if possible) before slicing.

FERMENTED FOODS

One of the earliest forms of food preservation and preparation known to man is fermentation. Before the advent of refrigeration, freezing, and even canning, fermentation was a way to keep perishable foods longer and to add flavor. However, there are even more benefits to fermented and cultured foods than that.

All my fellow Laura Ingalls Wilder fans will remember the talk of barrels or crocks of pickles. Some of you may even remember your grandparents or great-grandparents having crocks, or large Mason jars, full of saltwater-brine pickles, where just the vegetable, salt, and water were used to make a pickle. You're about to learn how to make them yourself, and as much as I love my home-canned pickles, there's a beauty to the fermented ones you'll want to try.

One of the great things about saltwater-brined (fermented) pickles is you can make as little or as much as you'd like at a time. You could do that with canned pickles, but I'm not about to go through all that work for one jar of pickles. When I have a small harvest of produce, I will ferment it.

If you're new to fermented pickles, don't expect them to taste exactly like a vinegar pickle. They're similar but have their own unique flavor. The best part about them is that they're teeming with beneficial microcultures and bacteria that help to limit pathogenic bacteria in our immune system. The enzymes in fermented food actually help predigest the food so that our bodies are better able to absorb the vitamins and minerals.

FERMENTED PICKLES

You'll need the following supplies to get started:

Glass Jar or Fermenting Crock: I personally prefer to use a Mason jar for all of my fermenting except for sauerkraut. Wide mouth is best so you can fit the fermenting weight inside with ease.

Water: I use our well water, which is considered hard. Though hard water isn't desired by most experts, I haven't had any issues. Filtered or distilled water is recommended if your tap water is treated with any type of chlorine.

Salt: Unrefined sea salt with no additives is recommended. Though canning salt doesn't have additives in it, it doesn't have all of the minerals that unrefined sea salt does. We want to give our microcultures as much food as possible. Gray, red, and pink sea salts are fine—just make sure you read the ingredients label for any additives, and stay away from those, including iodine.

Weight: You'll need some type of weight to keep the pickles beneath the brine level. You can purchase fermenting weights or use any clean weight that will fit inside the jar. I've used old baby food jars filled with a bit of the pickling liquid to act as a weight.

Optional but highly recommended:

I know our ancestors didn't have these, but since this is a modern guide to old-fashioned living, I highly recommend getting an airlock system for fermenting. My first summer of fermenting I didn't have an airlock system. I ended up losing gallons of pickles due to an overgrowth of mold. Please, let me save you the headache.

Airlock systems are fairly inexpensive and you'll use them over and over again. They allow the gasses from the fermentation to escape without allowing oxygen and yeast in, which result in an overload of bad microorganisms to the good and a potential fungal or mold overgrowth. I have both a Perfect Pickler System as well as the silicone nipple systems that fit directly on top of your Mason jar and use the metal band to hold it in place.

Cabbage-based ferments, such as sauerkraut and kimchi, I have found don't require an airlock system on in order to have success.

To make the brine, pour 2 tablespoons of salt into 4 cups (1 quart) of barely warm water. Stir until salt is completely dissolved.

Take fresh, rinsed, and clean vegetables and pack them into your clean container to a 2-inch headspace (the space between the top of the vegetables and the very top of the jar).

Pour the brine over the vegetables to a 1-inch headspace. You want to make sure the vegetables are completely submerged, as any pieces exposed above the brine will mold. Add your weight of choice to the jar to help keep all your veggies beneath the surface. As they ferment they tend to rise.

Place your lid on. If you're using an airlock system, follow the instructions that come with it; if not, use a regular canning lid and band. Just know as the gasses build up, you'll need to "burp" the jar (quickly unscrew the band to release the gasses) every day or so. The disadvantage to this is, no matter how superfast we are, some oxygen will get in, but many people have success with this method.

Put your jar in a warm location but not in direct sunlight. Ideally, 70° is best, but down to 65° will do. The colder temperature may require a few extra days of fermentation. However, you don't want the temperature to go above 74°, as warmer temps cause yeast and bad bacteria to take over.

After a day or so, you'll notice the brine will turn cloudy and little bubbles will begin to form. Congratulations, you have fermentation! It's really cool to watch. Allow the vegetables to ferment for four days.

After four days, go ahead and do a taste test. If they're tangy enough for you, then put a regular metal canning lid and band on and move them to the fridge for long-term storage. If they're not quite there flavor-wise, allow them to continue fermenting up to 10 days—basically, until they taste strong enough to you.

Occasionally, a film will start to form over the top of the brine. Take a spoon and skim off the film. If it's at the end of the ferment, go ahead and put the jar in the fridge. If it needs to continue fermenting, replace the lid and keep fermenting. Most times the film doesn't grow back.

Sometimes a piece of vegetable will rise to the surface, despite the weight. If it's exposed above the brine level, it will begin to discolor, and if not removed, it will mold. Remove any pieces that become exposed and reposition your weight.

Once you move the jars to the fridge, fermentation will continue, but the cold slows it down a ton. Fermented vegetables will keep in the fridge for months. They're not considered shelf stable, so don't keep them on the pantry shelf like you would canned pickles. *They must be stored in the fridge or another cool environment, preferably 55° or cooler, but not freezing.*

I generally let most of my vegetables ferment seven days for that magic flavor place, but this will depend upon your palate and the warmth of your room.

I prefer most of my pickled vegetables to be garlic and dill flavor, especially green beans, green tomatoes, and cucumbers. I add 2 to 3 peeled and smashed cloves of garlic to each quart-size jar (increase ratio according to container size) and 2 heads fresh dill or a tablespoon dried dill, plus your favorite spices. I like a teaspoon of mustard seed too. Adjust the dill to your taste preferences.

If you're making dilly green beans, the Perfect Pickler, Inc. recommends that you blanch the beans in boiling water for 2 minutes, let cool, and then proceed as normal.

When making fermented cucumber pickles, many people like to add a couple of grape leaves to the jar, as it's thought the tannins in the leaf will help create a crisper pickle. Feel free to add your favorite spices like mustard seeds and whole black peppercorns for flavor.

It's also recommended that you always snip off the blossom end of your cucumbers to remove an enzyme that creates mushy pickles. I usually remove both ends to help get the brine down in the cucumber (and in case you're not sure which end was the blossom end if you didn't pick them yourself). Make sure you're choosing fresh pickling cucumbers. Waxy cucumbers or English cucumbers don't make good pickles.

When fermenting bright green vegetables like green beans, cucumbers, and green tomatoes, you'll notice the color change to a duller green as the fermentation takes place. This is normal and just shows the enzymes are doing their work.

SAUERKRAUT

Sauerkraut can be made with either purple or green cabbage. A fresh head of cabbage is best, because you need the moisture content in the leaves to create your brine.

Using an old earthenware crock works great for sauerkraut, but you can also use a wide-mouth Mason jar or even a large glass bowl.

1 head green or purple cabbage

1 T. unrefined sea salt

Remove the outer leaves and core of cabbage. Chop or shred into the desired size pieces for your sauerkraut. A food processor can make quick work of the cabbage if you're going for shredded.

Many folks will pound their cabbage to release the juices, but my friend Wardeh Harmon (author of *The Complete Idiot's Guide to Fermenting Foods* and founder of TraditionalCookingSchool.com) shares this method for a no-pound sauerkraut and is what we've always used for ours.

Place the cabbage in a large bowl and sprinkle with the sea salt. Let sit for about 30 minutes and then give it a good stir. You'll begin to see juices form, but you need enough liquid to cover the cabbage when it's put in a jar, so stir it up and let it sit for another 30 to 40 minutes. If you have any live cultured sauerkraut already in the fridge, you can use a cup of the brine to help inoculate the new batch.

Mason Jar Method

Take a clean wide-mouth Mason jar and pack the cabbage tightly into it. Keep pushing down on the cabbage so that the juice rises to cover the surface. If you're not using an airlock system but just a regular canning lid, make sure you burp the jar (untighten the band) to release the gasses every so often. You'll see the metal lid start to bulge or become firm if they're starting to build up and know it's time to burp the baby . . . er, jar. Place the weight inside to keep the cabbage beneath the brine.

Fermenting Crock or Large Bowl Method

You will need a weight to keep the juices above the surface of the cabbage. Use a plate that covers the entire surface area of the crock or bowl. Fill a small Mason jar with water and place it on the plate to act as a weight. Make sure you can see the liquid above the cabbage.

Allow the sauerkraut to ferment for one to two weeks. We've found one week doesn't have that tangy flavor for us, so two weeks is about the sweet spot. Many people believe sauerkraut should ferment for a full four weeks for the maximum amount of good bacteria. This is up to you, but regardless, after it's reached the desired flavor, you must transfer it to the fridge.

If a film develops, you can skim that off. But if you see white or pink mold, discard and start over.

Yield: approximately 4 cups

YOGURT

Most of us are familiar with having yogurt in our home, but many store-bought yogurts aren't very healthy with all the additives they contain. It's much cheaper and healthier to make homemade yogurt. Do not use ultra-pasteurized milk if you're able, and preferably nonhomogenized as well, though if you can't find sources for these, regular milk will work.

- 4 to 6 cups milk
- ¼ cup yogurt (with live cultures) or yogurt starter

Pour the milk into a saucepan. On medium-low heat, bring the milk to 160° to 175°. Allowing the milk to heat at 175° for 15 minutes will result in a thicker yogurt. When you heat the milk, a layer of scalded milk will form on top. Skim this off with a spoon.

Allow the milk to cool to 110° and pour it into a clean Mason jar. Add starter and mix in thoroughly. If you add the culture before the milk is cooled, you'll kill it. If you add the culture into cold milk, you'll also kill it. It just likes to be warm—not hot, not cold. Anyone else thinking of Goldilocks right now?

Put a lid on the jar. I use plastic lids for Mason jars or save ones from peanut butter jars. (I have used a regular canning lid and band, but I prefer to save those for my actual canning.) I tend to use my Mason jars for everything from leftovers to cups on the go, so the plastic lids are great, as keeping track of bands drives me crazy.

Keep yogurt between 100° and 110° for 4 to 6 hours. There are a few ways to keep your yogurt warm. You can purchase a yogurt maker, but I prefer the more frugal route when possible. I've filled my slow cooker with three inches of water and turned it on the "keep warm" setting with the lid off. This setting keeps the water at 110°. Another option is to wrap your jars in a thick bath towel and put them in the oven. The oven works as a natural incubator. Just don't forget your yogurt is in the oven and turn it on! Other people will use a small ice chest, put extra jars of hot water in it, and use it to keep the yogurt warm. All these options work well.

After 5 hours, check to see if the yogurt is thick. I let my yogurt ferment for close to a full 24 hours to remove more of the milk sugars. Just remember, the longer it ferments, the tangier it gets. Once it's reached the desired thickness, store the yogurt in the fridge for up to one week—if you don't gobble it up within a day or two.

If your yogurt separates too much, with a lot of whey (watery liquid) on top, then your yogurt was a little too hot while fermenting. Try keeping it slightly cooler. You can either stir the whey back into the yogurt or drain it to use as liquid in cooking or fermenting.

You can use the plain yogurt in place of sour cream and mayonnaise in many cooking and baking recipes. Make sure to save ¼ cup of your fresh yogurt as starter for your next batch. I freeze my starter so I don't have to remember to save it later and so that the starter is at its strongest point, which is right after it's been fed.

If you and your family are used to store-bought yogurt, you will probably need to add some type of sweetener if eating plain.

Sweetener options:

- Drizzle in some raw honey (not for children under a year)
- Maple syrup
- Jam or jelly for a fruity, sweet option
- Stevia extract (I use the liquid version, and it mixes in great)

MASTER SMOOTHIE RECIPE

½ cup yogurt
½ cup water or milk of choice
½ cup frozen or fresh berries or a whole, small peach or banana
Sweetener of choice to taste (I use 6 drops liquid stevia)
¼ tsp. cinnamon (optional, depending upon fruit)
4 ice cubes

Place all ingredients in a high-powered blender and blend until smooth and frothy. Pour into a Mason jar and bottoms up!

Optional add-ins:

- 1 scoop protein powder of your choice
- ½ scoop gelatin (I only use organic or grass-fed brands for this)
- 1 T. cooked pumpkin with a dash of nutmeg
- ¼ to ½ cup frozen greens or spinach
- 1 T. almond or peanut butter
- 1 T. cocoa powder
- 1 T. ground flax seed
- 1 T. chia seeds

Yield: approximately 1½ cups

OATMEAL YOGURT BOWL

For a single serving, bring water to a boil in a small saucepan. Stir in oats, reduce heat to low, and cover. Cook for 7 minutes. Remove from heat and stir in vanilla and butter. Then add yogurt, salt, fruit, sweetener of choice, cinnamon, and nuts.

- ½ cup water
- ¼ cup rolled oats (not instant)
- ½ tsp. vanilla extract
- Pat of butter
- ¼ cup yogurt
- Dash of salt
- ¼ cup fresh or frozen fruit
- Sweetener of choice
- Healthy sprinkle of cinnamon
- 1 T. finely chopped nuts (optional)

GRANOLA

There's little that goes better with yogurt than granola—it's the creaminess of the yogurt against the crunch of the granola. Granola is extremely easy to make at home.

Preheat oven to 275°. Mix all the ingredients together, except dried fruit or chocolate, in a large bowl. Pour into a large, rimmed baking sheet.

Bake for 45 to 55 minutes until golden brown and toasted. Stir the granola every 15 to 20 minutes to prevent burning. Take out of the oven, and if you're adding dried fruit, go ahead and mix it all in together.

Allow to cool completely before adding chocolate and storing in an airtight container, if you don't eat it all at once. You can eat it as cereal, mix it in with yogurt, or snitch a few handfuls all by itself.

Yield: 5 to 6 cups (depending on how many add-ins you used)

- 3 cups rolled oats (not instant)
- 1 cup chopped nuts (pecans are my favorite)
- ½ cup honey or maple syrup
- 2 T. brown sugar (if you're avoiding refined sugar, omit)
- ¼ cup melted coconut oil or avocado oil
- ½ tsp. sea salt
- 1 tsp. vanilla extract
- ½ tsp. ground cinnamon (optional)
- 2 cups any combination of the following:
  - sunflower seeds
  - shredded coconut
  - extra chopped or ground nuts of choice
  - dried fruit of choice (add in after granola is cooked)
  - mini chocolate chips or chunks (add in after granola is cooked and cooled, not before)

BUTTERMILK

1 quart cold milk

¼ cup live cultured buttermilk (you can also purchase starter cultures online)

Buttermilk is held in high regard by bakers because of the wonderful flaky effect it has on baked goods. The reason for this is the acid, which creates pockets in the dough as it's baking, creating a light, flakier texture.

Buttermilk is the easiest cultured food to make. And it's a lot cheaper to make at home than to buy. One of the great things about cultured buttermilk is you can, of course, use it in your baked goods, though when it's cooked, you're losing the probiotic benefit due to the heat. But it will still treat your baked goods well.

Seriously, if you can pour cold milk in a jar and stir in a ¼ cup of starter, you're good to go. No heating anything up or fishing out any cultures. You can also use cultured buttermilk to just drink straight up (my father's preferred method), in a smoothie, or in homemade ranch dressing (my favorite).

You may use any milk you desire. My grandmother had raw milk, and that's preferred by some, but cost and ease of purchasing raw milk (it's illegal in some states) may not make this an option. I prefer organic non-homogenized milk, but have had success with regular milk as well. Totally up to you, my friend.

Pour the milk into a clean quart-size Mason jar. Stir in the starter culture or live cultured buttermilk. Cover with cheesecloth or a coffee filter and secure with a rubber band—or use my go-to, a metal canning band. Place in a warm area—around 70° is preferred. Allow to culture for 12 to 18 hours. The colder the room, the longer it will take the culture to set. Check it at 12 hours and see if it's firm. It will look set like yogurt.

Then place in the fridge for 6 to 8 hours to finish up before using. If you want it to be thinner, like milk, stir it briskly. The wonderful thing about cultured milk products is they keep longer. Your buttermilk will be good for 2 to 3 weeks in the fridge. But remember to always reserve ¼ cup for your next batch.

Now be prepared to make the best buttermilk recipes ever. Seriously, if you've used the substitute of lemon or vinegar in milk for buttermilk recipes, ain't nothing compared to the real thing.

Let's get to putting that buttermilk to use, shall we?

OVERNIGHT BUTTERMILK PANCAKES

The night before, combine the flour and buttermilk, cover the bowl with a towel, and let sit on the counter 8 to 12 hours or overnight. In the morning, stir in the butter, salt, sugar, egg, baking soda, and vanilla to the flour and buttermilk. Add a wee bit more buttermilk if the batter is too thick.

- 2 cups flour
- 2 cups buttermilk
- 4 T. melted butter
- ½ tsp. sea salt
- 3 T. brown sugar
- 1 egg
- 1 tsp. baking soda
- 1 tsp. vanilla

Heat a griddle or cast-iron skillet over medium heat with a teaspoon of butter. When butter is melted and skillet is hot, pour out pancakes to desired size. The batter is a little bit thick, but they make amazingly light and fluffy pancakes.

You can make these in the morning, without doing the soak. But the overnight soak helps aid digestion.

Yield: 8 servings

OATMEAL PANCAKES

Speaking of pancakes and oatmeal, these are one of my absolute favorite pancakes of all time. I've even been known to snitch one off the plate and eat it plain because I simply can't wait to put the toppings on before getting a bite. They're so good they don't need syrup.

- 2 cups milk
- 1½ cups old-fashioned oats
- 2 eggs
- ½ cup melted butter, coconut oil, or avocado oil
- ¾ cup flour
- 1 T. brown sugar or omit for sugar-free (stevia works well in this)
- 2½ tsp. baking powder
- 1 tsp. sea salt
- ½ tsp. cinnamon
- 1 tsp. vanilla

This recipe comes from my mother. With the addition of oatmeal, these are higher in both fiber and protein, making them a healthier choice than just a regular pancake recipe.

The recipe below also has a soaked variation. Soaked recipes go back to traditional cooking of sourdough and cultured food—the days before refrigeration. People made buttermilk, yogurt, and kefir because it kept their milk products longer. There are also some health benefits to soaked foods. It's thought that a soaked flour or grain recipe helps break down the phytic acid in the flour and oats, making it easier for us to digest.

For a soaked option, take a cup of yogurt (this replaces one of the cups of milk in the recipe) and mix with 1 cup of milk, 1½ cups oats, and ¾ cup flour in a bowl the night before. Cover with a towel and let sit overnight. In the morning, prepare as normal. You can also use two cups of real cultured buttermilk or dairy kefir.

Pour milk over oats and let sit 2 minutes. Meanwhile, beat eggs and butter or oil together. Add the rest of the dry ingredients and egg mixture to the milk and oats. Fry in hot oil, about 2 minutes on each side or until golden brown. Top with warm applesauce, buttermilk syrup (page 22), or jam or jelly of choice.

Yield: 8 to 10 servings

MILK KEFIR

Up to 4 cups cold milk
1 to 2 tsp. kefir grains

If you've never heard of kefir before, don't worry. I had never heard of it either as a child or young adult. Most sources show kefir originated in the North Caucasus Mountains. Kefir look like small grains (but they don't actually contain any grain or gluten) that consist of colonies of good yeast and bacteria, aka probiotics. Kefir grains have a much higher amount and more diverse types of the good bacteria and yeast than yogurt—like up to five times more.

I'm here to let you in on a little secret: kefir is easier to make than yogurt, though it is a daily commitment.

If you can get grains from a friend or someone local, that will be your best bet, as you can skip the rehydrating step, and if it's a friend, you generally won't have to buy them. Otherwise I've ordered mine from Cultures for Health online. If you order your grains online, they'll come to you dehydrated, which will involve you slowly waking them up over a week until they reach full strength, hence the local recommendation if possible.

Don't worry—if you go the online route, they'll come with detailed instructions on how to rehydrate them. That's how I started mine. Once you have plumped and hydrated kefir grains, you're ready to go.

Pour milk into a clean glass jar. Add in the kefir grains and stir with a wooden or plastic spoon. Note: It's recommended to not use aluminum utensils with your kefir.

Cover the jar with cheesecloth or a coffee filter (I think you have the drill down by now) and secure. Set the jar in a warm area but not in direct sunlight, and allow to culture for 24 hours. You'll notice the milk thickening up.

When my grains were in their infancy, it took them almost 2 weeks before they thickened up the milk in 24 hours, so don't be discouraged if they're a little slow to come to maturity. Just keep adding new milk and give them a little extra time.

TRADITIONAL LIVING TIP

Back in my grandmother's day when they milked the cow every morning, they had gallons of fresh, raw milk. They lived far off the road, down a dirt lane and over a creek. No electricity, which meant no refrigerator, and no indoor bathroom, but a good milk cow. (The outhouse is still standing.)

One of the benefits of culturing your food is it naturally preserves it. In the past, food wasn't allowed to go to waste. Culturing the cream and milk allowed folks who couldn't afford electricity to keep their dairy products longer. The culturing provides the same benefit for us today. A quart of yogurt or dairy kefir will keep much longer in the fridge than a quart of plain milk.

If after 24 hours the milk isn't thickening up, let it go another 4 to 8 hours, especially if your kitchen is on the cooler side.

Strain out the kefir grains and start a new batch with fresh milk in a clean jar. Store your freshly made kefir in the fridge or enjoy immediately. You can purchase a small strainer (plastic is advised) or use cheesecloth. If your kefir is thick, it can take a while to strain through. I've found it faster and easier to wash my hands and just fish the grains out with my fingers. Some will be on the bottom while a few are on top, at least with my grains.

The grains do need fresh milk after every fermentation, usually every 24 hours, but if you're going on vacation or need a break, you can feed them fresh milk and put them in the fridge for a week or two. It is hard on them if you do this too frequently, but every now and then should be fine.

Many folks use kefir just like yogurt in smoothies, eating, cooking, and baking. I like to take mine and add ¼ cup fruit or berries to 1 cup of kefir, whirl it in the blender, and let it sit for a few hours before drinking. The fruit sweetens it up a little bit and makes a healthy snack. The extra fermentation makes it slightly effervescent. And come summertime you can use it to make berry kefir popsicles. Yum.

SOUR CREAM

We know cultured foods are better for us, and they've proven to be less expensive for me to make at home. Did you know making homemade cultured sour cream is just as easy as making yogurt? Sour cream is thicker because we're using cream, and there's a higher fat content.

You can purchase a sour cream culture starter, but I simply use my yogurt in cream to make sour cream. A dollop on baked potatoes, chili, homemade nachos, scrambled eggs—you name it, and now it contains the goodness of live cultures.

Without a refrigerator, cream and butter would naturally culture. If you have raw cream/milk (which is what my grandparents had back in the day), the making of sour cream is incredibly easy. Note: Option 1 method will only work with raw cream/milk. *If the milk has been heated or pasteurized, you cannot use this method.*

Option 1: Raw Cream

Separate your raw cream from the milk. The cream rises to the top, and is thick and a slightly different color. Spoon it off into a clean Mason jar. Place a layer of cheesecloth or a coffee filter over the top and secure it with a rubber band or canning ring. Let it sit 24 to 48 hours in a warm area. The warmer your house (think summer months or near a heat source), the faster it will culture.

Option 2: Pasteurized Cream

To make sour cream with store-bought pasteurized cream (I prefer to not use ultra-high-temperature [UHT] treated milk or cream), you'll need cream and some type of starter culture. The good news is you can use either milk kefir or yogurt as your starter.

The reason we heat the milk when making yogurt, sour cream, and cheese is the heat denatures the whey protein, creating a thicker, smoother, and creamier product.

Heat the cream to 180° and then let it cool to about 80° (basically room temperature). Pour the cooled cream into a glass Mason jar and add in 1 tablespoon live culture, either yogurt or milk kefir, to 1 cup cream. Stir and cover with cheesecloth or a coffee filter; secure with a rubber band or metal screw-down band.

Let sit at room temperature for 12 to 24 hours, until you see it's thickened up and set. The longer it cultures, the thicker it will become. Due to using grass-fed cream with all the lovely yellow color, my sour cream isn't white but a gorgeous buttery color.

Store in the fridge and enjoy your probiotic-rich sour cream! Just remember to save 1 or 2 tablespoons to use in the next batch, or you can keep using your kefir or yogurt.

HOMEMADE MAYONNAISE

- 1 whole egg
- 1 tsp. prepared mustard
- ½ tsp. salt
- 2 tsp. lemon juice
- 1 tsp. organic white vinegar
- ¾ cup oil of choice (we prefer avocado or cold-pressed grape seed oil for a neutral flavor)

If you enjoyed the sour cream, wait until you try this mayonnaise! While it's not a cultured recipe, this is a staple in our fridge. And by staple, I mean we're not allowed to run out. My husband eats it on everything. A dollop on top of chili is just the thing, and instead of bread and butter, my husband loves bread and mayonnaise. Let me tell you, don't mess with a man and his mayo.

This was one of the last holdouts of store-bought products, mainly because my husband insisted on a certain brand name and nothing else. I admire his loyalty, but when going over the ingredients list and cost, I was determined to come up with a homemade version. The main ingredient in store-bought mayonnaise is soy oil. I have issues with this for a couple of reasons. First, soy is a major genetically modified crop, and the oil is usually hydrogenated. Second, soy contains phytoestrogens and endocrine-disrupting compounds.[1] It tends to be in tons of commercially processed foods, so I try to limit our consumption of it whenever I can.

This version contains only recognizable ingredients, and you can whip up a jar of homemade mayonnaise in less than three minutes. No more running to the store.

Crack the egg into a pint-size wide-mouth Mason jar. Add the mustard, salt, lemon juice, and white vinegar. Add oil on top and allow it to sit for a few seconds so the ingredients separate and the oil floats on top.

Gently place your immersion blender into the jar until it's to the bottom. Turn the immersion blender on and leave it at the bottom until the mayonnaise begins to emulsify. Slowly bring the immersion blender up and back down, incorporating the remaining oil until all the contents are thick, creamy, and completely emulsified.

Add a lid to the jar and store it in the refrigerator for up to two weeks.

This has the perfect tang to it. I've tried using olive oil, but found it had too strong of a flavor for our liking.

I know many people are shocked to see a raw egg in mayonnaise, but the addition of the vinegar and lemon juice add acid to help kill bacteria. We use a fresh egg from our chickens, so I don't worry about it, as I know our flock is healthy.

Yield: 1½ cups

I'm always amazed at how the old-fashioned methods seem to turn me back toward Jesus. When we create a healthy culture, the good things overcome the bad; they actually take the things in front of them and transform them into something better. Let's look for every opportunity to live our lives this way—to let the bad "ferment" into something beautiful and delicious, teeming with the love of Jesus!

PRESERVE

If you'd asked me a decade ago what preserving meant, I would have said it's the art of keeping food in an edible state long after it's been harvested. In a broader context of homesteading and traditional living, I would classify it as a way of preserving a way of life.

Both of those statements are true, but now, preserving has a much deeper meaning for me. In the past two years, my father-in-law and grandmother-in-law passed away, and my own father has been diagnosed with fast-progressing Alzheimer's disease.

The preserving and serving of their favorite recipes are a bridge to loved ones that surpasses time. When I open a jar of strawberry jam, for a moment Grandma Lucille is beside us in the kitchen. I hear her voice walking me through the steps of jam making every summer. Every time I reach for a jar of mustard pickles, the teasing voice of my father-in-law reaches past the fingers of death and fills the moment. I hope one day my own grandchildren and great-grandchildren will make recipes to feed their families and remember me.

Beyond personal ties, preserving food at home is a way many people are turning to preserve the integrity of their food. Sadly, many ingredients are being allowed into our food system that pose health risks, and many people, in order to escape them, are finding they have to preserve food themselves.

One of my favorite things to teach and share is food preservation. It is one of the greatest skill sets one can learn for resilience and health, and is the ultimate in batch cooking when it comes to canning.

This chapter is a highlight of my favorite go-to recipes shared from my book, *Everything Worth Preserving: The Complete Guide for Food Preservation at Home.*

There are nine different ways one can preserve food, but what comes to mind for most people is jars of home-canned food.

When it comes to food preservation, especially canning, there are safety considerations. The most notable is botulism. Botulism is a form of food poisoning, but unlike E. coli or salmonella where you mostly have severe stomach upset, botulism is a neurotoxin and deadly. Botulism is tasteless, odorless, and sightless, so one shouldn't rely on "I'll know if it's gone bad because I'll be able to detect it" train of thought. However, if you follow up-to-date and tested procedures and recipes, botulism is easy to avoid. Please read that again: easy to avoid.

The main thing to understand is to never alter a canning recipe or skip a step in the procedure; they are there for a reason. Second, knowing the difference between acidic and nonacidic foods determines if they can be safely canned using a water bath and/or steam canner or if they must be pressure canned.

Botulism *cannot* grow in an acidic environment of 4.6 or lower on the pH scale. This is why you see fruit and pickled vegetables safely water bath canned, but meats, vegetables, and broths pressure canned. When canning under pressure, you reach internal temperatures of 248°, which cannot be reached via a boiling water bath, no matter how long you boil it. For nonacidic foods, the higher temperature is required to ensure any botulism spores that may be present are killed.

All the recipes and procedures I use are from updated and tested resources. I do not adhere to nor share any "rebel" canning. If you've never canned before, I've included a step-by-step tutorial for both water bath and pressure canning, followed by favorite recipes. Enjoy!

WATER BATH CANNING TUTORIAL

Water bath canning is what many folks remember their grandparents or parents doing. It's an excellent starting place for acidic foods because you can use any pot that's deep enough to cover the top of the jars with at least one inch of water. Your large pot of boiling water is what we're referencing as a canner in this tutorial, whether it's a large pot you own or if you purchased a specific water bath canning pot.

1. Place the canning rack in the bottom of the canner (if you are using a large pot, either use canning bands to create a rack or twist up a towel and place it in the bottom of the pot). Add enough water to ensure there is one to two inches of water over the top of the filled jars. Heat the water to 140°F (60°C) for raw pack/180°F (82°C) for hot pack. Prepare jars, lids, and bands by washing them in hot water. While the canner is heating up, begin preparing the food to go in the jars. One at a time fill your hot jars using a funnel to indicated headspace.
2. Measure using either a ruler or headspace tool to appropriate headspace. This is the amount of space from the top of the food to the rim of the jar. Remove air bubbles by inserting a spatula or bubble remover between the food and jar. Slide up and down around the inside circumference of the jar two to three times. Add more food if needed to maintain headspace indicated in the recipe.
3. Wipe the rim clean and thread the jar with a damp cloth to remove any food particles (these can impede a seal). Place lid on jar, then the band, and screw the band down to fingertip tight.
4. Take filled jar of food and put into prepared canner. Repeat until all jars are filled and in canner. Make sure water covers jars by one to two inches. Two inches is recommended for processing times over 30 minutes.
5. With the lid on, bring the water to a full boil. Start processing time only once a full boil is reached. Keep the lid on during the processing time. Process at a full boil for complete recipe time, then

turn off heat. Remove the lid and wait 5 minutes before removing jars.

6. Remove jars from the canner and place upright onto a folded towel. Leave jars to cool for 12 to 24 hours before checking the seal; do not retighten or touch bands.
7. Check lids to ensure a seal. Lids should not give when pressed in the center and should hold when the jar is lifted by the lid only. Remove bands, wipe down jars and lids, and wipe dry. Label and store in a cool, dry, dark area.

PRESSURE-CANNING TUTORIAL

1. Make sure canning rack is in place before placing jars inside. Add 2 to 3 inches water to pressure canner and heat to 140°F (60°C) for raw pack/180°F (82°C) for hot pack. Prepare jars, lids, and bands by washing them in hot water; keep jars hot. While the canner is heating up, begin preparing the food to go in the jars.
2. Measure using either a ruler or headspace tool to appropriate headspace. This is the amount of space from the top of the food to the rim of the jar. Remove air bubbles by inserting a spatula or bubble remover between the food and jar. Slide up and down around the inside circumference of the jar two to three times. Add more food if needed to maintain headspace indicated in the recipe.
3. Wipe the rim clean and thread the jar with a damp cloth to remove any food particles (these can impede a seal). Place lid on jar, then the band, and screw the band down to fingertip tight. Take the filled jar of food and put into prepared canner; repeat until all jars are filled and in canner.
4. Visually check the lid and make sure the vent pipe is clear by holding it up to a light. Place lid on pressure canner and lock lid into place. Adjust heat to medium, and once a steady stream of steam is coming out of vent pipe, set timer for 10 minutes and let canner exhaust.
5. After 10 minutes, place weighted pressure gauge onto vent pipe on pounds of pressure indicated for specific recipe and your altitude.
6. Only begin timer when weighted gauge begins to jiggle and hiss and/or your dial gauge has reached the proper PSI.
7. After processing time, turn off the heat and let the canner reduce pressure naturally (this generally takes 30 to 45 minutes depending on the size of your pressure canner). Once pressure is reduced to zero, wait 5 minutes. Remove the weight and wait 10 minutes, then carefully remove the lid with it facing away from you to protect you from any steam. Let jars sit in the open canner for 10 minutes to reduce siphoning.
8. Remove jars from the canner and place upright onto a folded towel. Leave jars to cool for 12 to 24 hours before checking the seal; do not retighten or touch bands.
9. Check lids to ensure a seal. Lids should not give when pressed in the center and should hold when the jar is lifted by the lid only. Remove bands, wipe down jars and lids, and wipe dry. Label and store in a cool, dry, dark area.

MUSTARD PICKLE RELISH

When my father-in-law found out I was a canner, he started talking about how much he loved Great-Grandma's mustard pickles and hadn't had them in years (sadly, she passed from the family long before I met and married my husband). I'd never heard of mustard pickle relish before and thought the recipe was long lost, as no one had made it in years. It was one of those family recipes that were the stuff of legends, it seemed.

Until my husband's grandma was going through her recipe books and found a copy of it from decades past. She no longer canned, so she passed it along to me. Honestly, as I scanned the ingredients for the mustard pickles, I wasn't sure what to expect by the finished product, but man, one spoonful and I was hooked.

The day of my father-in-law's funeral I stood in our pantry, grabbing items for the memorial lunch. I thought I'd used the last jar of mustard pickles months earlier, but as I shuffled jars around to grab some cherry jelly for the meatball glaze, there in the back, a golden yellow jar of mustard pickles shone. I wrapped my fingers around the jar, stood in the middle of my pantry, and ugly cried, grateful I had a jar to serve in his memory. These are things truly worth preserving.

- 6 cups washed and diced pickling cucumbers
- 2 cups diced onion
- 1 cup canning/pickling salt
- 8 cups cold water
- 4 T. sugar
- 6 T. dry mustard
- 2 T. dry turmeric
- 2 tsp. celery salt (you can use regular salt, but the celery salt adds to the flavor)
- 2 T. Clear Jel (optional, but produces a thicker relish)
- ½ cup water
- 4 cups vinegar (5% acidity)

Place cucumbers and onions in a large stainless steel or glass bowl.

Mix canning/pickling salt with the 8 cups of cold water (double this as needed if doing a larger batch of pickles). Pour over top of cucumbers and onions, adding more cold water if necessary to cover the tops of the cucumbers. Use a clean plate and place on top of the cucumbers to keep them under the surface of the cold salt water. Fill a pint-size Mason jar with water, cover it, and set it on top of the plate to act as a weight. Put the bowl in the fridge overnight or for 12 hours.

After soaking cucumbers and onions, pour out salt water and rinse thoroughly with cold water and allow cucumbers and onions to drain.

Prepare jars, lids, and bands by washing them in hot water, and get the water bath or steam canner heating up; keep jars hot.

In a large stainless-steel pot, combine sugar, dry mustard, turmeric, celery salt, and Clear Jel, then pour in ½ cup of water, whisking until combined and smooth. Pour in vinegar and bring to a full boil while stirring. Once mixture has reached a full boil, lower heat to a simmer and stir until it thickens up, then add the cucumbers and onions and bring to a boil. When it reaches a boil with the vegetables added, keep at a low boil and cook for 15 minutes, stirring as needed.

In hot, sterilized jars, pack the relish/pickle mixture to ½-inch headspace. Remove air bubbles and add more product if needed to keep the ½-inch headspace. Clean the rims, put on lids and bands, and screw down to fingertip tight.

Place filled jars into your water bath or steam canner. Process pints for 10 minutes.* Remove canner lid and wait 5 minutes. Place jars on the counter on a folded kitchen towel. Cool for 24 hours, check the seals, and then store.

**Note: Altitude adjustments:* If you're 1,001 to 3,000 feet, increase processing time by 5 minutes; 3,001 to 6,000 feet, increase processing time by 10 minutes; if above 6,001 feet, increase processing time by 15 minutes.

Yield: approximately 4 pints

The first time I tried making jam, I ended up with jars of strawberry syrup. I thought the jam seemed awfully liquid as I ladled into the jars to can, but reasoned with myself it would thicken up during the canning and cooling process.

The next morning, I discovered none of my jars of jam had set. When I lamented to my husband, he asked, "Are you sure you didn't do something wrong?"

Rest assured he went unharmed. I thought for sure it was the box of pectin, but in humble mode, I went down to Grandma Lucille's house for a proper jam-making lesson.

One of the things I did wrong was pulling the jam off the stove and jarring it before it had reached the gelling point. There are three ways to tell if your jam has reached the gelling point. You can use any of the three tests on page 118 to ensure you're not making syrup when your goal is jam.

NO-SUGAR STRAWBERRY JAM

I first learned to make strawberry jam from my husband's Grandma Lucille. As I became more of an ingredient sleuth, I wasn't comfortable using most brands of pectin, not to mention many required as much sugar, if not more, than the berries.

Then I landed on Pomona's Pectin. This pectin allows you to use much smaller amounts of sweetener—or in this recipe's case, no sugar—than other brands because it relies on calcium for the gelling factor. You can use honey or, for a no-sugar option, stevia.

Pomona's Pectin includes calcium powder in the box to make calcium water (necessary for using Pomona's Pectin) as well as powdered pectin (not a GMO-based pectin source), which makes it the only store-bought pectin I use.

- 2 to 3 lbs. fresh strawberries
- 1 T. calcium water; see Pomona's Pectin box for instructions.
- ¾ cup water or fruit juice
- 1 T. powdered pectin, Pomona's brand
- Stevia concentrate (optional; I used 5 dropperfuls)

Wash, hull, and halve your strawberries.

Prepare jars, lids, and bands by washing them in hot water, and get the water bath or steam canner heating up; keep jars hot.

Place strawberries into a blender (or food processor, or mash by hand) and lightly mash to your preferred thickness.

Once berries are mashed, measure how much you have (this will determine how much pectin and calcium water you need). My total was 6 cups.

Place the mashed strawberries in a pot over medium heat and bring to a low boil.

Add calcium water to the pot of mashed strawberries.

In a separate small saucepan, bring ¾ cup water or juice to a boil. Add just-off-the-boil water/juice and pectin powder to a blender, vent the lid, and blend for 1 to 2 minutes until the powder is fully dissolved.

When fruit is at a boil, add pectin water/juice. Stir and return to a full boil.

Add stevia to taste if using; too much can sometimes taste bitter, so add in increments.

Continue stirring to avoid scorching and cook for 1 to 2 minutes.

Using a funnel, ladle jam into jars, filling to a ¼-inch headspace. Use bubble remover to remove any bubbles and recheck headspace and top off, if needed.

Wipe the rims of each jar with a damp towel, add the two-part canning lid, and tighten to fingertip tight (as tight as you can get them using your fingertips only).

Process jars for 10 minutes.*

For steam canners: Leave the lid on for 5 minutes, then remove lid and wait an additional 5 minutes before removing jars to a towel-lined counter.

For water bath canners: Remove the lid and wait 5 minutes before removing jars to a towel-lined counter.

Wait 24 hours before removing bands, wiping jars, labeling, and storing.

**Note: Altitude adjustments for water or steam canner:* If you're 1,001 to 3,000 feet, increase processing time by 5 minutes; 3,001 to 6,000 feet, increase processing time by 10 minutes; if above 6,001 feet, increase processing time by 15 minutes.

Yield: approximately 6½ to 7 cups of jam

GEL TESTS: THREE WAYS TO TEST YOUR JAM "SET" OR "GELLED"

The sheet test (the one I use most often)**:**

- Take a large metal spoon and put it in the fridge or freezer when you begin making your jam. Dip the spoon into the boiling jam and hold it up so that the spoon is sideways and the jam can drip off the side/edge of the spoon. If it just runs off, it's not ready. Large drops mean you're almost there, and the sheeting is when the jelly/jam drips off the spoon in one sheet, instead of individual drops, hence the name "sheet test."

The cold plate test:

- Put a saucer or small plate in the freezer. Put a small spoonful of jam on the chilled plate and put it in the freezer for a minute. Pull it out and push against the edge of the jam with the tip of your finger. If you can run your finger through it and it stays separated and/or the surface shows wrinkles where you've pushed it, then it's done.

The candy thermometer test:

- Use a candy thermometer, making sure you don't touch the bottom of the pan (directly on the heat source) with the end of the thermometer. The goal is 220°F (104°C). It's important to note that if you're at high altitude, 1,000 feet above sea level, then you need to subtract 2° for every 1,000 feet above sea level.

When you're doing these tests, pull your jam onto a cool burner so you don't overcook it if it's indeed at the gel stage.

CHERRY JAM WITHOUT PECTIN (LOW SUGAR)

- 5 cups sweet cherries
- ½ cup water
- 2½ cups sugar (can use between 2½ and 3 cups depending on how sweet your cherries are and your preference)
- 5 T. lime or lemon juice from concentrate

My grandmother Revonda was born in 1914. She raised children through the Great Depression and lived without electricity or indoor plumbing for decades. She never purchased a box of store-bought pectin in her life. She taught my mother how to make homemade jam and jelly without store-bought pectin, and I have converted many recipes using her techniques, including this delightful recipe.

Wash, remove stems, and *pit cherries*. A cherry pitter is highly advised.

Prepare jars, lids, and bands by washing them in hot water, and get the water bath or steam canner heating up; keep jars hot.

Roughly chop up the cherries. Place chopped cherries in a large stock pot. Add ½ cup water. Bring to a boil and allow to simmer for 15 minutes, stirring occasionally. You'll see the cherries begin to break down and thicken.

Stir in sugar and lime juice or lemon juice, mixing well. Bring to a full rolling boil, stirring constantly. Sugar will scorch quickly if not kept moving. Boil, uncovered, till thick, about 25 minutes.

Use the gel test to ensure jam has reached the gel point. Once confirmed, turn off the heat and, using a funnel, ladle jam into jars to a ¼-inch headspace.

Wipe rims with a damp towel; put on lids and bands. Submerge in hot water bath and process for 15 minutes.*

Turn off heat, remove canner lid, and wait 5 minutes before moving jars to a folded towel. Let sit for at least 12 hours before checking seals on jars. Then store in a cool, dark place for up to a year.

**Note: Altitude adjustments for water or steam canner:* If you're 1,001 to 3,000 feet, increase processing time by 5 minutes; 3,001 to 6,000 feet, increase processing time by 10 minutes; if above 6,001 feet, increase processing time by 15 minutes.

Yield: 2 pints or 4 eight-ounce jelly jars

PRESSURE CANNING

Pressure canning tends to intimidate folks, but my pressure canner is one of my favorite tools. It opens the door to so many different options for shelf-stable food, including vegetables and meats, than water bath canning.

Of all the items I can, the one I use every single week and the base for so many dishes is broth. Broth is extremely economical to make at home. I always have jars on my shelf, ready to go at a moment's notice.

When canning broth, as instructed below, you do need to skim off the fat. I've been asked if canning destroys the nutritional benefits of the broth. Even after canning, my broth (when put back in the fridge) still gels just as strongly as it did before canning. This is my litmus test.

I'm much more confident in my homemade and home-canned broth than I am in any store-bought alternative. If the high temps of roasting the bones (which is much higher than the canning temperature) didn't destroy the properties, I don't believe canning them for the short processing time does either.

HOW TO MAKE YOUR BROTH

1. Place your bones (some people prefer to use just bones with bits of meat left on them; others prefer to put a whole chicken that has been cut up with the meat still on; I use soup bones with meat for my beef broth) into your pot or slow cooker. If you want to add vegetables, you may, but see our chart on processing times when using vegetables and meat together, or you may use all vegetables.
2. Add 1 to 2 tablespoons of apple cider vinegar or white vinegar. This will help break down the bones, releasing the gelatin and collagen.
3. Measure out how much water you're pouring in to cover the bones, meat, and vegetables. This will be approximately how much liquid you get back out (minus a cup or so) so you know how many jars to prepare for canning.
4. For the **slow cooker method**, turn bones mixture on low and let it cook for 24 hours. For the **stovetop method**, bring ingredients to a low boil and boil for 2 hours. In an **Instant Pot**, cook on high pressure for 1 hour. Some broth aficionados say broth must simmer for 72 hours. I always get a wonderful gel on mine regardless.
5. When broth is cooked, strain through a fine strainer, or you can line a strainer with cheesecloth. I use a fine mesh strainer and don't mind if tiny bits of meat filter through (we're talking itty bitty).
6. Place broth into the fridge until the fat layer on the top of the broth is white and turns completely solid. Skim off this fat and discard or save for another use.

I toss odd and end pieces of vegetables into a freezer container for broth making, such as the ends of celery, onion skins, ends of carrots, or any other small amounts of vegetables I'd normally discard. We're straining the broth and not eating the vegetables, so I don't care if it's the odd and end pieces. This is also very frugal.

CANNING THE BROTH

1. Prepare jars, lids, and bands by washing them in hot water, and get pressure canner heating up; keep jars hot.
2. Place strained and skimmed broth back into a large pot and bring to a boil. Fill jars with broth to a 1-inch headspace. Wipe down the rim of the jar. Place lid and band on and screw down to fingertip tight.
3. Place into the prepared canner on the rack. Check that the vent pipe is clear and lock the lid into place and bring to a boil. Allow steam to vent for 10 minutes and then close the vent. For broth made strictly from bones, process at 10 pounds of pressure: pint jars for 20 minutes and quart jars for 25 minutes (see chart for broths made with vegetables). If using a dial-gauge-only pressure canner, use 11 pounds PSI. Follow pressure level according to your altitude and type of gauge.*
4. Turn off heat and allow pressure to reduce to zero naturally. When pressure is completely reduced, remove the lid, and wait an additional 10 minutes. Remove jars, place on towels in a draft-free area, cool for 24 hours, check seals, and store.

**Note: Altitude Adjustments:* If your altitude is 1,001 feet above sea level and you're using a weighted gauge pressure canner, increase your weight to 15 pounds. For a dial gauge pressure canner, you'll increase by 1 PSI for every 2,000-foot increment: starting at 2,001 feet above sea level to 4,000 is 12 PSI; 4,001 to 6,000 is 13 PSI; up to 8,000 feet above sea level is 15 PSI.

Processing Times for Broth

BROTH TYPE	POUNDS OF PRESSURE *see above note for altitude adjustments	PROCESSING TIMES:	
		PINT JARS	QUART JARS
BEEF BONES	10	20 minutes	25 minutes
CHICKEN BONES	10	20 minutes	25 minutes
VEGETABLE https://www.bernardin.ca/recipes/en/vegetable-stock.htm	10	30 minutes	35 minutes
COMBINATION OF BEEF AND VEGETABLE https://www.bernardin.ca/recipes/en/beef-stock.htm?Lang=EN-US	10	20 minutes	25 minutes
COMBINATION OF CHICKEN AND VEGETABLE https://www.bernardin.ca/recipes/en/chicken-stock.htm	10	20 minutes	25 minutes
VEGETABLE BROTH OR YOUR OWN COMBINATION OF CHICKEN/BEEF AND VEGETABLES IF NOT FROM AN ABOVE TESTED RECIPE	10	60 minutes	75 minutes

Safety Notes: There is no tested time or recipe for canning fish stock or fish broth that I have seen.

Note: Vegetable broth has a longer processing time. If you're adding vegetables to your meat, then it's a combination recipe and should be canned to the longest processing ingredient. Consult recipes from the *Ball Complete Book of Home Preserving* and the Bernardin website, if desired; I've included links above that have some specified vegetable amounts with Bernardin's chicken and beef stock and a shorter processing time. If you're following Bernardin's exact recipe, then it's fine to go the shorter 20-minute processing time, but if you're adding in vegetables to taste (which is what I do), you must process for a longer time.

I prefer to have both pint and quart sizes on hand for varying recipes. I can in pints when it's a smaller batch and quarts when I make a larger batch. Enjoy your jars of home-canned nourishing goodness!

TRADITIONAL LIVING TIP

Using the bones for a second batch of broth is a frugal practice. In the case of beef bones, I reuse them almost every time.

For smaller bones like chicken, I do a test. I push on the bones and if they crumble (are completely soft), then I don't reuse them. They've given me all their gelatin and collagen at this point. I find this happens when using my Instant Pot due to its effectiveness.

Always use fresh vegetables and herbs on the second batch; only the bones are reused. And if you're worried that the second batch will be weaker, consider adding extra vegetables and herbs.

PRESSURE-CANNED GREEN BEANS (RAW PACK METHOD)

The very first item I learned how to can by myself as a newlywed was green beans. My family has been seed saving their own strain of heirloom green pole beans for more than five generations and over a hundred years. My entire life we've grown and preserved these beans. And homegrown and home-canned green beans taste nothing like store-bought or store canned. I confess, neither myself nor my children can eat store-bought green beans. They've no flavor.

14 pounds for 7 quarts / 9 pounds for 9 pints
Green beans
Salt

In the dead of winter when there's no fresh vegetables from the garden, we rely on green beans as a staple vegetable at the dinner table.

Green beans are one of the vegetables safe to use the raw pack canning method with. This makes them a quick canning project, and with my large All-American canner, I can process nineteen pint jars at once, making stocking the pantry quick work.

Wash beans and trim ends (remove strings on string varieties). Leave whole or snap into 1-inch pieces.

Prepare pressure canner (for more information, see page 120). Prepare jars, lids, and bands by washing them in hot water.

Fill hot jars with snapped beans, leaving a 1-inch headspace.

Add salt (1 teaspoon for quarts and ½ teaspoon for pints).

Add boiling water, leaving 1-inch headspace. Remove air bubbles and add more water if needed to maintain 1-inch headspace.

Wipe rims, put lids and bands on to fingertip tight.

When all the jars are filled and in the canner, place the lid on your pressure canner. Turn heat to high and allow steam to vent through the vent pipe for 10 minutes. After 10 minutes, place the weighted pressure gauge on at 10 pounds pressure* and process pint jars for 20 minutes and quart jars for 25 minutes. If using a dial-gauge-only pressure canner, use 11 pounds PSI. Follow pressure level according to your altitude and type of gauge (see chart page 121).

Turn off heat and allow pressure to reduce to zero naturally. When pressure is completely reduced, remove the lid and wait an additional 10 minutes. Remove jars, place on towels in a draft-free area, cool for 24 hours, check seals, and store.

**Note: Altitude Adjustments:* If your altitude is 1,001 feet above sea level and you're using a weighted gauge pressure canner, increase your weight to 15 lbs. For a dial gauge pressure canner, you'll increase by 1 PSI for every 2,000-foot increment; starting at 2,001 feet above sea level to 4,000 is 12 PSI; 4,001 to 6,000 is 13 PSI; up to 8,000 feet above sea level is 15 PSI.

Ball

HOW TO MAKE TOMATO SAUCE

Tomato sauce is one of the most versatile items you'll have in your pantry and food storage. It's probably my favorite tomato product, and if I only had to pick a top few (I don't think I could pick just one) then it would be on my top favorite list of home-canned items.

Tomato sauce can be turned into pasta sauce, pizza sauce, ketchup, added to soups, stews, chili, and casseroles, and of course used as tomato sauce in recipes.

Traditionally, tomato sauce took much longer to make than canning regular tomatoes, but with the help of modern appliances such as a blender, you can have homemade tomato sauce ready to can much faster than ever before.

While you can use any type of tomato, a paste tomato will reduce the boiling time and produce a thicker sauce much faster. My preference is San Marzano Lungo or Amish Paste tomatoes.

There are a few options when it comes to removing the skins on your tomatoes and making sauce.

1. ***Traditional water blanching:*** Immerse your tomatoes into boiling water for a minute or so, plunge into cold water, and remove the skins. Chop tomatoes, remove stems, cores, and any blemished areas and simmer in a large pot.
2. ***Food mill or sieve:*** Chop tomatoes into quarters and place into a large pot. Crush tomatoes as they're reaching a boil and continue adding new layers of tomatoes. Once they're all in the pot, let boil for 5 minutes. Then process mixture through your food mill or sieve to remove skins and seeds. Place the remaining sauce back into the pot on the stove and heat to a boil.
3. ***Freeze your tomatoes whole:*** Pop your ripe tomatoes into the freezer, then thaw, and rinse under warm water. The skins fall off; scoop out seeds. Place in a blender and puree, or if you don't have a blender, chop, put in a large pot, mash with a potato masher, and bring to a boil.
4. ***Roast your tomatoes:*** Roast tomatoes on low broil for 30 to 45 minutes, until skins are beginning to blacken and shrivel. Allow to cool for 15 minutes (cool enough to handle), then remove the skins, puree up the skinless tomato, put straight in a pot, and cook down to sauce or run through a sieve/food mill to remove the seeds.

To prevent the tomatoes from separating, as soon as you've cut them, they need to be heated. Tomatoes contain an enzyme that when exposed to air begins to break down the pectin (which results in separation, where you see a layer of liquid and then the tomato flesh/sauce), and heat inactivates this enzyme. This is why many instructions only have you cut a few tomatoes at a time before adding them to the pot. If they do separate, it's not a safety issue; just mix back together before heating and serving or cooking.

Always use stainless steel or a nonreactive pot when cooking tomato products.

No matter which of the above methods you use, bring tomatoes to a boil over medium heat, and let the sauce simmer until some of the water has evaporated and sauce has reached its desired thickness. Using a paste tomato will result in a thicker sauce faster. Stir often so it doesn't burn or scorch. You can let the sauce reduce by half if you wish for thickness or only reduce by a third—up to you!

CANNED TOMATO SAUCE

Thin Sauce:

Average of 5 pounds tomatoes per quart or 2½ pounds per pint.

Thicker Sauce:

6½ pounds tomatoes per quart or 3¼ pounds per pint

Tomatoes

Bottled lemon juice or citric acid

Salt (optional) ½ teaspoon to pint jar or 1 teaspoon per quart

Herbs/spices (optional)

Rinse tomatoes, choose the peeling method from page 125, and prepare sauce. Once sauce has reached desired thickness, prepare jars, lids, and bands by washing them in hot water, and get the water bath, steam, or pressure canner heating up.

Add lemon juice or citric acid, optional salt, and optional herbs to each jar, then fill with hot tomato sauce according to the canning method below.

Acid amounts to add to jar based on size:

Bottled lemon juice: 1 T. per pint | 2 T. per quart jar

Citric acid: ¼ tsp. per pint jar | ½ tsp. per quart jar

Note: Headspace is different for water bath and pressure canning. While the National Center of Home Food Preservation uses the same headspace, Ball does not. Both are tested sources (which means they're both safe), but I've found when pressure canning I have less siphoning using the headspace recommendations from Ball.

Water bath or steam canner instructions

Fill jars to a ½-inch headspace. Run a spatula around the jar circumference to remove air bubbles. Add more tomato sauce if needed to keep ½-inch headspace. Wipe the rim of the jars clean, place the lid and band on. Screw down to fingertip tight and place jars in a water bath or steam canner. Process pints for 35 minutes and quarts for 40 minutes* (if you're 1,000 feet or higher above sea level, you will need to use a hot water bath and not the steam canner).

Remove canner lid and wait 5 minutes. Remove jars, place on towels in a draft-free area, cool for 24 hours, check seals, and store.

Pressure canner instructions

Fill jars to a 1-inch headspace. Run a spatula around the jar circumference to remove air bubbles. Add more tomato sauce if needed to keep 1-inch headspace.

Wipe the rim of the jars clean, place the lid and band on. Screw down to fingertip tight and place jars in canner. When all the jars are filled and in the canner, place the lid on your pressure canner. Check the vent pipe is clear and lock the lid into place. Turn heat to high and allow steam to vent through the vent pipe for 10 minutes, then close the vent. After 10 minutes, place the weighted pressure gauge on at 10 pounds pressure* and process pint and quart jars for 15 minutes. If using a dial-gauge-only pressure canner, use 11 pounds PSI. Follow pressure level according to your altitude and type of gauge (see chart at beginning of chapter).

Turn off heat and allow pressure to reduce to zero naturally. When pressure is completely reduced, remove the lid, and wait an additional 10 minutes. Remove jars, place on towels in a draft-free area, cool for 24 hours, check seals, and store.

**Note: Altitude adjustments for water or steam canner:* If you're 1,001 to 3,000 feet, increase processing time by 5 minutes; 3,001 to 6,000 feet, increase processing time by 10 minutes; if above 6,001 feet, increase processing time by 15 minutes.

**Note: Altitude adjustments for pressure canner:* If your altitude is 1,001 feet above sea level and you're using a weighted gauge pressure canner, increase your weight to 15 lbs. For a dial gauge pressure canner, you'll increase by 1 PSI for every 2,000-foot increment; starting at 2,001 feet above sea level to 4,000 is 12 PSI; 4,001 to 6,000 is 13 PSI; up to 8,000 feet above sea level at 15 PSI.

Flavor options:

- Add to the jar 1 fresh basil leaf, free of blemishes.
- Add to the jar 2 teaspoons dried herbs. Examples: ½ teaspoon dried basil, ½ teaspoon dried rosemary, ½ teaspoon dried oregano, ½ teaspoon dried thyme, or any combination of dried herbs you prefer.
- You can sub out one of the ½ teaspoons of dried herbs for hot red pepper flakes if you like a little heat; however, I would try it with ¼ teaspoon first to make sure it's not too hot.

RAW-PACKED TOMATOES WITHOUT LIQUID

While you may can tomatoes packed in water, I want all the delicious tomato flavor I can get. This recipe produces a delicious base for soups, stews, and chilis. This is what I use in the Meatball Minestrone soup on page 63.

Average of 3 pounds tomatoes per quart or 1½ pounds tomatoes per pint

Salt (optional)

Bottled lemon juice or citric acid

Prepare jars, lids, and bands by washing them in hot water, and get the water bath or pressure canner heating up; keep jars hot.

Peel tomatoes by blanching in boiling water for 30 to 60 seconds or until the skin starts to crack. Immerse tomatoes in cold water and slip off the skins. Remove cores and any bruised or blemished spots (sometimes they show up more after blanching). You can leave tomatoes whole, in halves, or quartered.

Add acid to each jar. If using bottled lemon juice: 1 T. per pint jar | 2 T. per quart jar. If using citric acid: add ¼ tsp. per pint jar | ½ tsp. per quart jar.

Pack raw tomatoes into prepared jars with a ½-inch headspace. Press tomatoes down tight until the juice in the tomato fills up the spaces between tomatoes and in the jar with juice. Add ½ teaspoon salt to pints or 1 teaspoon to quart, if desired.

Remove air bubbles, recheck headspace, and add more tomatoes if needed. Wipe down the rim of the jar. Place lid and band on and screw down to fingertip tight.

Place into the prepared canner on the rack.

To process in a water bath, make sure jars are completely submerged beneath the water. Bring to a boil and process both pints and quarts for 85 minutes. Remove canner lid and wait 5 minutes. Remove jars, place on towels in a draft-free area, cool for 24 hours, check seals, and store.*

To process in a pressure canner (my favorite), place jars inside pressure canner. Check the vent pipe is clear and lock the lid into place and bring to a boil. Allow steam to vent for 10 minutes and then close the vent. Process pint and quart jars at 10 pounds of pressure for 25 minutes. If using a dial-gauge-only pressure canner, use 11 pounds PSI.*

Turn off heat and allow pressure to reduce to zero naturally. When pressure is completely reduced, remove the lid and wait an additional 10 minutes. Remove jars, place on towels in a draft-free area, cool for 24 hours, check seals, and store.

**Note: Altitude adjustments for water bath canner:* If you're 1,001 to 3,000 feet, increase processing time by 5 minutes; 3,001 to 6,000 feet, increase processing time by 10 minutes; if above 6,001 feet, increase processing time by 15 minutes.

**Note: Altitude adjustments for pressure canner:* If your altitude is 1,001 feet above sea level and you're using a weighted gauge pressure canner, increase your weight to 15 lbs. For a dial gauge pressure canner, you'll increase by 1 PSI for every 2,000-foot increment; starting at 2,001 feet above sea level to

4,000 is 12 PSI; 4,001 to 6,000 is 13 PSI; up to 8,000 feet above sea level at 15 PSI.

DEHYDRATING

Dehydrating food is one of the oldest forms of food preservation there is. Though electric dehydrators are quite nice, you can dehydrate food without one by using warm air.

Long before the days of electricity, food was preserved using dehydration. My father fondly recalls strings of leather britches decorating their attic bedroom.

LEATHER BRITCHES

Leather britches are green beans that have been preserved by stringing and drying, rather than canning or other forms of preservation.

The great thing about this method of preservation is that you don't have to heat up your house with a pressure canner or even a dehydrator to preserve them safely.

During the Great Depression, my grandmother did can some food, but they had a limited number of jars, so she had to choose what food went into jars versus other forms of food preservation that were available to her.

Traditionally, leather britches were done with a greasy bean, an heirloom bean that is slick without fuzz on the pod. Any hardy, non-fuzzy green bean will dry well and make great leather britches. It's best to choose a variety that has thicker skin and larger beans.

Use beans that aren't overripe. They should be in the perfect eating stage, tender and crisp when snapped. Some green beans are referred to as string beans because they have a long, fibrous "string" that grows on one side of the bean. Green beans are also referred to as snap beans because of the noise they make when you're snapping the ends off the beans. If the variety of bean that you have has the string, it needs to be removed. No one likes a piece of floss-like material in their mouth while enjoying dinner!

HOW TO MAKE LEATHER BRITCHES

1. Give the beans a quick rinse, then string them by snapping off one end and pulling the string-like membrane off the bean. Then snap the other end of the bean off.
2. Grab an older sewing needle and a long piece of thread and double thread your needle. The beans can get heavy if doing a long strand, so doubling the thread is highly recommended. Tie off a large knot at the end of the string. If the knot is too small, the beans will just slip right over it.
3. Take the bean and poke the needle through the middle of the bean. I like to poke through one of the actual beans rather than just through the green fleshy part; this will help the beans stay in place.
4. Continue stringing your beans until you have a nice tall stack of beans. I like to do mine in about one- to two-foot sections, but ultimately, it depends on how many beans you're harvesting at a time for how long your strand will get OR how much your family will eat at one sitting.
5. Make a big loop at the top of the string and hang it from a hook where it's out of the way, preferably in a warm, dry area with good airflow.
6. As the beans dry, they will start to look leathery, hence the name, "Leather Britches."
7. Store them in a cool, dark, dry area of your home.

Leather britches need to be rehydrated before cooking. Cover 4 cups of leather britches with 6 cups hot water (make sure they're covered by a couple of inches) and let soak for 2 hours, or until the beans are soft and pliable.

Rinse them and place the beans in the insert pot of a pressure cooker with enough water to cover by a couple of inches, and add 1 slice chopped bacon, 1 teaspoon salt, and 1 clove minced garlic. Cook on high for 20 minutes. Let the pressure release naturally for 15 minutes, then manually release any remaining pressure.

CHAPTER 5

THRIVE

I have lived my entire life on the same road in the shadow of the North Cascade Range. Across the river we have a post office that is open four hours a day during the week. The gas station closed down almost a decade ago, and the nearest town is more than ten miles away.

Most of the places are referred to by the last name of the original owner or settler of the land, not by the address. For example, one of our parcels of land on the deed is referred to as the Banner place, because that was the last name of the man from whom my grandparents purchased it. My dad's field and barn are referred to as Fruehling's, because that's the name of the old farmer he purchased it from years before I was born. You'd think after this many decades we'd refer to it by my dad's name, but that's not the way of it up here.

I remember my first overnight trip to the large, bustling city of Seattle. A friend and her sister took me out to dinner downtown and we strolled through the streets afterward. They had both grown up in the city and were quite comfortable with the throngs of people.

We crisscrossed through traffic, and they read the streets like I could read the mountain ridges and landmarks back home. Which was a good thing, because I don't think I could have found my way from one block to the next, let alone back to where we were staying.

There was no need for a flashlight or headlamp. Storefronts, streetlights, and stoplights lit up the crosswalks. I stopped in the middle of the sidewalk.

"What's the matter?" my friend asked.

I stared up at the sky. "It never gets dark here, does it?"

She followed my gaze upward. The glow from the city stretched far into the sky. "I guess it doesn't, not really."

We continued on, the soles of our shoes slapping the pavement. No worries about stepping into mud or other barnyard concerns.

My eyes kept glancing toward the sky, my subconscious working to decide if it really was nighttime or not. Trying to go to sleep with all the lights and noise was an all-night affair. I'm used to the yip of a coyote, the serenade of frogs in the summer, and the only outside light from the wash of a full moon.

I thrive in a country environment, where "street smarts" include knowing how to tell when rain is moving down the mountain, recognizing when a storm is blowing in over the ridge, and keeping an eye out when you find bear scat around.

I'm clueless in the city, but others thrive there. They know not to ever pull out your money and feed a parking meter when you're standing by yourself and someone is eyeballing you. No matter where we find ourselves in life, be it the busy corner of a sprawling metropolis or a quiet back pasture corner, we can thrive. We only need someone to show us the tools, the way of the land, so to speak, in order to grow.

The Merriam-Webster Dictionary defines the word "thrive" as "to progress toward or realize a goal despite or because of circumstances."

I don't know about you, but I kind of love that this definition includes that last part of the line—"despite or because of circumstances." Because each of us has battles in our lives.

They may not be the same battles. My battlefield might be things from the past while yours is a diagnosis from the lab. But no matter what our battle may look like, each of us knows the pain and the crushingness that comes in the thick of it.

Here's the thing, though—when we have Jesus on our side, it doesn't matter what's on that battlefield. We're going to thrive. We're going to conquer that "despite" part because He conquered it when He died on the cross for our sins.

Remember when I shared about my thyroid issues? That was a battlefield for me. I felt like I was literally slogging through rubber boot–sucking mud every day for months on end.

Despite that, He led me to the point where I learned to lean on His strength because I had none of my own left. He also led me to a doctor who could help me with both prescription and natural medicines so I could thrive again.

What I love about herbal and natural medicine is we're just beginning to understand how the things God made in this world work together. While herbalism as a way of helping heal the body has been around long before the recent rise of modern medicine, we now have the science to see how or why they help with certain things.

GROWING YOUR OWN HERBS

One of my favorite things about using herbs is that you can grow many of them yourself with very little space, making them truly self-sustainable and free!

For the most part, herbs do well in small spaces and grow quite well in a container. Even my apartment- or yard-challenged friends can still grow their own herbs.

Many herbs are better suited to containers because of their invasive nature. Unless you want herbs gone wild all over your homestead (which isn't always a bad thing), you'll want to plant mint, lemon balm, oregano, and thyme in containers if you're limited in space or like a manicured garden with everything in its spot. They spread by sending out runners via their root systems, so a container helps keep them from sprawling.

But many people like to use thyme as a ground cover. It's a wonderful thing to have your landscaping be the foundations of your medicine cabinet, flavor your food, and offer such a pleasing array of foliage and flowers for the eye.

You can pick any size container—I prefer whiskey barrels that can hold multiple herbs, and smaller pots for individual herbs. Make sure there's enough room for the roots to spread out and down. If the container is outside, make sure there are adequate drain holes in the bottom. For larger containers, fill the bottom with sticks, branches, and leaves. These will break down over time, creating more soil, but allowing you to use less soil initially (we're using hügelkultur principals in a container).

Fill the rest of the way up with rich potting soil and compost. Because the dirt in the container won't receive food from surrounding soil like in regular gardens, you'll want to give it a boost of fertilizer and good compost on the top every year.

You can grow many herbs from seeds or purchase small starter plants from nurseries or plant stores. Many herbs will reseed themselves for the following year, most notably cilantro and dill.

To start seeds indoors you'll need to know your average last frost date to calculate when to begin growing your herbs from seed. You can type into Google your zip code and "first and last average frost date" if you don't know yours already.

You'll need small seed-starting containers and potting soil. This is one of the few times I recommend purchasing organic potting soil. Just like human infants, baby seedlings are more susceptible to viruses and pathogens in the dirt that may be lurking in your regular garden soil. If you've ever lost seedlings before to dampening off (where baby seedlings slump over, shrivel up, and die), this is probably your culprit.

You can pasteurize soil at home by heating it up in your oven, but I find it more practical to purchase it.

Pick your container. If you're reusing containers from previous plants, make sure you sterilize them by soaking them in a solution of 1 part bleach to 10 parts water for 20 minutes. Allow to dry before using.

My favorite options are to use old egg cartons (though they do tend to require a bit more watering as they're porous) or old plastic clamshell containers from store-bought produce.

Fill your container with soil, place the seeds on the surface, and wet the soil. To mimic rain and avoid the washing away of soil, I fill a spray bottle with warm water and mist my seeds. Cover with plastic to trap the moisture. This is where the clamshells come in handy, because you can simply close the lid.

Keep the soil moist, and don't allow it to dry out until your seeds have sprouted. Depending upon the seed type, this can take anywhere from 2 to 14 days. Most seeds require a soil temperature of 60° or warmer. You can use special seed-starting heat mats or place plant starts next to a heater vent or your wood stove. Check them morning and night and mist with your spray bottle to keep them moist but not soaking wet.

Once the seeds sprout, remove the plastic covering and move to an area with adequate light.

GROW LIGHTS

For most people, a sunny windowsill, even if it's a southern exposure, doesn't provide enough light for strong seedlings. Grow lights allow you to mimic the sun. That means you can use full-spectrum lights, either LED or fluorescent, to grow strong plants. The different spectrums mean the different light wavelengths.

Grow lights don't produce as much strength and intensity as sunlight. This means the amount of time that you have your lights on is going to be longer than if your seedlings were outside. Vegetables typically require at least six-plus hours of full sunlight. For grow lights, you'll need between 12 to 16 hours of light. LED lights are more intense than fluorescents so they don't need to be on as long, only needing 12 to 14 hours.

Because LED lights are stronger and more intense, they don't need to be as close to the plants. If they're too close they can burn the tops of the plants, turning them white or light brown in color. How far above should LED grow lights be?

That depends on the wattage of the bulb. Remember to always go by what your plants are telling you. If they're bleaching, move the bulb farther away. If seedlings are weak/reaching/leggy, move the bulb closer.

LIGHT SPECTRUMS

1. Blue: important for strong root growth as well as photosynthesis.
2. Red: encourages stem growth, flowering, fruit, and chlorophyll production.
3. Green: helps with photosynthesis, although not quite as important. It becomes more important when a plant is bigger because the green light is able to get down to the lower canopy and reach those lower leaves, thus allowing them to produce energy to help the plant grow.
4. Yellow: by itself, yellow doesn't play a crucial role. When yellow is paired with the other colors, it increases the plant's ability to bounce back from stress.

TRANSPLANTING OUTDOORS

The second biggest mistake people make when growing their own seedlings, next to not sterilizing, is not exposing their seedlings to movement. Outdoors they have the rain hitting their leaves and the wind moving their stems. This results in a stronger plant.

Seedlings indoors are wimps. They need the stimuli to become strong. It reminds me of the

adversities and hard times in my own life, because these are always the times when I do the most growing and my faith gets a super shot of maturity.

An easy way to mimic the outdoors for your seedlings is to gently run your hand over the top of the plants whenever you walk by. You could put a small fan on them, but I'd rather not have to use any more electricity than necessary.

When you're ready to transplant your seedlings outdoors, make sure you harden them off. This is a process of taking them outdoors for longer periods of time each day over a week before planting them in their permanent spot. If you don't take this step, you'll end up putting your seedlings into shock and most likely killing them.

Find a spot that is sheltered from hard winds and doesn't get too hot. Put your seedlings outdoors for one hour the first day. Increase their time outdoors by two hours each day over a week.

When transplanting, dig a hole twice as wide if possible but the same depth as the container the plant is in. If the roots are bound together, take the edge of your spade and gently break them up so they can easily spread out and find food for the plant. Fill in the hole with soil and make sure the soil is at the same line on the stem as it was in the container (an exception to this is tomatoes, which need to be planted deeper than their seedling pot level). Water well.

GROW BASIL INDOORS

You can keep some herbs in the house as long as they get adequate sunlight or are under a grow light. Many folks will bring in their basil or other tender herbs so they can harvest them all year long. Never fear; no matter how cold your climate is, you can have year-round herbs via a windowsill herb garden. And are you ready for this? You can grow basil without any dirt! I've successfully grown basil indoors through the winter in just water!

Step 1: Have you ever been at the grocery store and seen those little packages of living basil? Buy one or two bunches (usually about three plants are inside each package). Growing basil in water during the winter months is actually preferable, as you don't have to worry about your soil molding.

Step 2: Choose a planter. You'll need a planter of some kind, and the most frugal option is to use something you already have at home. I have a thing for Mason jars, especially the vintage blue ones. Make sure your jar is washed and rinsed well. The quart size work best, as they're taller and offer more support for the basil.

Step 3: Add water. Put about an inch of water in the bottom of your jar. (Note: If you're on city water or have chlorine in your water, you'll need to use untreated water.) You don't have to add liquid silica, but because silica is normally found in soil, the addition of it will help the cell structure of your plant. It's available at most nurseries and plant stores. It comes very concentrated, so just a drop is all you'll need in each jar.

Step 4: Place your basil plants in the water. Find the warmest and sunniest window in your home, which is usually a southern exposure side of the house. Because your plants have been inside a store with very little sunlight, don't be alarmed if the leaves seem wilted and shriveled the first few days. Place the plant in the window and wait a week. All but one of mine perked up after some TLC in the sunlight.

Be sure you don't place the basil against the glass or allow the leaves to touch it. The glass will be quite a bit cooler than the air and can kill the plant, especially during nighttime temps. If an exceptionally cold night is in the forecast, you should move your plants out of the windowsill onto the counter where it's warmer overnight.

Replace the water every week or two.

Once your basil is doing well in its new home, you'll want to harvest it. Now, harvesting basil isn't hard, but here are a few tips to ensure the continued growth of your herbs. Contrary to what you'd think, leave the large bottom leaves of basil alone. These are what feed your plant.

When you've got pairs of leaves at the top of your plant in a few tiers, pinch off leaves directly above a pair. This will cause two new shoots to grow, creating more leaves and a bushier, stronger plant.

FAVORITE PERENNIAL HERBS

Some herbs are perennials and will come back every year. These are some of my favorites, as they require planting only once and not as much care. If your area gets extremely cold, some perennial herbs may act as annuals, meaning you'll have to replant them each spring if you don't cover them up or bring them inside during the cold months.

Some herbs are annuals, but due to their self-seeding nature, they act as a perennial and you generally don't have to replant them manually each year.

Knowing your gardening zone and microclimates on your property and yard is key. To discover your gardening zone (this will tell you if a perennial will survive your winter temperatures), simply type in your zip code and gardening zone into your favorite search engine.

Microclimates are areas in your yard that are naturally warmer or colder than other areas and can be used to your advantage. For example, rosemary doesn't generally overwinter well in my area. However, I've had one plant in a large dark-colored container right next to our back deck in southern exposure—the warmest part of our homestead—winter over for ten years straight without doing a thing to it. But I've had rosemary in other locations on our land that didn't make it through winter.

Chamomile

There are two types of chamomile: Roman chamomile is a perennial, whereas German chamomile is an annual, but it tends to self-seed, so it acts as a perennial. German chamomile has more studies done on it and is generally used more overall than Roman chamomile. Hardy to zone 4.

Chives

Chives are excellent as a container herb or planted directly in the ground. Chive plants will spread out, so when a plant gets too big, simply take a sharp, pointed shovel and divide it. It will die back during the winter and send up new shoots in the spring. Hardy in zones 3–9.

Comfrey

Comfrey has a long root system, making it tolerable to both hot and cold weather. It is often planted under fruit trees. Just be aware that the plant is almost impossible to eradicate or remove once it's established. It produces pretty purple and violet blossoms. Hardy in zones 3–9.

Echinacea

Also called coneflower, this plant has beautiful blooms and will come back year after year. Echinacea makes a pretty bouquet as well. It prefers full sun but will tolerate some shade. Hardy in zones 3–9.

Horehound

White horehound, or common horehound, is a flowering perennial in the mint family. Its flowers create little round balls, making a whimsical addition to beds and flower arrangements. Hardy in zones 3–9.

Lavender

A beautiful addition to your landscaping and flower beds, lavender prefers full sun and well-draining soil, doesn't like to have its roots wet, and does well in raised beds or rock gardens. In the early spring, trim back the plant to a few inches tall. Hardy in zones 5–9.

Lemon balm

This perennial herb in the mint family dies back in the winter but comes back in the spring. Its bright green leaves are hard to miss and smell delightfully of lemons, unless you get the lime variety, which of course smells like lime. Hardy in zones 4–9.

Marshmallow

Althea officinalis is a perennial flowering herb that's part of the mallow family. It grows best in zones 5 through 8 but will grow down to zone 3 with some insulation. It produces a tall stalk with pale pink blossoms up and down it. Hardy in zones 3–9.

Rosemary

This perennial does best in full sun with well-draining soil but will tolerate some shade. Some varieties are more cold tolerant than others. Hardy in zones 8–9.

Oregano

Oregano prefers full sun, but if your area gets really hot, afternoon shade won't bother it. It tends to spread, so either keep it trimmed, which helps create a bushier plant, or plant in an area where you don't mind if it spreads out. Hardy in zones 4–9.

Sage

Sage likes a good amount of sun but tolerates afternoon shade. It's a gorgeous addition to landscaping because its leaves are a beautiful silver green and quite soft to the touch. It does well in containers or in the garden ground. It's fairly hardy, and I can harvest fresh leaves well into December in our zone 7. Hardy in zones 4–10.

Thyme

Thyme also likes full sun and holds up well to drought or low water. I like a low-maintenance plant, and thyme fits the bill nicely. It also will make a home in either a container or the garden. Hardy in zones 5–9.

Annual Herb Seed Starting Chart

HERB	DAYS TO GERMINATE	WEEKS TO START BEFORE LAST FROST	WHEN TO PLANT OUT-DOORS	WHEN TO DIRECT SOW
BASIL	5 to 10 Days	4 to 8 weeks	2 to 3 weeks after last frost, can stagger plant all summer	2 to 4 weeks after last frost
CALENDULA	5 to 15 days	6 to 8 weeks	1 to 2 weeks after last frost	After last frost
GERMAN CHAMOMILE	7 to 14 days	4 to 8 weeks	1 week after last frost	2 to 4 weeks before last frost
CILANTRO/CORIANDER	5 to 10 days	4 to 8 weeks	Right at last frost	2 weeks before last frost
DILL	10 to 14 days	It does better direct sown		4 weeks after last frost or when soil temperature is 60 to 70°
SUMMER SAVORY	2 to 3 weeks	6 to 8 weeks	After danger of last frost has passed	1 week after average last frost date

HOW TO HARVEST HERBS

To keep most herbs from getting leggy, you'll want to pinch off the leaves from the top of the plant, not the bottom. This can be done as needed for cooking or when the plant begins to get too big.

I use my hands if I'm just collecting a few leaves for a recipe. But if harvesting a larger amount, sharp scissors or gardening shears are best. Remember, we don't want to crush or bruise the leaves before use. We want all that flavor in our food.

HOW TO DRY YOUR OWN HERBS

Pick herbs in the morning, right after the dew is gone. They have the highest concentration of oils in their leaves at this time of day. Basil is the exception and can be picked a bit later in the morning.

Lightly rinse your herbs to remove any dust or other unseen debris. I'm sure you practice organic gardening at home, so we don't have to worry about any icky chemicals or pesticides. Place herbs on an absorbent towel to suck up the rinse water.

Be careful not to crush or bruise your herbs before drying. You'll lose the oils if this happens, and that is where the flavors are concentrated. If possible, dry herbs on the stalk and remove the leaves after they're dry for storing.

There are two ways to dry herbs: a dehydrator or the old-fashioned hanging method. If the weather is damp or has high humidity, you may want to go with the dehydrator method.

Old-fashioned method: Tie the ends of no more than four to five stalks of herbs together. Hang the bunches upside down in a warm, dry area, out of direct sunlight. Allow to dry until leaves crumble at your touch. Depending upon the moisture content in your leaves and the climate, this can take anywhere from a week to a month. Check periodically for any mildew or mold growth. Discard if mold or mildew are present. We tried putting our herbs in a pillowcase and hanging it to keep dust away, but there wasn't enough air flow and they ended up molding. However, using a paper bag works wonderfully; it allows adequate air flow but keeps dust off the herbs.

Dehydrator method: Place your herbs in a single layer on your dehydrator tray, making sure they're not touching. Because the herbs will shrink dramatically when dried, I use my fruit leather screens. You want to make sure there's enough room between the herbs for the air to circulate. Dehydrate your herbs at 95°, which is the lowest possible setting on my dehydrator. Check them at 12 hours. One year, we had excessive rain, and it took 24 hours for my herbs to dry. Because herbs don't seem to transfer flavors when drying, you can dry them together. I've had four trays going at once with chocolate mint, spearmint, oregano, basil, and thyme.

Once herbs are dry, place them into a clean, dry jar. It's best to not crush or crumble your herbs until use, as this increases the surface area, making them break down faster and release the medicinal oils. I prefer glass jars, as plastic containers seem to affect the flavor of the herbs over time.

Common Herbs and Their Uses

	CULINARY USE	MEDICINAL USE
ARNICA	Do not take by mouth or internally, as this can cause serious side effects.	This has been used for centuries in topical salves for aiding bruises, sprains, and sore muscles. You'll find it in many topical gels or ointments even on store shelves.
BASIL	Basil is one of the most popular flavorings in Italian dishes and is great when used in soups, dressings, and salads. Especially a favorite paired with sliced tomatoes and mozzarella cheese.	Basil is used to help aid digestion and also has antibacterial properties.
CALENDULA	Calendula can be used in tea and has been used to color butter and cheese.	This is a wonderful herb for the skin and basically an all-around work horse. It has anti-inflammatory and antiseptic properties, which makes it a great candidate for multiple skin issues and also for wound care. It smells wonderful and also has history as a dye due to its orange blossom. Because calendula is considered a gentle herb, you'll find it in a lot of natural products for children. (Always check before using any herb or essential oils on children.)
CARDAMOM	This is a strong spice, so a little goes a long way. It's often paired in fruit desserts or custards, similar to cinnamon, and is a highlight in many Indian dishes.	Cardamom can be used as a digestive aid.

	CULINARY USE	MEDICINAL USE
CAYENNE	Cayenne adds heat to any dish and is commonly used in Mexican recipes.	You'll find this spice in pain relief creams on the pharmacy store shelf as capsaicin cream, used to help aid the relief of muscle, nerve, and joint pain. Never apply to open wounds or skin to avoid burning the skin or causing blisters. Use a small amount and lower strength when first using topically. As a medicinal spice it helps aid digestion, is thought to help boost the metabolism, and might help prevent blood clotting. Caution: Don't use prior to surgical procedures, if you're on blood thinning medications, or if you have a blood clotting disorder.
CHAMOMILE	This herb is commonly used to make a soothing tea.	This little white flower plant is another common garden plant. It's been around for centuries and is used to support feelings of calmness and to aid nervous stomachs. Many people enjoy chamomile as a bedtime tea. Chamomile is often used in wound care to help promote healing. Recent studies show it can help improve cardiovascular conditions and support immune systems.[2]
CHILI POWDER	Chili powder is used in almost every Mexican dish and often added to other dishes for flavor. It's the base of many homemade spice mixes.	See *cayenne*. Make sure your chili powder doesn't contain any other additives before using.
CHIVES	Chives are one of our favorite herbs to add to potatoes, eggs, casseroles, salads, meats, and soups. They're a member of the allium (onion) family and are delicious both fresh and dried.	Chives are used to help aid digestion and also contain vitamins C and A.
CINNAMON	Cinnamon is used in a variety of baked goods. It pairs well with fruit and pumpkin. I've even used it to flavor some stews or chili. It's a warm spice and is probably one of the most used in many a pantry.	Medicinally, cinnamon is a powerful little spice. It's used to help aid digestion and also has antiviral and antifungal properties. Cassia cinnamon has large amounts of the compound coumarin and can harm the liver in large doses. [3]
COMFREY	Comfrey should not be taken internally without the recommendation of a medical professional.	A common medicinal plant, often known as bone-knit, comfrey also contains chemicals called pyrrolizidine alkaloids that can damage the liver and lungs and is not advised for internal use.[4] Topically, comfrey reduces inflammation from sprains and broken bones. The leaves and roots of the comfrey plant contain allantoin, which is a substance that helps new skin cells grow.
CORIANDER	Coriander is the seeds from cilantro. The leaves of cilantro are used mainly fresh for flavoring salsas and pico de gallo. The seed is used mainly in Mexican dishes after it's ground up, but also is used in Indian curry dishes.	Coriander is used to help aid digestion, and studies have found it effective in killing some parasites.[5]

	CULINARY USE	MEDICINAL USE
CUMIN	Cumin is traditional in many Mexican and Indian dishes.	Cumin has been proven to help boost the immune system[6] as well as having many antioxidant properties.
CURRY	Curry is found in many Indian recipes and cuisine. It's actually a blend of many spices, with turmeric as the base. Usually it includes cumin, turmeric, coriander, black pepper, fenugreek, red pepper, ginger, celery, and cardamom.	Curry may help reduce inflammation, aids digestion, and may help blood sugar levels.
DANDELION	Dandelions send down a long taproot, making them hard to eradicate from your yard but excellent come harvest time. Pull the plant up by the root, rinse off the dirt, and dehydrate for storage. In the spring when the leaves are young, you can add them to salads or any other dish as salad greens. The blossoms can be dipped in batter and fried. The roots are a powerhouse as well.	Dandelion is thought to aid with digestion, and has traditionally been used in the past for liver issues and as a diuretic.[7]
ECHINACEA	This herb is commonly used to make a soothing tea.	This is one of the herbs I use frequently once my kids start back to school and cough and cold season go into overdrive. Echinacea is used for its ability to help support the immune system.
GARLIC	Garlic is used daily in our home. In fact, we grow about 70 bulbs of garlic every year and we're of the opinion that if a recipe calls for garlic, always double or triple the amount.	Medicinally, garlic may cover the widest range of ailments. Garlic contains a chemical called allicin. It is used to treat many conditions related to the heart and blood system, including blood pressure and cholesterol, cancer, bacterial and viral infections, topically to the skin, common cold symptoms, and stomach ailments.[8]
GINGER	Ginger is a main spice in baking, especially gingerbread, apple, and pumpkin recipes. A little goes a long way, as it can have a bit of a kick to it.	Ginger is thought to help all sorts of stomach ailments, including nausea and vomiting, pain, and inflammation, and it also has antibacterial properties as well as immune support.[9] This is also one that you shouldn't use if you're on blood thinning medications or have blood clotting disorders.
LAVENDER	The blossoms should be harvested before they begin to dry out, or when they first start to open. They can be added to teas or used in baking.	Lavender is probably the most commonly used herb for its calming and soothing properties. I put a drop of lavender essential oil on my pillow every night when I go to bed. I also make lavender sachets for my husband's truck and keep dried bunches of it around the house. Lavender works well to help soothe the skin and is often used in preparations for burn relief and pain. The blossoms can be infused into oil for salves and creams.

	CULINARY USE	MEDICINAL USE
LEMON BALM	Harvest lemon balm early in the season before the heat of summer evaporates most of the oils.	Lemon balm is probably best known as an aid in reducing stress and promoting relaxation. It also has antiviral and antispasmodic properties, and use is associated with fevers and coughs.
MARSHMALLOW ROOT	Used to flavor candies.	Marshmallow root can help soothe a sore throat and ease the swelling and pain of mucus membranes in the respiratory tract.[10]
MUSTARD	Mustard is commonly used in many of our pickling brines and condiments, especially mustard for sandwiches and added in powdered form to homemade barbecue sauces.	Mustard is surprisingly strong in antioxidants and is antibacterial. So much so, that research shows mustard can help fight and may prevent certain types of cancer.[11] Mustard is a longtime standby for helping aid respiratory symptoms.
NUTMEG	Nutmeg is another favorite spice when it comes to baking. It completes my trinity of baking spices with cinnamon and ginger.	Nutmeg is thought to help aid digestion symptoms and to contain some antibacterial and antifungal properties.[12]
OREGANO	Oregano is the base for many Mexican and Italian dishes. It pairs well with tomato-based recipes, beef, and chicken.	Oregano is used to help aid the digestion system, possibly help reduce cough, and has antifungal, antibacterial, and antiviral properties. It also helps eliminate parasites.
PEPPERMINT	Peppermint is a wildly prolific plant, best suited to a container. I often bruise a few leaves and toss them in my water bottle for a flavor pick-me-up.	Peppermint can soothe an upset stomach and help support bowel function. Though peppermint is known for its use with stomach issues, if you have GERD or acid reflux, peppermint can help relax the sphincter muscle, allowing acid from your stomach to climb up to the esophagus, making symptoms worse. If you're feeling congested, just the scent of peppermint oil can help with congestion. Just make sure you don't get the peppermint oil on your skin, as it will sting and burn.
PLANTAIN	The young leaves can be eaten raw in salads. The older leaves are tougher and stringier, and they can be simmered in soups and stews.	Plantain is known to help aid the healing of wounds, skin abrasions, and swelling, and is thought to have antibacterial and antifungal properties.[13]
RED RASPBERRY LEAF	To prepare as a tea, steep the dried leaves in a cup of just-off-the-boil water for 10 minutes; strain and drink. We harvest our own leaves from our red raspberry patch. They have a very mild flavor.	This is commonly used for women's issues, from relieving menstrual cramps to hormonal migraines.

	CULINARY USE	MEDICINAL USE
ROSEMARY	Rosemary is a particularly fragrant herb. I rarely roast a whole chicken or turkey without the use of rosemary. I pluck a couple of fresh stalks and put them in the cavity of the bird. Whenever I'm making broth or stock, rosemary goes into the mix. It's rare I make a soup that a bit of rosemary doesn't jump in the pot as well. Rosemary pairs well with just about every type of red meat.	Rosemary is commonly used for digestion issues, hair loss, and has anti-inflammatory and analgesic properties.
SAGE	This silvery-green leaf herb is one of my favorites because it's easy to grow, lasts almost a year in my garden, and is just so tasty. I use sage with my meatballs, meatloaf, and many a soup and broth.	Sage is used to support digestive problems and supports mind and mental performance.[14] It can decrease milk when nursing, so a sage tea can be soothing when weaning. Of course, it's not recommended to use any herb medicinally when breastfeeding without first checking with your medical professional. Sage helps decrease secretions and extra mucus and is often used to help aid sore mouth, throat, and swollen nasal passages.
STINGING NETTLE	In the spring when the leaves are young, they can be added to soups and stews or sautéed in butter and garlic as a side dish. Once they're cooked the leaves no longer sting, so no worries. Make sure you wear gloves and long-sleeved shirts when harvesting. They really do live up to their name.	Stinging nettles are thought to help with decreasing inflammation and increasing urine output.[15]
THYME	Thyme is used as a flavoring in many dishes, especially Italian.	Thyme supports the immune system during cough and cold season. It can also help soothe a sore throat.
TURMERIC	This spice is typically found in Indian and Asian dishes and is known for its bright yellow color.	Turmeric is a wonderful addition to add to your chicken soup, as it helps boost the immune system and is now becoming more widely known for its antioxidant and anti-inflammatory properties. However, it can be harder for the body to put that turmeric to work and absorb it unless you eat it with fat or black pepper.[16]

CULINARY USES OF HERBS

Now let's put those spices to use. If you're using fresh herbs in a recipe that calls for dried herbs, you'll need to use three times the amount of fresh herbs the recipe calls for.

If you've ever plunked down money for those little seasoning mix packets at the store or not been able to make a recipe because you didn't have one of those little packets, then this section is just for you. Many of those seasoning packets contain anticaking agents and ingredients made from GMO crops in the form of both corn and soy, just to name a few reasons I don't buy them. Plus, when one is making them at home, one can customize the flavor to their tastes, grow a good portion of the ingredients themselves, and save a ton of money by making their own. Whew, that's a whole lot of reasons to love these recipes.

Feel free to double or triple these recipes, but remember, when we're mixing spices and herbs, it's best to keep them to smaller batches (I wouldn't do a quart-size jar) at a time so you use it up before it starts caking. While the shelf life of spices and herbs is quite long—one to two years if they're kept dry and away from heat and light—the best flavor will be within six months of mixing. If they start to clump up (remember, there is no silicone dioxide or other anticaking agents in these babies), simply take the end of a spoon and break up the largest clumps and stir. Make sure you're not storing them right above your stove where heat and moisture will contribute to faster caking.

Thoroughly combine all the ingredients in a bowl first to ensure even mixing (or shake really well in the jar if there's enough room). Spoon the mixed blend into your container of choice. Whenever I'm pouring anything, I use a funnel if possible. Put a lid on it and label your jar. That's it—you're set to go.

TACO SEASONING

Combine all the ingredients into a glass jar. When making tacos, brown 1 pound of ground beef (or cubed chicken), drain off fat, stir in ½ cup water and 2 tablespoons of taco seasoning, or to taste. Stir well, until all the meat is coated, and allow to simmer for 1 to 2 minutes.

¼ cup chili powder
2 T. cumin
1 T. onion powder
1 T. garlic powder
1 tsp. dried oregano
2 tsp. paprika
1 T. salt
2 tsp. ground black pepper
½ tsp. crushed red pepper flakes (or to taste)

CHILI SEASONING

Combine all ingredients in a glass jar. Use 4 tablespoons of the mix to one pot of chili. This recipe is what I use in our 4½-quart slow cooker.

¼ cup chili powder
¼ cup cumin powder
2½ T. onion powder
2½ T. garlic powder
1½ T. paprika
1½ T. dried oregano
2 T. sea salt
1 tsp. ground black pepper
1 tsp. crushed red pepper flakes (or to taste)

ITALIAN SEASONING

Mix all ingredients in a bowl and transfer to a sealable container. Use this to taste in spaghetti sauce, pizza, stew, soups (especially tomato), or even sprinkle on butter when making garlic bread.

¼ cup basil
2 T. oregano
2 T. thyme
2 T. marjoram
2 T. rosemary
1 T. sage
1 tsp. garlic granules (optional)

RANCH DRESSING

Mix all the ingredients and place in a glass jar.

For ranch dip: Use 2 tablespoons (or to taste) of the mix with 2 tablespoons mayo and ¾ cup yogurt (or sour cream).

For ranch dressing: Use 1 tablespoon mix with ⅓ cup mayonnaise and ⅓ cup buttermilk (for a traditional flavor) or sub in ⅓ cup regular milk. You can add more mayo to make it thicker or more milk for a runnier dressing.

Add a tablespoon of dry mix to your popcorn for homemade ranch popcorn, but be warned, it's slightly addictive.

- 2 T. dried parsley
- 5 tsp. dill weed
- 1 T. chives
- 1 T. onion powder
- 1 T. garlic powder
- 1 tsp. salt
- ½ tsp. basil
- ¼ tsp. ground black pepper

POPCORN SEASONING

Sprinkle onto popcorn to desired taste (melted butter drizzled on the popcorn first is a must at our house).

- 1 T. nutritional yeast
- ½ T. powdered cheddar cheese (optional)
- 1 to 2 tsp. sea salt
- ½ T. garlic powder
- Dash of paprika or chili powder

BASIL PESTO

Add garlic to taste in this recipe. The amount you use will depend on the size of your cloves—I always think more is better! The pine nuts are a traditional pesto ingredient, but since they add so much to the cost, I rarely include them.

Place all the ingredients in a high-powered blender or food processor. Start with the smaller amount of olive oil and add more if needed to blend well. Process until smooth and well blended.

Cover tightly and store in the fridge, or freeze. Many people like to freeze pesto in an ice cube tray—once frozen, pop out the cubes of pesto and keep in a freezer container to add to sauces when cooking. My friend Julie puts her pesto in a gallon freezer bag and lays it flat to freeze in a thin single layer, and then breaks off however much she needs when cooking.

Yield: 1¼ cups

- 2 cups fresh basil leaves
- 2 to 6 cloves peeled garlic
- Pinch of sea salt
- ¾ to 1 cup olive oil
- ½ cup freshly grated Parmesan cheese
- ¼ cup pine nuts (optional)

MEDICINAL USES OF HERBS

Many of your kitchen/culinary herbs are medicinal herbs as well. The difference is the amount, frequency, and application of use.

When I first started my journey into herbs and natural medicine, I approached it very much from a typical Western medicine viewpoint. I wanted to know the herbal equivalent of Tylenol. While there are herbs known for use with headaches, pain, and fevers, herbalism is very much treating the body holistically, not simply throwing a Band-Aid on a symptom like much of Western medicine.

Our bodies are incredibly complex. Even biblically we know all parts affect the other: "So the body is not made up of one part but of many" (1 Corinthians 12:14). So why do we throw that out when we treat the body?

As an herbalist, I've had to undo much of my prior medical training from my pharmacy tech days. We need to understand why the body reacts a certain way instead of immediately trying to stop the action. For example, analgesics are the largest purchased class of over-the-counter medications in the United States.

But why does inflammation (which is a source of pain for many) occur in the body? What is the purpose? Instead of taking something that temporarily blocks our pain receptor or temporarily reduces the inflammation, what if we addressed the core issue that's causing it to begin with?

While I've greatly simplified things here, this is the difference between a holistic and herbal approach versus what most people are accustomed to. But because of my background, both as a Christian and in my pharmacy training, I want to know exactly how that herb works, its mechanisms in the body, and safety precautions.

I am here to tell you herbs are the basis of our medicine cabinet here in my home. They are extremely effective. Most of the time when people tell me herbs don't work, it's because they lack the proper understanding of using them.

Many herbs will already be "hiding" in your regular seasonings in your pantry, but some will have strictly medicinal purposes only. Please, do your research and confirm with your medical professionals before using herbs medicinally, as they can counteract other medicines you may be taking.

There's a bit of misconception with folks that because something is natural, it's safe. That is not true, my friends. Many herbs and natural spices have true effects on the body and can interact with certain medications or medical conditions.

For example, my daughter has a blood clotting disorder—Von Willebrand disease, to be exact. She must stay away from ginger, so no ginger honey or even candied ginger for her.

While I don't want to scare you away from using herbs, I do want you to be responsible and use good judgment. I believe we're blessed to live in a day and age where we have the benefit of both modern and traditional medicines.

Growing up, I rarely went to the doctor. We didn't have insurance, and unless you were really sick, you toughed it out. Luckily, I didn't have many illnesses or need of the doctor often.

After going through GERD and stomach acid issues, including an endoscopy and biopsy of my upper stomach and esophagus, I discovered that my healing came from changing my diet and the things we used in our home.

It sparked our journey to *The Made-from-Scratch Life* and seeking out alternative and natural ways in both our health and home. Herbs weren't something we used in my home growing up, except for occasional culinary purposes.

On my own, I began diving into natural medicine and herbal uses. What I'm sharing with you are truths I've learned on my journey and the herbs we use in our home.

In case you haven't noticed, I'm kind of fascinated by the old way of doing things. While having a special fondness for the pioneers during the American Old West days due to the Laura Ingalls Wilder books, my appreciation goes back much further.

When we look at the ancient cities and the way people lived before our modern conveniences, I'm humbled at how good we have it now. Most of us aren't hiking outside to find clean water or even to an outdoor well to heave on a rope to get a bucket of water (at least in first-world countries and most of Western civilization). We flip a little lever on our faucet and both hot and cold water come rushing into our homes.

Can you imagine being able to treat someone only with various roots and leaves? In modern society, what a typical mother or wife knows about using medicinal plants in her area is virtually forgotten. It wasn't passed down in my family, and it may not have been in yours either.

While I firmly believe in using modern medicine (it saved my life when I had an ectopic pregnancy) and think it can be a wonderful gift God has given us, I also believe in using the natural plants He created. After all, God is the master herbalist; He made them all.

The first place we look to for herb use is in our pantry cupboard. Most of us have a few (or not so few) bottles of dried herbs we use to tasty up a dish. Did you know that many of those herbs not only serve to make our food taste better, but oftentimes those tasty bits have beneficial medicinal properties as well?

While much of modern Western medicine doesn't use herbs in general medical practice, Germany uses herbs in their regular medicine with their German Commission E, a scientific advisory board that evaluates the safety and efficacy of the herbs used for licensed medical practitioners in Germany. Your regular doctor may or may not recommend herbs, but licensed naturopaths will.

For those of you wishing to dive deeper into herbalism, I recommend starting with my course, *Practical Home Herbalism*, which you'll find listed under classes on my website at MelissaKNorris.com.

HERBAL TEA INFUSIONS

As you step into the world of herbs, you'll likely hear terminology thrown around. The first and easiest form is one most of us are familiar with—and that is tea, also referred to as an infusion. We're infusing water with the essence of herbs. Infusions and teas are best suited to the leaves and flowers of a plant.

Choose your herb or herbs of choice to make your tea or infusion. If you have a tea ball or empty tea bags, fill them with your herbs (usually 1 to 2 teaspoons worth) and bring water to a boil. Pour just-off-the-boil water on top of the herbs and allow to steep for at least 5 minutes or up to 15 minutes. The longer it steeps, the stronger it will be. Strain out herbs, add any sweetener if using, such as honey, and sip.

When I have a cold coming, I make this tea to help aid my sore throat and relieve my stuffed-up nose.

1½ tsp. fresh sage leaves (or ¾ tsp. dried)
¾ tsp. marshmallow root
2 tsp. raw honey

Place herbs in a tea bag or tea ball. Pour just-off-the-boil water into your cup and allow to steep for 10 minutes. Remove the herbs and stir in the honey. Sip and enjoy!

Note: Never give raw honey to children under one year of age due to the risk of botulism.

DECOCTIONS

This method takes longer but is similar to making a tea or infusion. This is usually the choice when using the roots, bark, or seeds of the plant.

Place your pieces of herbs into the bottom of a small saucepan, usually about 2 tablespoons worth. Cover with 2 to 4 cups of water. Bring to a gentle boil over medium-low heat. Allow to simmer for 15 to 30 minutes, then strain, allow to cool to a safe sipping temperature, and drink.

Note: You can still use the roots or bark when making an infusion or tea; it just won't be as strong as a decoction. I often make tea blends with both leaves and roots or bark.

HERBAL TINCTURES

While *tincture* sounds very official, it's really the same thing as making your own extracts. To get started, you'll need a clean glass jar, herbs, and alcohol.

Let's chat a minute about alcohol. There can be strong feelings about the use of alcohol. In the case of tinctures or extracts, it helps preserve the herbs and give a long shelf life. It's also the vehicle that extracts the good properties from the herb. Most times, only a small amount of the tincture is used at a time, and when added to a hot beverage, the heat evaporates the alcohol, leaving the herb behind. Alcohol is needed because its strong solvency helps extract some herbs, especially those made from the bark or roots. (*If you're uncomfortable using alcohol, keep reading for instructions on making vinegar- and glycerin-based tinctures, but know you won't be able to fully extract some of the medicinal properties. If you're comfortable taking pharmaceuticals, I view medicinal tinctures as no different.*)

What's the best alcohol to use?

Some people prefer to use vodka because it is clear and relatively tasteless. If you're concerned about GMOs or gluten, because most commercially made vodka is made from grains (although some specialty ones are made from potatoes and even grapes), then search out a local organic brand.

The proof of the alcohol matters when making tinctures. An 80 proof vodka or rum means it's only 40 percent alcohol. A 100 proof is 50 percent alcohol. A 195 proof is 95 percent alcohol. (Everclear is the only commonly available brand I know of that comes this strong.)

ALCOHOL RATIO FOR TINCTURES

The folk method of tincture making is when people eyeball the amount of herb matter in a jar and then top it off. To ensure you're getting enough herb matter to solvent ratio and the proper strength, I highly recommend using a food scale. When using fresh herb matter (not dried) you should use the highest proof alcohol you have to avoid mold growth due to the higher water content of the fresh herbs.

Fresh herb tinctures are in a 1:2 ratio, meaning 1 part fresh herb by weight to 2 parts alcohol in volume. If you had 1 ounce of herb, you would use 2 ounces of alcohol.

Dried herb tinctures use a 1:5 ratio, so if you had 1 ounce of dried herbs you would use 5 ounces of alcohol.

The percentage of alcohol varies based on the herb you're using. Most *materia medica* books (the collected body of knowledge of therapeutic plant uses) will list the alcohol percentage needed for the herbal tincture.

For example: echinacea tincture is 65 percent alcohol/35 percent water. The only way to get to this ratio is to use 95 percent alcohol (we just round up to 100 percent even though it's technically 95 percent when doing the math). For a 5-ounce tincture you would use 3.25 ounces 100 proof and 1.75 ounces water to equal 5 ounces of total liquid.

Most tinctures call for at least 50 percent to 65 percent alcohol, which means you'll need at least

100 proof or 195 proof diluted to the proper ratio. If the above math makes your head swim or you're unable to find 100 proof, the highest proof vodka you can find is sufficient in most cases.

HOW TO MAKE A TINCTURE

Chop up or grind the herb and add it to the jar, then cover with the alcohol following the method chosen (folk or by weight). Store the tincture in a dark cupboard or area away from direct sunlight and try to remember to shake it daily. When using dried herb matter, check the liquid level after two days to make sure there's still an inch of liquid covering the top of the herbs. Add more liquid if the herbs have soaked it all up.

Tinctures can steep anywhere from two to six weeks depending on the herb. After steeping, line a fine wire mesh colander with cheesecloth and place over a large bowl. Pour the herbs and liquid into it. Wrap the cheesecloth around the dried herbs and wring/squeeze to get all the liquid from the herbs out.

Pour into tincture bottles, label, and store in a cool dark area for up to six years. If you don't have enough tincture bottles, simply leave tincture in the Mason jar in a dark cupboard and fill tincture bottles as needed.

Vinegar Tinctures

Follow the above instructions, but use vinegar instead of the alcohol. In her book *Medicinal Herbs: A Beginner's Guide*, herbalist Rosemary Gladstar recommends warming the vinegar before using to help release the herbal constituents. Raw apple cider vinegar is commonly used as a natural health tonic, and as long as you just warm it, you won't destroy any of the good stuff and will add more goodness to your tincture.

Fire Cider isn't technically a tincture (especially when it comes to dosing), but it is an infused vinegar. Fire Cider is an old-timey natural remedy to help boost the immune system, but it really aids the sinuses when you come down with the sniffles and are congested. There are many variations of this recipe, most notably made popular by Rosemary Gladstar, and the beauty of it is you can make it your own based on what you have on hand.

The base of Fire Cider is usually onion, horseradish root, garlic, ginger root, hot pepper, and apple cider vinegar, with other herbs and roots tossed in based on preference and availability.

Medicinal properties by ingredient:

Onion: High in vitamin C, onion has anti-inflammatory and antioxidant properties.

Garlic: It has demonstrated antiviral properties in vitro against rhinovirus and several other strains.[17] When participants of this study took 180 mg of allicin (the organic compound found in garlic) daily, they reported 64 percent fewer colds, and symptom duration was reduced by 70 percent.

Horseradish root: Aids in improving the immune system and alleviating respiratory conditions. The German Commission E has approved horseradish for respiratory infections. Precautions: should not be used in pregnancy/nursing or for those with thyroid issues.

Ginger root: Anti-inflammatory and warming properties that stimulate the circulatory system. Ginger root also has antiviral properties for the flu and cold viruses. Use with caution if you are on blood thinning medications or have a blood clotting disorder.

Hot peppers: We're after the capsaicin found in jalapeños and cayenne pepper to name a few. Capsaicin improves the circulatory system, but it also has antiviral and antimicrobial properties, as well as vitamin C. Use caution with using capsaicin-containing peppers: consult a medical professional before use if pregnant or nursing; have blood clotting disorders; are on blood thinning medications; or are on blood pressure medications, stomach acid medication, and/or theophylline.

Glycerin Tinctures

If you don't want to use alcohol or vinegar, you can make tinctures with glycerin. Make sure you always use a non-GMO food-grade glycerin that is made from vegetable oil and is naturally sweet. Some glycerin is only for external or body care use.

You also need to dilute your glycerin with distilled water before pouring over your herbs. It's best to use distilled water so you don't introduce contaminants. Use 3 parts glycerin to 1 part distilled water. Store in refrigerator for up to one year.

HOW TO USE HERBAL TINCTURES

Herbal tinctures can be taken straight, but due to their potency, most herbalists recommend you dilute them in tea, water, or juice.

Tinctures are generally measured by dropperfuls (the little glass droppers with the rubber bulb on the end) or a teaspoonful, depending upon the herb used in the tincture and the form.

Please review the herb, use, and dosage before using your tinctures medicinally. Visit the Resource page at https://melissaknorris.com/books/hand-made/#bonus where you can find more in-depth information.

TRADITIONAL LIVING TIP

Put those spent herbs to use, not in the garbage. They can be added to your compost pile. If you have livestock, chickens love the leftover berries from making elderberry syrup.

FIRE CIDER MASTER RECIPE

- 1 medium onion, diced
- ½ cup diced horseradish root
- ½ cup diced ginger root
- ¼ cup crushed/diced garlic
- ¼ tsp. cayenne pepper
- 1 to 2 T. fresh thyme or rosemary (optional)
- 2 diced jalapeños (optional)
- Raw apple cider vinegar
- ¼ cup raw honey (optional)

In a clean quart-size Mason jar, place all of your chopped ingredients. Pour apple cider vinegar over contents until completely submerged.

Use a weight if needed to keep the contents under the vinegar. Place a lid on and shake. Try to shake once daily and allow mixture to steep for 2 to 4 weeks.

Strain out the solids. Stir in the ¼ cup raw honey if using.

Use as needed. Some people will use a shot (1½ ounces or slightly less than a ¼ cup) diluted in hot broth or water once a day during cold or flu season; others use it several times a day when they feel symptoms coming on.

Note: Feel free to swap out or omit ingredients, and make this your own. Just remember to do your due diligence on researching each herb or item for any precautions or interactions when using it medicinally.

HERB-INFUSED OIL

- ¾ to 1 cup dried leaves or blossoms
- Oil of choice (extra virgin olive oil, jojoba oil, or avocado oil)

Making an infused herb oil is an excellent way to increase the medicinal properties of your homemade salves and balms. I make several different kinds of herbal oils to have on hand.

I've found the best containers are Mason jars, but any glass container with a lid will do.

Fill a quart-size (4-cup volume) Mason jar with your leaves or blossoms. Pour in the oil to cover the herbs by 1 inch. If using a smaller jar, make sure you leave at least a ½-inch headspace, because the dried herbs absorb the oil and expand.

Place a lid on the jar and shake well. Set the jar in a warm, sunny window.

Shake the jar once a day to help infuse the oil. If the oil level drops below the herbs, add more oil until they're completely submerged.

After 4 to 6 weeks, strain the oil through cheesecloth or a fine-mesh sieve. Store your herb-infused oil in a glass bottle in a dark and cool place, making sure you label it with the type of herbs and the date made. The oil should last for up to a year. You can add a few drops of vitamin E oil to help prolong the shelf life.

Note: It's always best to use dried herbs and plants rather than fresh to avoid moisture and bacteria growth in your infused oil.

FAST HERB-INFUSED OIL

Am I the only one who doesn't always plan ahead? Sometimes we need a way to do something that doesn't take four to six weeks. This is the method you can use to make herb-infused oil in just a day. You'll just need a slow cooker or a double boiler.

Measure out the herbs into a glass Mason jar. Cover the herbs by 2 inches with oil. Place the Mason jar into your slow cooker, filled with about 2 inches of water. (You can also place the Mason jar in a saucepan with water on low heat as a double boiler.) The goal is to have the warm water surround the jar, effectively heating the oil to draw the properties from the herbs into the oil. Bring up to a low heat, preferably between 95° to 120°F. We want as many of the medicinal properties to remain in the herbs as possible.

Allow to infuse until the oil has taken on the scent and color of the herbs, preferably for at least 2 to 8 hours, but the longer the better, provided the heat is low. Even on low my slow cooker tends to get pretty hot, so using a cooking thermometer to test the temperature periodically is a great idea. To keep the temperature lower, leave the lid off when using your slow cooker. I actually found that the "keep warm" setting worked best on my model to keep temps right around 100°.

When the oil is finished infusing, take it off the heat and allow it to cool. Strain the oil through cheesecloth. Store your herb-infused oil in a glass bottle in a dark and cool place, making sure you label it with the type of herbs and the date made. The oil should last for up to a year. You can add a few drops of vitamin E oil to help prolong the shelf life.

THE ELDER

Even many people who don't know much about herbs have heard of elderberry. It's a great herb with multiple uses, though most people are more familiar with elderberry syrup, but the elderflower has many medicinal properties as well.

Elderberry grows in almost all areas of the United States and Europe. There are two varieties of elderberry, *Sambucus nigra* (European elder and produces a black-colored berry) and *Sambucus canadensis* (American elder and produces a blue-colored berry). There are more clinical studies with the *Sambucus nigra*, simply because Europe uses herbs in their mainstream medical practices and the United States does not, but the studies on *Sambucus canadensis* show both have medicinal properties, and most herbalists will use either variety.

Contrary to popular social media sharing, all parts of the elder plant can be used, but the ripe berries (avoid consuming unripe) should be cooked before consuming to avoid stomach upset. The bark and root are commonly stated to leave out of any syrup making because they have both emetic and purgative properties (aka nausea, vomiting, and diarrhea).

You may also see quite a few online sources citing a specific incident from the 1980s where a group in California consumed large amounts of fresh elderberry juice that was pressed with the leaves and bark, and of the twenty-five people in the group, eight were taken to the hospital. I've seen this story misquoted, saying the ailments were due to cyanide levels, but the victims' arterial blood gasses and serum cyanide levels were later reported as normal; that part tends to get left out in the telling. The moral of the story is don't drink five glasses of raw elderberry juice.

Most people can consume elderberry just fine, especially once cooked. (Though as with any substance, some are much more sensitive to it than others, so if you experience any stomach issues, back off the dose.) Anytime you try something new, herb or food, take a small amount to first see how it affects you and if you have any type of reaction.

When dealing with cold or flu symptoms (it can be hard to tell which is which when you first feel the telltale signs of being sick), I've found starting sooner rather than later tends to make a big difference on how effective the remedy is, along with the dosing. The good news is, elderberries and elderflowers have been tested and show antiviral properties against influenza A and B (various strains) among other viruses and bacteria, including *Staphylococcus aureus* and *Streptococcus pyogenes* among other strains. You can see why so many turn to this plant for cold, flu, and respiratory infections.

You'll see some overlap in the medicinal properties of both the flower and the berry, but here's a snapshot.

Properties (berries): antiviral, immunomodulating, antioxidant rich, inflammatory modulating

Properties (flowers): antiviral, antibacterial, anti-inflammatory, relaxing nervine, relaxing diaphoretic (induces sweating), diuretic, skin protectant, antioxidant rich

The elderflower can be made into a tincture or a tea. Because elderflowers are diaphoretic, they are often used to support the body during a fever, as sweating is a natural defense when we get too hot.

ELDERFLOWER TEA

To brew, steep dried elderflowers/blossoms in 8 ounces of water just off the boil for 10 to 15 minutes. Strain and add honey to taste, if you wish. Consume throughout the day. Enjoy!

- 2 to 3 tsp. dried elderflowers/blossoms
- 1 cup water

Daily Dose: 10 to 15 grams daily (German E Commission), 6 to 12 grams daily dried flower or infusion

Cautions: Don't use without consulting a medical professional if you have an autoimmune disease or are on autoimmune medications. Too much may cause nausea, vomiting, and abdominal distress.

ELDERBERRY SYRUP

One of the reasons elderberry syrup is so popular is because you can make it ahead of time and have it on hand in the fridge. The other reason: it's syrup, which means even those folks with a picky palate (be it young or old) can be coaxed into taking it. The beauty of this recipe is we're incorporating honey, and raw honey has its own medicinal properties, making this a double dose of goodness.

- ½ cup dried elderberries
- 1½ cups water
- 1 T. raw apple cider vinegar
- ¼ cup honey

Place dried elderberries and water in a saucepan and bring to a simmer. Cook for 30 minutes and mash the berries toward the end to help them release more juice. Add more water if berries soak up too much so you have enough syrup left to strain at the end.

Strain syrup, making sure to push down on the berries to extract all the juice.

After it's cooled slightly but is still warm, add in apple cider vinegar and honey.

Stir well and store in fridge for up to 6 weeks.

Yield: approximately 6 ounces

Doses

Preventive: Take 1 tablespoon daily as a preventive measure a few days before high exposure activity and then seven days after suspected exposure. Example: I have a flight coming up and will begin using it three days before, during my trip, and seven days after I get home.

Symptoms present: When feeling symptoms, more frequent doses throughout the day are needed. A tablespoon every couple of hours while awake is recommended.

Safety precautions: Use with caution if you have an autoimmune disorder, and consult with your doctor and pharmacist.

SALVES AND BALMS

Making a homemade salve for the skin is much easier than most people think. They're a great way to fill your medicine cabinet and are much cheaper to make at home than purchasing; plus, you get to control the ingredients.

A balm is typically firmer than a salve—I use 3 parts oil to 1 part beeswax. A salve is typically softer and can have a ratio of 2 parts oil to 1 part beeswax, or even 2 parts oil with a cocoa or shea butter base and very little, if any, beeswax.

You will need a tin or glass container to store your salves and balms. I recommend going with a smaller Mason jar that allows you to get your fingers all the way to the bottom to scoop out the last of the salve and balm. Jelly jars work great.

When you're ready to make your salve, place the oil and beeswax in a double boiler or a large Pyrex glass measuring bowl over a smaller saucepan. Place a few inches of water in the lower pot, and heat to a low boil.

Place a spoon or small saucer in the freezer.

Stir the oil and beeswax together until it's completely melted and in a liquid state. Test your salve by dropping a few drops onto the frozen spoon or saucer and placing it back in the freezer or fridge for a minute to see what the final texture of your batch will be once cooled. If you'd prefer a firmer texture, add more beeswax. For a softer texture, add more oil.

Remove from heat and add in any essential oils if using, stir, and pour into desired containers. Allow salve to cool and set. Store salve in a dark and cool space when not in immediate use for the longest shelf life.

LIP BALM

1 T. infused avocado oil (0.45 oz. by weight; see page 160)

1 T. cocoa butter (0.45 oz. by weight)

1 T. beeswax (0.45 oz. by weight)

8 to 10 drops essential oil (optional)

Using your infused herbal oil in this recipe will give it another scent boost as well as medicinal properties. Some of my top choices of infused oils for lip balm are peppermint, calendula, or lavender.

When making homemade salves, lotions, and balms, it really is best to get a small food scale so you can measure your ingredients by weight instead of volume to be accurate. However, lip balm is a smaller recipe, so you can usually get away with measuring instead of weighing.

The cocoa butter gives this a nice smell and pairs nicely with spearmint or orange essential oil. Please make sure you use an essential oil and brand that is safe for external use before ever adding it to your products.

To be able to test the consistency of your lip balm, place a saucer or small bowl in the freezer before you begin. Using a double boiler, or a small saucepan with a large Pyrex glass measuring bowl on top, heat the first three ingredients on medium-low heat, stirring frequently. When everything is liquefied, remove from heat and stir in essential oils if using.

To test the consistency of the lip balm, take a small amount and place it on the cold saucer or plate. It will harden very fast. Rub it on your lips to test.

Add a small amount more oil to the mixture if your test sample is too firm. If it's too soft, add a small amount of beeswax. Test again until it's reached your desired state. It's much easier to make adjustments this way, because once it's in the tubes, you're kind of stuck.

Immediately begin filling your containers, because the balm will start to cool and solidify rather quickly.

Fill lip balm containers three-fourths of the way full and allow to slightly cool. This takes only a minute or two and prevents a tunnel or hole forming in the top of your lip balm. Once the balm has cooled (it will start to harden and lighten in color), fill to the top of the container. Allow to cool, place lid on, and use. I keep the pot simmering so I can set the balm back on if it starts to cool too much before I top off the tubes.

A glass eyedropper is helpful for filling the containers. I keep a dedicated one for making balm, as it's pretty much impossible to clean it out thoroughly. If the balm hardens inside the dropper, let it simmer in the water for a few minutes, expel the liquid, and dry before the next use. (You never want to introduce any water into your lip balm, as this can encourage bacteria growth.)

If you use the pouring method, some of the lip balm will harden along the spout and side of the glass. Hold the Pyrex on its side above the steam of the double broiler until the balm is melted to get every last drop; be careful, it's hot and steamy. Immediately pour into your last container.

Yield: 8 lip balm tubes

SKIN-SOOTHING SALVE

- 1 oz. calendula-infused oil
- 1 oz. lavender-infused oil
- 1 oz. coconut oil or shea butter
- 1 oz. beeswax
- 10 to 15 drops lavender essential oil (optional)

Combine oils and beeswax in a double boiler over low heat and melt. When everything is liquefied, stir and remove from heat. Allow to cool slightly and stir in essential oil. Pour into a tin or small jelly jar and allow to cool.

There are many herbs to choose from to infuse your oils with in the making of the salves. The addition of essential oils can also be used—just do your due diligence. Also, make sure and test a small area of skin when using a new herb in case you have allergies.

Popular Herb Choices:

- Arnica and peppermint for sore joints and muscles
- Chamomile, calendula, comfrey, and plantain for skin issues

You can use a single herb or combine them to your preference. It's up to you!

PEPPERMINT CHOCOLATE BODY LOTION

- 2 oz. peppermint-infused olive oil (may sub in any other oil of your choice)
- 2 oz. shea butter
- 2 oz. cocoa butter
- 2 oz. coconut oil
- 10 to 15 drops peppermint essential oil (optional)

We know our skin is our biggest organ, and it absorbs what we put on it. Many of the lotions and creams you buy at the store have preservatives, fillers, and not-so-nice ingredients in them.

I don't know about you, but whenever I use store-bought lotion, it seems my skin never stays moisturized for long. I'm having to constantly reapply.

When you look at the ingredient list on most store-bought products, one of the first things listed is water. Water is a filler ingredient, and it also causes the need for more preservatives in order to keep it from growing bacteria and to stay shelf stable. Plus, while water is essential for us to consume, it doesn't help moisturize our skin on the outside.

This homemade lotion can be made with just a few ingredients in very little time, and because we're not using fillers, it's ultra-moisturizing to the skin. I like the addition of peppermint to this homemade lotion (it's really a cream) because peppermint is soothing to irritated skin and it smells divine with the cocoa butter. But you can customize this to any scents and herbs you wish. That's the true beauty of handmade.

Heat water in bottom of your double boiler or in small saucepan with Pyrex glass bowl on top.

Measure out your oils and butters and place them in the top of the double boiler. Stir frequently until melted.

Remove from heat and pour into a food processor bowl or your stand mixer bowl. Move to the fridge to cool.

After 20 to 30 minutes, when oil is cooled but not solidified, add the drops of peppermint essential oil (don't worry about stirring it in; it will be fully whipped in the final stage). Place back in fridge until oil has softly set.

You want it to be soft enough that you can poke your finger in it but not so soft there's still liquid beneath the surface.

When oil is set, place the bowl on the food processor or stand mixer and blend for about 4 minutes, until the oils turn creamy and soft. You may need to stop partway through to scrape down the sides. When finished, place into a glass container.

This is greasier than regular lotion when you first put it on, but it soaks in within a few minutes and leaves the skin super soft. If you're in the dead of summer or live where it's really hot, you may want to store this in the fridge if it starts to melt. I haven't had that issue.

Other popular scent combinations you may wish to try would be lavender or sweet orange. Sweet orange is not considered to be phototoxic like many of the citrus oils. Always use citrus oils with care if applying to the skin, as most can cause serious burns due to phototoxicity.

Popular oil choices:

Jojoba oil: This oil is a great choice for the skin, as it is extremely close to our natural sebum, making it a great oil for topical use.

Fractionated coconut oil: Fractionated coconut oil stays in a liquid state no matter the temperature. Nonfractionated coconut oil melts at 78°, so if your room temperature is cooler than that, it's in a solid state.

Avocado oil: This oil is high in vitamins E and C, as well as fatty acids—all wonderful components for the skin.

BATH SALTS

One of the easiest ways to use your herbs is to make herbal bath salts. Many times when we think of using herbs we think of cooking, teas, and tinctures. However, your skin is your biggest organ, and it absorbs whatever it contacts.

Bath salts aren't anything new, but they're much cheaper to make at home, and you can choose what herbal and essential oil blend you'd like to make. Taking a warm bath in the evening is a great way to help relax before bedtime.

A warm bath is thought to raise your body temperature, so when you get out and your body temperature falls (which happens naturally in the evening as your body prepares for rest), it may help your body become ready for sleep. The warm water also helps to relax stressed, tired, and sore muscles.

Adding bath salts puts aromatherapy into play with the addition of the herbs. Epsom salts are the main ingredient in bath salts. They're large crystals of magnesium sulfate. Our bodies need a proper level of magnesium to function properly. And some studies show magnesium may offer help with insomnia.[18]

Magnesium is one of the most important minerals in our bodies and helps regulate hundreds of enzymes in our bodies. It helps the proper function of our cardiovascular and endocrine systems as well as our brain and neurotransmission.[19] To sum up, it's a pretty big deal in keeping us healthy on a whole lot of levels.

An Epsom salt bath can help increase your magnesium levels. Plus, any excuse to lounge in the tub for a half hour or so is a definite plus in my book.

You can use straight Epsom salts, especially if you're sensitive to scents, but it's fun to create different scent combinations, and these make great gifts to give. You can choose to use essential oils, herbs, or a combination to create your bath salts.

Epsom salts can be found at almost any grocery store or pharmacy. You can purchase them in large bags or small containers. I keep a two-pound bag on hand.

Baking soda (sodium bicarbonate) is added to help soothe irritated skin, act as a water conditioner, and help leave skin feeling extra silky.

BATH SALTS

3 to 4 T. herbs of choice (optional)
Sea salt (optional)
2 cups Epsom salts
½ cup baking soda
10 to 20 drops essential oil (optional)

Wash and rinse fresh herbs and let dry on an absorbent towel. Some favorite herbs for aiding relaxation are calendula, chamomile, and lavender. Rosemary and peppermint are good choices to help soothe tired and sore muscles. Chop finely with a sharp knife and stir into sea salt. Once combined, add to your Epsom salts. You can play around and do half sea salt and half Epsom salts, or adjust the ratio to your liking.

Mix all ingredients together and store in a clean Mason jar. Add 1 cup to bathwater. To help dissolve the salts, pour them under the running water while the bathtub is filling.

Never add essential oils directly to bathwater, as they won't disperse. By adding them to the Epsom salts first, they're able to dissolve into the water. Otherwise, you'll create an oil slick on top of the water. Always use essential oils with caution—less is more. Some oils, like peppermint, cinnamon, and other warm oils, can burn the skin if applied directly without dilution (and some should never be applied to the skin or used in the bath). Do some research on the essential oil you select.

BEESWAX CANDLES

Not only are candles a simple light source and a good visual reminder of the power of God, but they're also simple to make at home.

Many of the candles you buy in the store have chemicals and toxic pollutants in them, which fill our homes and air. They might smell good, but we don't see the invisible vapors being released into our homes.

When we look back to the days of old, we see that candles were frequently used. One of the beauties of a candle is they can easily be made at home using ingredients one could produce off their own land if needed.

While there are many waxes available, I wanted my homemade candles to be made from natural ingredients. Almost any fat source will burn, though some aren't going to smell very nice, and though we're after function, a pleasant end product is also a plus.

Beeswax is our first ingredient. If you have honeybee hives, you'll be able to harvest your own beeswax. However, most of us aren't beekeepers. You can purchase beeswax online from various retailers, in craft stores, and often from co-ops or health food stores. I'm lucky enough to have two local beekeepers in our area and can purchase beeswax from them.

If you purchase beeswax from a store, beeswax sold in pellet form is the easiest for measuring and melting quickly. Beeswax from a local beekeeper will come in larger hard blocks. You can chop small chunks off with a knife. I've also tried grating it, which works somewhat. Another option is to melt the beeswax over a double boiler and pour it into smaller molds for quick use later.

The next ingredient in our candles is the fat source. While beeswax will burn all by itself, it does burn hot. Adding in another fat source helps make a softer candle and helps keep the wax from cracking (because we want them to look pretty too, right?), and my two choices are lard and coconut oil. The pioneers of old often used tallow (beef fat) or lard to make candles, without the addition of other waxes. As much as I love our home-rendered lard for baking and cooking, I don't necessarily want to smell animal fat burning when I light my candles. The beeswax naturally smells of honey when it's heated. Score! In fact, when I was making up a batch recently, my husband came in and said, "That smells awesome."

Beeswax is hard when cooled but turns to liquid when heated. If beeswax is melted at too high of a temperature, it can become discolored and also scorch or burn. This usually happens when it reaches a temperature of 185°. We want our beeswax to smell like honey when it's burning, not burned wax. To avoid all of this, you will want to melt the waxes and oils in a double boiler. If you have made my other herb-infused or body care recipes, you're familiar with the double boiler, or a makeshift version. If you don't have an official double boiler, they're easy to make. I don't like having to purchase something if I can use things I already have to get the job done.

Fill a saucepan with 2 inches of water. You'll need a smaller vessel, preferably either a metal pouring pot (they're shaped more like a pitcher, as they have tall sides) or a Pyrex measuring cup or a Mason jar. For candle making with a double boiler, I have a measuring cup and a Mason jar I leave as my dedicated wax/oil melting pots. That way I don't have to worry about cleaning out the melted and reset wax and oils.

The smaller container needs to be small enough that the water can surround the sides. You don't want the container actually touching the bottom of the pan, however, because then it's directly against the heat source. To avoid this, I put a few canning bands in the bottom of the pot to act as a shelf for my pouring pot. Works like a charm.

Bring the water to a boil then turn it down to a simmer—a gentle boil. Put your pot/jar with the measured beeswax down into the water. The smaller the chunks of beeswax, the faster they will melt. Stir occasionally using a metal spoon until all the beeswax is almost melted. Now add in your fat source, which will melt much quicker than the beeswax did. Once completely melted, remove from heat, and immediately stir in any essential oils or fragrance oils you'd like to use. Pour your wax into the candle containers.

(Remember, if you ever do have beeswax or any other oil catch on fire in your kitchen, do not ever try to put it out with water. This will only cause the fire to spread. You need to smother it—put a lid on the pot, or your surest bet is to use a fire extinguisher. I've never had this happen to me, but it's always best to be prepared ahead of time.)

Next up we need a wick source. Many store-bought candles use wicks with either a lead or metal wire in the center. I don't know about you, but I don't really want the toxins from burning lead or metals floating around the air in my home. We use all-cotton wicks, without any metals or lead.

Choosing the size of your wick (meaning thickness, not length) will depend upon the diameter of the container you're using for your candle. A regular-mouth Mason jar has an opening of just more than 1½ inches when measured from the inside of the jar, not the outer rim. They flare out a bit at the shoulder of the jar on the pint sizes to almost 2 inches.

I really like the smaller eight-ounce jelly jars for candles. The small-size natural paper wicks from CandleScience perform very nicely for me in these jars. If you're using a larger diameter container, you'll likely want to increase the size of your wick.

You'll want to do a few test jars before making a large batch to make sure you have the correct wick size for your beeswax and container. After candles have cured for at least 24 hours, trim the wick to ¼-inch length above the surface of the wax.

Light the candle and let it burn for two hours. At the end of the two hours, the wax should be nearly or all the way melted to the sides of the jar. If there is a lot of soot or mushrooming of the wick, it's probably too big. On the other hand, if the melted wax isn't reaching out to the sides of the container, the wick may be too small.

Candle Size Guidelines

These are the guidelines I follow when testing out a new jar size for a candle. We don't want the full weight of the jar in wax, as it would be too much. For instance, if you have an eight-ounce jar, you don't want a total of eight ounces of wax and fat. I do three-quarters of the total container capacity, meaning an eight-ounce jar would need six ounces of combined wax and fat. For a six-ounce jar I would use four and half ounces of wax and fat.

Then I break down the amount of beeswax to the amount of either coconut oil or lard. I use two-thirds beeswax and one-third fat. This means that for the eight-ounce jars I use four ounces of beeswax and two ounces of fat. The largest jar size I've used to date is eight ounces.

Formula for amount of wax and fat per jar = ¾ of the total jar capacity

Formula for wax and fat ratio = ⅔ wax + ⅓ fat source

HOMEMADE JAR CANDLE

8-oz. glass jelly jar
4 oz. beeswax
2 oz. coconut oil or lard
1 wick
Wick centering device (optional)

Center your wick. If you purchased wicks with adhesive tabs, then attach the wick base to the center of the jar. If not, use a hot glue gun and attach it to the center of the jar. Use a candlewick centering device to help center the wick and to keep tension on the wick when pouring the wax and letting it cool. Note: You can also use a pencil: Tape the end of the wick to the pencil and roll it until it's taut, with the pencil resting lengthwise across the top of the jar. However, you wouldn't want to put the pencil in the oven, so this step will need to be done right before pouring.

Preheat your oven to 170°. Put your jelly jar on a cookie sheet and place it in the oven to warm up. (The heat does melt the hot glue a bit, but I just push it down right before pouring and haven't had a problem.)

Heat up water in the bottom of your double boiler. While the double boiler is heating, measure out the beeswax into your melting container. When double boiler is boiling, adjust heat to a simmer and place your melting container inside. Stir occasionally, and keep an eye on your melting wax. When the wax is almost fully melted, add in the coconut oil or lard. This process will take about 20 to 30 minutes total, depending upon the size of your beeswax chunks or pellets.

When wax is fully melted, remove melting container from the heat. Add in any fragrances if using, and stir well to incorporate them. Many people use only essential oils so the scent is not synthetic, but beeswax doesn't throw other scents (meaning the candles don't give a lot of scent when burning), and because the beeswax already smells like honey, I choose not to add the extra expense of fragrance. This is totally up to you!

With a hot pad or oven mitt (the jars aren't extremely hot at 170°, but I wouldn't grab them barehanded), take your jars out of the oven and pour your candles. Turn off the oven.

Place candles back in the now-turned-off oven and allow to cool in the warm environment. When using this method of slowly cooling the wax, I haven't experienced any cracks in the finished candle. I did experiment with poking relief holes in the wax but found it wasn't needed when cooling in the warm oven, so now I skip the step of having to do a re-pour.

When candles are cooled to solid, remove from the oven and allow to cure for at least 24 hours. Trim the wick to ¼ inch above the surface of the candle, and enjoy!

One note regarding cleanup: I use a dedicated spoon and melting containers to avoid having to get all the wax out. But if you have a utensil that needs to be used for something else, pour just-off-the-boil water over it, then wipe clean with a paper towel you can throw away. You don't want beeswax water going through your pipes.

Yield: 1 candle

SOAP

The pioneers of old made almost everything by hand. The sheer amount of knowledge these folks possessed is astounding. So much of what we purchase today was commonly made at home.

One of those items is soap. Back in the day, the pioneers made their own lye from wood ash and rendered the fat from their beef (tallow) and pigs (lard) to mix with it. Many people today still make soap with lye (you can't make soap without it) and fat, but they don't make their own lye; they purchase it from the store. Lye is caustic and needs to be used with care given to safety and proper procedure.

Always wear safety goggles, long-sleeved shirts, long pants, and rubber gloves when mixing your lye water and throughout the soapmaking process. Use a room with good ventilation, and make sure no small children or pets are present. Have vinegar on the counter, as it neutralizes lye.

For those just getting into soapmaking, one of the easiest ways to make soap is to use the melt-and-pour method. You purchase a base of lye and oils that's already been through the saponification process and is fully cured.

This means you get to use the soap sooner without the curing process and don't have to worry about getting ratios just right or having a failed batch. If you're wanting a project to use with the kids, this is a much safer route.

You can purchase the base in one- or two-pound increments or all the way up to ten or twenty pounds for making large batches.

This lets you create your own scents and colors (if you wish to add color powder), and though some of the work has been done for you, it's still much cheaper than purchasing a handmade bar of soap at the store or craft fair.

There are many options for the melt-and-pour bases including goat's milk, shea butter, clear, glycerin, and cocoa butter. Make sure to check the ingredients list for soy or gluten. I prefer to use non-soy and GMO-free ingredients, even in our skin care. For the exact items I use, visit the Resource page at https://melissaknorris.com/books/hand-made/#bonus.

Your basic supplies for melt-and-pour soap are:

- melt-and-pour base
- a scale if you are using fragrance, essential oils, or colorant
- thermometer
- *Additive options:* essential oils (only use oils suitable for contact with the skin); dried herbs (finely chopped); oatmeal (finely chopped); honey

The following recipe shows how to make melt-and-pour soap. You can simply double this if you have a two-pound melt-and-pour base.

LEMON-LIME SOAP

- 1 lb. (16 oz.) melt-and-pour goat's milk soap base
- 4.5 grams lime essential oil
- 3.5 grams lemon essential oil
- ½ tsp. dried zest of lime and lemon

Prepare your mold. You can purchase soap molds, line any suitably sized container with freezer paper, use silicone muffin cups, or line a bread pan with freezer paper. For a one-pound batch I use my 7 × 4 × 2-inch loaf pan.

Sprinkle the dried zest on the bottom of the prepared mold. Alternatively, you can mix the zest into the soap instead of just placing it in the mold.

Place two inches of water in the bottom of a saucepan with a canning band in the center and bring to a boil. Chop up the melt-and-pour base into even pieces and put in a melting container. A Pyrex measuring bowl or quart-size Mason jar work well.

Turn the water down to a simmer and place your melting container filled with the chopped melt-and-pour base on top of the canning band, creating a shelf. Stir until the chunks of the melt-and-pour base are completely melted. Make sure mixture doesn't exceed 140° or it can burn. Remove from the heat and place on a hot pad.

Measure out your essential oils.

Let melt-and-pour base cool slightly before adding your scents—about 120° is preferred. As it cools, the top may form a film—just stir every 3 to 4 minutes to stir in the film. When the melted base has cooled to about 120°, add the essential oil.

Stir in desired scents and additives, mixing well. Pour into prepared molds and allow to set and cool for 24 hours. Remove from molds and cut into bars if needed.

To cut bars, use a ruler and mark every 1 or 2 inches by making a score mark with a knife. I prefer a 1-inch bar of soap. Then use a sharp knife and slice at your measurements.

I don't have decades of soapmaking experience under my belt, but I have the next best thing. My mother makes her own soap, and one of my good friends, Julie, and her friend Karen have been making their own soap together for more than sixteen years. There is something to be said for years of experience, and I was super excited when Julie and Karen offered to give me some hands-on lessons and share their knowledge and expertise with you in this book.

The beauty of homemade soap is being able to control the ingredients and scents that go into it. And let's be honest, being able to say you make your own soap is pretty awesome.

Melt-and-pour methods have already done the work with lye for you, and cold and hot process methods are when you mix the lye in yourself.

HANDMADE SOAP (COLD PROCESS METHOD)

The cold process requires curing time before being able to use the soap. We do use heat, but we don't "cook" the soap as long, and it does its curing during the cooling process, hence the cold method name.

To start with, you're going to need some basic tools and ingredients:

Large pot	Lye	Large spoon
Food scale	Oil/fat source	Safety goggles
Two Pyrex or heat-safe measuring bowls for making the lye water	Distilled water	Safety rubber gloves
One large heat-safe bowl to measure the oils and fat	Vinegar	Soap mold
Plastic or silicone spatula	Essential oils (optional for scent)	Freezer paper
Immersion blender	Coloring powder (optional for color)	

WHERE TO PURCHASE YOUR INGREDIENTS

You used to be able to purchase lye at the grocery store, but many stores no longer carry it, as it was used to make illegal substances and can be dangerous if not handled properly. You can order lye online at soapmaking websites such as Brambleberry.com or Amazon. The lye (sodium hydroxide) is the type used for making solid bars of soap.

The recipe I'm sharing with you from Julie and Karen uses olive oil, palm oil, and coconut oil. You can use other oils, such as lard, tallow, or cocoa butter, just to name a few. Always start with a recipe from a reliable source when first starting out. As you become more comfortable and experienced, you may create your own recipes with the oils and fats you have on hand. You can find a soap calculator through an online search.

You'll need a scale to measure out your ingredients. This recipe is done in grams and creates twenty one-inch-thick bars of soap for a mold that is 3 × 20 inches long and 3.5 inches deep, or approximately a six-pound batch.

Many soap makers prefer a wooden mold. Karen's father helped them make their molds, but you can also find wooden soap molds for sale online or in soap shops. My mother lines a shoe box with freezer paper or plastic wrap, and I've even used lined bread loaf pans. Get creative—as long as the container can be lined and will hold the full batch, use it!

COLD PROCESS OATMEAL HONEY SOAP

384 grams palm oil
439 grams coconut oil
576 grams olive oil
200 grams lye
462 grams distilled water
40 to 60 grams essential oil (optional)
½ tsp. colorant powder (optional)
½ cup finely ground oats (optional)
3 oz. warm honey (optional)

1. Put the containers of palm and coconut oil in a sink or dishwashing tub full of hot water to melt the oils to liquid state.
2. Line the soap mold with freezer paper or waxed paper. Leave the edges long so you can wrap it over and easily pull up when it's time to remove the soap.
3. Put on your safety glasses and gloves. Wear long sleeves and pants when working with lye and making soap.
4. Carefully measure the lye into one of the heat-safe bowls, preferably with a pour spout, and set aside. Measure the distilled water into a heat-safe bowl (when you add the lye it will get HOT). Put the measured distilled water on your stovetop *with the exhaust fan on.*
5. Slowly (do not dump it all in at once) *pour the lye* into the distilled water. *Never* pour the water into the lye; it can result in an eruption of lye and cause dangerous burns.
6. Stir the lye into the water and stay at arm's length—you don't want to inhale the fumes. You'll see the fumes as the lye is mixed in. Stir until the lye is dissolved into the water. Make sure this is done in a well-ventilated area, not a small room, and preferably under an exhaust fan. It's not advised to have pets or small children running around during this time. Once the lye is completely dissolved in the water, it will be 180°.
7. When the oils have started to melt enough to pour, turn on your scale and measure out your oils. Put a large pot on the stove over low heat and pour in the measured palm and coconut oil; continue stirring until the oils are fully melted, usually around 120° to 125°. Be sure the pot has been washed well, as any particles of food or other substances could contaminate your soap. Safety note: It's advised to have dedicated soapmaking tools and utensils to avoid cross-contamination with your food or accidental ingestion of the lye.
8. Keep an eye on the temperature of your oil and lye. They both need to cool down to 90° in order to mix the lye with the oils. Place the container with the lye mixture in the sink in a small amount of cold water.
9. It's much faster and easier to use an infrared (point and shoot) thermometer. If you're relying on a regular cooking or candy thermometer, you'll want to use two. Otherwise, when going back and forth between the oil and the lye, you'll have to thoroughly wash, rinse, and dry it every single time (see, just get the infrared).
10. Pour the olive oil into the other oils to help cool it down faster. Usually the addition of the olive oil will drop the temperature by approximately 20°. When both the lye and the oil are cooled to

90° (it's more important for the two of them to be the same temperature rather than exactly 90°), slowly pour the lye into the oils while constantly stirring the oils with the immersion blender, but do not turn on the blender yet; just use it as a spoon. Don't stir directly into the stream of the lye, but try to cover the entire pot.

11. Once all the lye is poured in, continue stirring with the immersion blender, only pulsing it with the blender every 30 seconds or so. If you use the blender continually, you'll reach the tracing point too soon and it will also introduce air pockets. Don't stop stirring, though, or your soap might not set.
12. The soap will begin to turn a creamy color and thicken up. Continue stirring and pulsing until it reaches the trace. The tracing point is when it becomes thick like pudding: lift your immersion blender slightly above the mixture so you can drizzle some of the liquid on top of the soap mixture. If it forms a line on top before dissolving back into the rest of the soap, then you've reached the tracing point. This generally takes about 5 minutes.
13. Once it's reached the trace, stir in any scents, colorants, or other items you're using in the soap. For honey oatmeal soap, pour in the oats and stir—you don't want any large clumps. Stir in honey and mix until combined well. The honey oatmeal soap makes a great exfoliator and doesn't require any added scents.
14. Pour into your prepared soap mold. Cover the top of the soap with the flap of waxed or freezer paper and put the lid on. Take a couple of thick towels or blankets and wrap the soap mold to keep the soap from cooling off too quickly during the next 24 hours. Try not to disturb it for the next 24 hours.
15. After a few days, the soap will be set enough to cut into bars. Cut the bars and spread them out on a surface to allow them to finish curing. The curing process will take a total of 4 to 6 weeks to finish the saponification. At the end of the curing process there won't be any active lye left.

Saponification is the process of the lye (an alkali ingredient) and fat or oil (your acidic ingredient) creating a chemical reaction that produces soap and glycerin. The wonderful thing about handmade soap is the glycerin isn't stripped out, leaving a softer soap that's more nourishing to the skin. This recipe is considered superfatted, which means there's enough fat in the recipe for extra fat to be present in the finished soap for more moisturizing.

Cleanup

Vinegar neutralizes the lye. Pour vinegar over the spoons, spatulas, and the immersion blender (after it's been unplugged, of course), and then wash with hot, soapy water, rinse, and let dry. Pour vinegar into the bowls and pots, swish it up all the sides, and then wash, rinse, and dry. You may wish to still wear gloves when washing out your utensils and pots.

FIVE OLD-TIME REMEDIES THAT WORK

I bet when you came down with the sniffles or common ailments as a child, your mother or grandmother had a bunch of different remedies she'd recommend. Some of them are plain odd and really have no place except for the fondness of telling the tale. But the following old-time remedies do have a place in our home.

1. *Chicken soup is good for a cold.* Grandma knew her stuff on this one. Chicken soup is good for a cold, and there's science to prove it, even though we homesteaders knew it before they did. *The New York Times* reports that chicken soup can help reduce upper respiratory symptoms.[20] Homemade chicken soup made with traditional bone broth and lots of vegetables is going to be even more beneficial. Whenever fall rolls around and we move into cold and flu season, I recommend stocking up on your stock. The addition of herbs like oregano, rosemary, and thyme will impart additional medicinal benefits.
2. *Baking soda for a bee sting.* My daughter was stung by a bee. The sting itself wasn't hurting (odd but very happy outcome); however, she was scratching it like crazy. I mixed up a paste of baking soda and water and applied it directly to the sting. It took away the itching and she was back to playing and running around in no time. *Note:* If you're allergic to bees or suspect an allergic reaction, get yourself to a doctor or emergency room immediately.
3. *Inhaling steam.* When your nose is congested and you feel like you can't breathe, take a hot shower or fill a sink or pot with hot water and make a tent. Take a towel and cover your head with it while leaning over the hot water, trapping the steam and allowing you to breathe it in for a few minutes. Make sure you use common sense and don't burn yourself. The steam will help loosen your congestion and allow you to cough up the ick easier. Many people like to add a few drops of peppermint or eucalyptus oil to the water, but even the hot water itself will help. You could also add crushed peppermint leaves to the water, making an herbal steam. Menthol (derived from the mint family) is often used in humidifiers and as aromatherapy, and you can try adding a vaporizer or diffusing the oil to help. However, some small children and others may have sensitivities to peppermint and especially eucalyptus, so it's not recommended to use this method with infants or small children. Watch for any signs of irritation when using this method of adding in the menthol family to your steam.
4. *Honey as a cough suppressant.* Who knew that sugar could be taken as medicine? But not just any old sugar. Only if you're using good raw honey can you call it medicine. A cup of warm honey tea with a bit of lemon doesn't only help warm you up, it actually relieves your cough. Honey is now being recommended as a cough suppressant in the medical community instead of over-the-counter products. (Again, we homesteaders were ahead of the curve on this one.) Is there anything cooler than being able to use your food storage as your medicine cabinet too? I prefer local raw honey for all the benefits it offers. If you can find a local beekeeper or local source, I'd go with that; otherwise, look for raw honey at your local co-op or grocery store. Many people like to infuse their

honey with herbs or spices for flavor and further medicinal properties. To retain all the benefits of honey, raw or unpasteurized honey is best. *Note:* Due to the risk of botulism, do not give honey to children who are less than one year old.

5. *Ginger for nausea and upset stomach.* If you had an upset stomach, there's a good chance your granny might have given you some ginger tea. For years people have used ginger to treat digestive and stomach ailments, and some studies have shown it to be beneficial while others aren't as conclusive. *Note:* Ginger may help soothe an upset stomach, but if you're on blood-thinning medications or have a blood clotting disorder, you should consult with a medical professional before using.

FIVE FORAGING RULES TO LIVE BY

1. *Only forage for food that you know for certain is safe.* Foraging is not the place to be a rebel or take risks. There are poisonous plants out there, and some have look-alikes. A field guide with photos is an excellent place to start, especially one that lists the poisonous look-alikes. Do not rely solely on a plant app for identification; they're not 100 percent correct.
2. *Only forage food in a safe area.* Not only do we need to know our food is safe, we need to know it's not been sprayed with chemicals or exposed to pollutants. Anything near a roadway is not a good candidate for foraging, nor are areas near crops unless you know the farmer or landowner hasn't or doesn't use spray.
3. *Be a good steward.* Don't forage on private property without asking for permission first. If you're granted permission, then make sure you leave the property as you found it. If gates are closed, leave them that way; if they're open, leave them that way.

   Also, know enough about the plant that you don't wipe it out. Now obviously, things like dandelions aren't going to be endangered from overforaging in a field or yard. But if you're picking morel mushrooms, you should know to always leave part of the stem in the ground to produce spores for next year's crop and to keep mushrooms in a breathable bag as you pick to leave spores behind and populate new areas.
4. *Properly prepare wild edibles.* You need to know the proper and safe way to prepare your foraged wild edible. For example, you should never eat wild mushrooms raw. You should always cook them thoroughly. For some plants, such as rhubarb, the fruit is safe to eat but not the leaves. Use a reliable source for cooking and eating instructions before consuming.
5. *Test a small amount first.* Don't eat a huge amount of a wild edible your first time out. Prepare a small amount and eat a few bites to see if you have a reaction. Even though it may be a perfectly safe wild edible, you could have an allergic reaction to it.

THREE PLANTS TO FORAGE

- **Dandelions** are one of spring's first gifts to the pollinators. The greens, flowers, and roots are all useful for various culinary and medicinal uses. The leaves and blossoms have antioxidant and anti-inflammatory properties, making them a great herb to infuse into oil for a topical salve.
- **Chickweed** is also great for both culinary and medicinal uses. All parts of the plant are edible.
- **Stinging Nettle:** This is one you'll want to learn how to identify to avoid those painful stings!

MEDICINAL BENEFITS OF DANDELION

One of my herbal mentors, Dr. Patrick Jones, put dandelions as one of his top wild herbs and each of the plant parts as listed below for their medicinal properties.

Dandelion greens: Dandelion greens are great for the kidneys. They make a good diuretic (increases urine output) alternative to over-the-counter remedies. The greens help with edema, bladder infections, and clearing out the system. They're packed with vitamins A and C, as well as potassium.

Dandelion roots: Dandelion roots are great for the liver. They're good for stimulating bile production and bile flow, improving digestion. They also soothe and protect the gut.

Dandelion flowers: The flowers are edible and have some great medicinal properties as well. They can be used to support lymphatic flow and for joint pain relief.

Ways to Use Dandelion

Dandelion greens can be consumed raw like you would use lettuce or spinach. Toss them into your smoothies or add them to soups.

Dandelion greens are best harvested when they're young and tender before the plant begins to flower (and especially before the flowers go to seed). Early spring is ideal.

Dandelion blossoms have a faint honey-like flavor. They can be added to many sweet dishes and teas.

Dandelion blossoms are best harvested just as they fully bloom (before they go to seed). You can also soak dandelion blossoms in olive oil (or any kind of oil) and rub the infusion onto arthritic joints for pain relief.

Dandelion roots make a great coffee alternative. The roots are helpful for flushing uric acid from the body. Those with gout may find dandelion helpful.

The roots of the plant are best harvested in the fall or early spring before the plant puts out new growth.

MEDICINAL BENEFITS OF CHICKWEED

All portions of the chickweed plant are edible. It is a diuretic, can be great when used externally for itchy skin, helps fight cellulite, and also has a cooling effect, which makes it great for hot summer days. It's also known for helping create movement in the lymphatic system.

Ways to Use Chickweed

Chickweed is pretty bland in flavor, but it can be added to a salad to give it some bulk (a great way to help stretch the grocery budget). You can add it to basil pesto, to smoothies, or even blended with water and used as the liquid to make egg noodles.

Chickweed is best harvested in spring through midsummer. If you wait too long into the summer, it might start to get a little bit bitter.

MEDICINAL BENEFITS OF STINGING NETTLE

Stinging nettles have many benefits:

- Helps alleviate seasonal allergies
- Helps alleviate joint pain and arthritis
- Aids the immune system
- Works as a kidney tonic
- Works as a diuretic
- Supports the urinary system

Ways to Use Stinging Nettle

One of my favorite ways to use fresh stinging nettles is to sauté them in a pan with some garlic and butter and then top the mixture with a fried egg.

Cooking nullifies their stinging ability, so stinging nettles can be used to replace any green in a cooked recipe. Try them in soups or stews, stir fries, or baked into a quiche or casserole.

Stinging nettles can also be made into a tea.

TRADITIONAL LIVING TIP

Take advantage of what nature has already provided. We now can order almost any herb or spice we wish with the internet and shipping, but before the advent of online shopping, cultures have used foraging for both food and medicine for centuries.

You can't get much more local and sustainable than foraging, though it is important to forage responsibly and not overforage an area, wiping out that plant, as we've seen happen with wild ginseng.

STINGING NETTLE TEA

Using Fresh or Freeze-Dried Nettle

2 tsp. dried stinging nettle leaves, or 2 T. fresh or freeze-dried

2 cups boiling water

Honey or other sweetener (optional)

Rinse a Mason jar in hot water to prep it for receiving boiling water. (This helps eliminate thermal shock and avoid the possibility of cracking your jar.)

Place stinging nettle leaves in the jar, then pour the boiling water over the leaves. Depending on your preference, you can add more water to make a weaker tea

Cover with a coffee filter or cheesecloth.

Once the tea has cooled slightly, you can add honey or another sweetener to taste, and stir to dissolve.

Let the leaves steep in the water for about 10 hours or overnight.

Strain and drink a cup at a time over the next two days. It's really good over ice!

Place a lid on the Mason jar and store your nettle tea in the fridge. Consume within three days for the most medicinal benefits.

Using Dried Nettles

Place the dried nettle leaves in a tea strainer and place the strainer in a mug.

Pour in boiling water, cover, and let it steep for 10 to 15 minutes.

Add honey or sweetener of choice; stir to dissolve.

Strain out and discard leaves.

Sip and enjoy!

HOMESPUN HOLIDAYS

One of my favorite things to do at Christmastime is to decorate. I love the colors swirling about and the memories attached to certain treasured ornaments or decorations. When I was a little girl, my mother had a Christmas music box shaped like the front of the house with a little blonde-haired girl in a red coat standing at the door with a small tree on the side that housed a tea light candle.

I pretended I was the little girl and adored winding up the music box (very carefully) to listen to it play. My mother gifted the music box to me when my daughter was small, and someday I'll pass it on to her.

Believe it or not, this homestead girl actually has a fake tree. We have a woodstove in our living room, and a live tree only lasts a few weeks before it becomes a fire hazard, no matter how much water we keep in it.

We wait until it gets dark and then we all go outside for the lighting.

We put our tree up two days after Thanksgiving, hence the need for a fake one. The kids and I spend the afternoon hanging up the ornaments and setting out our favorite decorations. Now that my son has graduated high school, I save his Mickey Mouse ornament from when he was a little boy for him to hang. They say it goes so fast, to enjoy the moments when they're little, but I believe it's one of those things you can't understand until you've gone through it.

Back to those lights. Why is it that when you put the lights away, every single strand works, but after you bring them all out, there's always that one that doesn't?

But the real finale is when we turn on the lights. My husband strings up the lights on the outside of the house, and we always position the Christmas tree in the front window so you can see the lights from it shining out as well. We wait until it gets dark and then we all go outside for the lighting. Thankfully, we've not had a Griswald moment, and we've never blinded our neighbors or had complete light failure.

One afternoon I glanced at our Christmas tree. The lights weren't on yet, as I tend not to plug them in until later in the day. All the ornaments were in place, the star crowning the top, and the red skirt draped around the bottom. It was pretty and all the components were there, but it didn't have the same impact.

Then I plugged in the lights. Ornaments gleamed, the icy snowflakes glittered, and the lights twinkled. It was as if the Christmas spirit itself had entered the room.

Then it hit me. That is our life and world without Jesus.

We can have all the right things in place. We can look the part, go to church, quote the Bible, say the things society says are good and right, but without the true light of Jesus, we're just a dull imitation.

Or on the flip side, we can be a complete mess, with our latest mistake sitting front and center on our chest like a scarlet letter. Like a Christmas tree with gaping holes, chipped ornaments, and an angel with a broken wing. But when those lights come on, we no longer see all of that.

Instead, the light of Jesus is multiplied in the ornaments, and despite the chips, we no longer see the bare spots. The glow of His love not only covers up our sins, it washes them away, and He takes those broken spots and makes them into one big, beautiful light that reaches out to light the lives of others.

It's when Jesus comes into our midst, makes a home in our hearts, and lights us from within that we see the true splendor we were meant to be. Have you ever noticed that those who really love God just seem to have this inner glow, no matter what their age or circumstances?

When Jesus spoke again to the people, He said, "I am the light of the world. Whoever follows me will never walk in darkness, but will have the light of life" (John 8:12).

How many of us have been like that unlit tree? God has already carefully chosen each decoration and facet about us. He's lovingly placed them just so in our lives, and He's waiting for us to turn on the light so we can see how beautiful we are and all the gifts He's given us.

I don't know about you, but sometimes I have a hard time seeing all the beauty He sees in me. I tend to focus on all the things I haven't gotten right, the times I've messed up, the shame of past sins instead of the grace and mercy of today.

Have you ever noticed that when one strand of lights on your tree burns out, it's all you can see?

Have you ever noticed that when one strand of lights on your tree burns out, it's all you can see? It doesn't matter that the rest of the strands are twinkling; your eye can't help but notice that one broken strand. Immediately you go to work trying to find the burned-out bulb to fix it. Or perhaps you're not a wasting-any-time type of girl and pull out a brand-new strand—no judgment here.

When we don't accept God's grace and mercy, we're walking around with burned-out lights on our tree.

God is longing to fix the strand. Immediately, He sees when one of His children is hurting or living in the shame of the past, but we have to trust Him enough to truly turn the light back on.

You are beautiful. Your past, your mistakes, your sins—all are washed white as snow once you accept Jesus as your Savior. He called you, knowing full well all the things you've done and all the things you will do, the good and the bad.

> *He chose us in him before the creation of the world to be holy and blameless in his sight (Ephesians 1:4).*

You are forgiven. You are called. You are His own and beloved. Turn the light on, my dear friend. Turn the light on.

BIRTHDAYS

It's funny how we view birthdays depending on our age. When we're little, we can't wait for our birthday and often proudly insert the half. I think my kids say they're "and a half" the day after their birthday.

Once we hit those middle years, sometimes we'd rather forget we've reached that milestone yet again.

Then as we gain some more wisdom with the years, we hopefully start to see that each birthday is a gift. God has given us another year to live out His plan for us. While it might not come in a box, wrapped in paper and tied with a bow, it is a gift, nonetheless. We get to decide what we'll do with said gift during the next 365 days—to let it sit on a shelf until the next year rolls around or make sure we get full life out of it.

When I was little, my birthday meant I got to pick what was for dinner. Choosing a favorite restaurant wasn't an option. This was our favorite homemade meal and dessert. We've carried the tradition on with our children, and it's fun to see which foods get swapped out as they grow older and which ones stay.

Another tradition surrounding birthdays since the day my kids were born is a homemade birthday cake. Some years they've tested Mom's decorating skills from a John Deere tractor cake to Mickey (and then Minnie) Mouse and even a Darth Vader cake.

We never purchase boxed cake mixes—but if you've made it this far in the book, I have a feeling you knew that was coming. Truthfully, you can make an awesome cake at home without worrying if you've got a mix in the cupboard or needing to run to the store.

CAKE MAKING TIPS:

1. Room temperature butter, eggs, and milk will give you a lighter-textured cake.
2. Sift the flour. Seriously, I know this seems so old school and who has time for it, but it really only takes a few minutes and the difference is notable.
3. Try using cake flour—but there's no need to buy it. Instead, for every cup of flour, place 2 tablespoons of cornstarch (I use only organic corn products) in the bottom of your measuring cup and then fill normally with all-purpose flour.
4. Grease and flour your pans beforehand.
5. Preheat your oven and make sure the rack is smack dab in the middle.

BIRTHDAY CAKE

This recipe is adapted from *Betty Crocker's Picture Cook Book.*

- ⅔ cup soft/room temperature butter
- 1¾ cups sugar
- 3 eggs
- 2 tsp. vanilla
- 2¾ cups flour
- 3 tsp. baking powder
- 1 tsp. salt
- 1¼ cups milk

Preheat oven to 350°. (If baking cupcakes, preheat oven to 400° and prepare cupcake pans for 2 dozen.) Grease and lightly flour two 9-inch cake pans or one 9 × 13-inch cake pan.

In a large mixing bowl (use either a stand mixer or hand mixer) mix the butter, sugar, eggs, and vanilla. Beat this until super fluffy, at least 5 minutes on high speed. Trust me on this part—it makes all the difference in the texture.

While the mixer is doing its thing, sift your flour. In another medium size bowl, stir together the sifted flour, baking powder, and salt.

Turn your mixer to low and alternate adding in small amounts of the milk and dry ingredients, adding about a third of each at a time. Continue mixing until fully combined and then pour batter into prepared pans.

- Bake 9-inch cakes for 35 to 40 minutes.
- Bake oblong cake for 45 to 50 minutes.
- Bake cupcakes for 18 to 20 minutes.

To check if cake is done, insert a toothpick in the center. If it comes out clean, take the cakes out of the oven. Let cool in pan for 10 minutes. After 10 minutes, run a knife between the edge of the pan and the cake, turn upside down onto wire racks, and allow to cool completely.

Frost when completely cooled.

BUTTERCREAM FROSTING

- ½ cup softened butter
- 3 cups powdered sugar
- Pinch of salt
- 1½ tsp. vanilla
- 2 to 3 T. cream

Using a stand mixer or hand electric mixer, beat butter until light and creamy. Add in powdered sugar, salt, and vanilla. Cream together on low until fully incorporated. Thin with cream, starting with 1 tablespoon at a time until it reaches desired consistency.

Variations:

- *Lemon frosting:* Omit vanilla and use lemon juice in place of the cream.
- *Chocolate frosting:* Use 2½ cups powdered sugar and ½ cup cocoa powder.

CHOCOLATE GRAVY

¼ cup melted butter
1 T. flour
½ cup sugar
¼ tsp. salt
½ cup cocoa powder
¾ cup boiling water
1 cup milk
½ tsp. vanilla

When you were growing up, did you have any favorite foods that weren't served very often? Whenever it showed up on the table, you knew it was something special.

My dad always talks about my grandmother serving biscuits with chocolate gravy on special days. His eyes light up at the memory. Unfortunately, I never got the recipe from my grandmother before she passed away, and I don't ever remember her serving it. My mom never made it either.

One year I was determined to surprise Dad with chocolate gravy for breakfast. Everyone should start their special day with a tasty surprise, right? I scoured my cookbooks and between a chocolate sauce recipe in my great-grandmother's *Watkins Cook Book* and a close friend, Sue Watts, who is an expert cook (everyone needs at least one or two friends in their life who are expert cooks), I tweaked the recipe a bit to make enough to smother biscuits.

I'm not sure who was more excited over the breakfast treat, Dad or me.

Blend the butter with the flour in a saucepan over medium heat. Add sugar, salt, and cocoa powder. Whisk in the boiling water and milk. Let the milk get hot and remove the pot from the stove. Stir in vanilla. If you let it boil, it may thicken up like pudding.

Serve warm over biscuits. If you have any left over, it makes a great chocolate sauce for homemade chocolate milk or to serve over ice cream. Store in a small Mason jar in the fridge.

CHOCOLATE DEPRESSION-ERA CRAZY CAKE

- 1½ cups flour
- 1 cup white sugar
- ¼ cup cocoa powder
- 1 tsp. baking soda
- ½ tsp. salt
- 1 tsp. vanilla extract
- 1 tsp. vinegar
- 6 T. oil (melted lard, coconut oil, or avocado oil would be my picks)
- ½ cup cold water
- ½ cup cold coffee

Need a chocolate cake? The answer is yes, one always needs a chocolate cake. This cake originated in the Great Depression, when eggs, butter, and dairy were scarce. It goes by a few names, including Wacky Cake or Crazy Cake.

In ode to my great-grandmother, I use some cold coffee, which is known to heighten the flavor of chocolate in baked goods. You can omit it if you like, but I never bake a chocolate cake without it.

You can double this recipe to make a layered cake or a 9 × 13-inch sheet cake.

Preheat oven to 350°. Mix dry ingredients in a mixing bowl until well combined.

Tradition has you make three wells (holes) in the dry ingredients. Pour the vanilla in one hole, vinegar in one hole, and oil in the third hole.

Now pour the cold water and brewed coffee over the entire thing and stir until just combined.

Pour into an ungreased 8 × 8-inch pan and bake for 30 to 40 minutes, or until a toothpick in the center comes out clean. When cool, spread with frosting of your choice!

After the candles are blown out, the last of the crumbs eaten, and the children are in bed, I have a special tradition that is as much for me as it is for them.

I pull out their baby books and remember back to the moment they entered the world—from the first sound of their cry to the way they took my breath away with a fierce love I'd never known before.

Every year I write them a letter. I share funny or cherished memories from the past 365 days, what they're learning, and what they mean to me. It's my place for me to tell them my hopes, prayers, and dreams for them for the coming year and the rest of their life. Then I tuck this letter into their baby book to give them someday when they're grown.

This can be done with grown children, small children, grandkids, or any special person in your life.

EASTER

Easter has always been one of my children's favorite holidays. Homemade rolls are always a highlight of any holiday. My husband's grandma was not only the family jam maker but a renowned baker, and she passed her dinner roll recipe to me.

One of my favorite roll recipes has always been crescent rolls because, let's face it, butter makes everything tastier. The recipe below is her original recipe for dinner rolls, but I also altered it just by the way you form and bake the rolls for a delicious homemade crescent roll recipe.

Either way you make it, this is sure to become a holiday must-have at your dinner table.

CRESCENT ROLLS

- ½ cup warm water (around 110°)
- 2¼ tsp. yeast
- ½ cup warm milk
- 1 egg
- ¼ cup butter, melted
- ¼ cup honey
- 3½ to 4 cups all-purpose or bread flour
- 1 tsp. salt
- 2 T. softened butter

Mix warm water and dry yeast in a bowl and stir to combine with a whisk. Set aside and allow the yeast to bloom (about 5 minutes; it will turn bubbly and foamy).

Add milk, egg, melted butter, and honey into the bowl and stir to combine.

Add flour and salt and mix by hand using a dough whisk until the dough pulls away from the sides of the bowl (can use a stand mixer for this step if desired).

Using the kneading attachment to your stand mixer (or kneading by hand on the countertop), knead dough on low for 7 to 8 minutes, then test the dough by doing the "windowpane" test. Take a golf ball–size piece of dough and, using pointer finger and thumb on each hand, slowly stretch dough. You should be able to stretch it thin enough before it breaks so that you can see light shining through the dough.

If the dough tears before you can get it thin enough to see light through it, let it rest for about four minutes, then knead it on low for another two minutes and do the windowpane test again.

Remove the dough from the bowl, add some oil to your bowl to keep the dough from sticking, then place the dough back into the bowl, giving it a quick turn so all sides are coated in oil.

Cover the bowl with a tea towel and place in a warm, draft-free area of your kitchen to rise for one hour (or until doubled in size).

Preheat oven to 400°.

Remove dough from the bowl and place on the countertop. If dough sticks to the counter, use a silicone baking mat to roll or sprinkle a small amount of flour on your surface.

Roll dough into a 12-inch circle, approximately ¼-inch thick. Spread softened butter over the surface, then cut into 16 pie-shaped (triangular) pieces. Beginning at the fat/circle end, roll up dough. Place on a rimmed baking sheet, point side underneath.

Bake for 12 to 15 minutes.

When golden on top, remove rolls from oven and, using a stick of butter, rub generously over the top of the rolls. Allow to cool until warm and enjoy!

TRADITIONAL DINNER ROLLS

This recipe uses the same dough as the crescent rolls. After the dough is formed but before the rise, follow these directions.

1 batch dough for Crescent Rolls

Divide the dough into 15 to 16 equal portions. You can get precise and weigh out your dough to ensure equally sized rolls, but I just eyeball it!

Take each section of dough and roll it into a ball. Pull each side of the dough down to create tension on the top surface. Place each ball of dough seam-side down into a greased pan (or well-seasoned cast-iron skillet), leaving adequate space between each roll to allow the rolls to double in size.

Cover rolls with a slightly damp tea towel and allow them to rise until double in size (about one hour).

Preheat oven to 400°. Bake rolls for 12 to 15 minutes.

Rolls should be just starting to turn golden brown on top when they're done.

When they're fresh out of the oven, take a stick of butter and rub it generously over the tops of the rolls.

If you can, it's best to let the rolls cool for 30 minutes before eating, otherwise the centers may turn a bit gummy!

TRADITIONAL LIVING TIP

Save your butter wrappers. They have enough butter left on them to grease a baking sheet or cake pan.

GREEN BEAN CASSEROLE

I know many people think of green bean casserole as a Thanksgiving dish, but we serve it at Easter and Christmas as well. However, using a condensed can of this and that never sat quite right with me, so I came up with this whole food version instead.

- 1¼ cups homemade cream of mushroom soup (see below)
- 4 cups green beans, canned, frozen and thawed and blanched, or fresh and blanched
- 3 to 6 slices bacon, cooked, cooled, and crumbled
- 1 T. Parmesan (optional)

Preheat the oven to 350°.

Grab a large cast-iron skillet and heat up your homemade cream of mushroom soup (see the following recipe).

Add green beans and stir gently until all beans are coated in the soup. Distribute them evenly in the pan.

Crumble bacon pieces all over the top of your casserole.

Bake until casserole is heated through and bubbly, about 20 to 25 minutes.

Add freshly grated Parmesan cheese over the top, if desired.

HOMEMADE "CREAM OF" SOUP

I've not bought a can of condensed anything soup in over sixteen years. There's no need when you can make a nourishing and delicious homemade version in minutes with pantry staples. You can adapt this for a mushroom or celery version; see variations listed below.

- 3 T. butter; for dairy-free, use lard or coconut oil
- 3 to 4 T. flour*
- ½ cup milk or cream
- ½ cup chicken broth
- ¼ tsp. salt
- Dash of pepper

In a saucepan over medium-low heat, melt butter (or fat of choice).

Whisk in flour. It will make a thick paste; continue whisking for about a minute to cook out the raw flour taste.

Slowly whisk in liquids. Bring to a simmer (barely a boil), adding more liquid if soup becomes too thick. It will thicken up more as it cools.

Remove from heat and stir in salt and pepper.

Variations:

- *Cream of celery substitute:* sauté ¼ cup of finely diced celery in butter before adding flour and other ingredients.
- *Cream of mushroom substitute:* sauté ¼ cup of finely chopped mushrooms in butter (or fat source) before adding flour and other ingredients.

Note: Organic cornstarch or xanthan gum work as gluten-free thickeners. Mix the cornstarch or xanthan gum into the cold broth until it is dissolved; do not add it to the melted fat or it will be clumpy.

THANKSGIVING

Thanksgiving is one of my favorite holidays. I love the focus of gratitude, family, and, let's be honest, the good eats.

A part of me really adores cooking a huge meal and having leftovers for days. Say I'm not the only one?

I've learned to bake my pies the day before, if possible, to have plenty of oven space for the bird. I usually make my pie crusts a few weeks ahead of time and freeze them. Like many of you, I work the day before Thanksgiving at my day job, so having the pie crusts and pies done ahead of time helps to lighten the load. After all, the whole point of Thanksgiving is to be thankful—not stressed out and overwhelmed.

We also have a potluck strategy in our family. Everyone brings at least one or two dishes to help out the host. Everyone in our family welcomes this policy, especially because we rotate who is the host every year.

If we're hosting, of course we roast a big old turkey, but even if we have the meal elsewhere, I still roast a turkey for us.

ROASTED TURKEY

1 whole turkey
1 to 2 onions
4 cloves garlic
Sea salt
3 sprigs fresh rosemary
4 to 5 leaves fresh sage
¼ cup butter
Pepper

To prepare the bird, thaw it in the fridge at least 2 days ahead of time if frozen (3 if it's a large bird).

Preheat oven to 325° and get out your roasting pan and rack.

Remove the giblets, neck, and gravy packet (because we're going to make real gravy). Rinse the inside and out of the birdie; dry well.

Peel the onions and cut into thick wedges. Peel and crush cloves of garlic to release the oils. Sprinkle the inside of the bird with sea salt. Stuff the cavity with onion, garlic, and fresh rosemary and sage.

Using kitchen twine, truss your turkey by tying the legs closed and wrapping around the tail.

Rub the butter all over the outside of the turkey. Sprinkle with more sea salt and the pepper. Place the bird *breast-side down* in the rack and roasting pan. Turn breast-side up the last quarter of the cooking time. A pair of cooking tongs is helpful with the turning, and an extra pair of hands to hold the pan in place, with oven mitts, of course. This keeps the breast from drying out and eliminates the need for aluminum foil.

Cook in preheated oven according to weight and time

Turkey is done when the internal temperature is 180° in the thigh and 165° in the breast. Make sure the thermometer is not touching the bone.

Place the turkey onto a platter and let it rest for 15 minutes before carving to retain the juices.

WEIGHT	COOK TIME (UNSTUFFED)
5–7 lbs.	2–2½ hrs.
7–9 lbs.	2½–3 hrs.
9–18 lbs.	3–3½ hrs.
18–22 lbs.	3½–4 hrs.
22–24 lbs.	4–4½ hrs.

TURKEY GRAVY

Drippings from turkey roasting pan
¼ cup flour
1 to 2 cups broth
Salt and pepper to taste

After you've put the turkey to rest on the platter, strain out the liquid from the bottom of the pan, and place your roasting pan over two burners on the stove on medium-high heat.

Add the flour to the drippings and stir to create a thin paste. When this begins to bubble, whisk while pouring in 1 cup strained broth (you can also use water or milk). Whisk the whole time. If it's too thick, add an additional cup. Allow it to cook for a couple of minutes to thicken up, if needed. Season with salt and pepper to taste.

ROASTED CARROTS

½ lb. carrots, rinsed, peeled, and chopped
2 T. coconut oil or butter
Sea salt to taste
2 T. brown sugar (optional)
Cinnamon to taste (optional)

I think carrots are an underappreciated vegetable. They're so versatile, but they rarely get to shine in cookbooks or at the table. They add gorgeous color when grated finely on top of a salad or added to soup. I have two picky eaters in my home who think they don't like carrots, but they never notice when I grate them into sauces or soups.

One of my favorite treats is roasted carrots. I've been known to eat an entire pan by myself. I'm a bit of a purist with my roasted carrots, whereas my mother prefers hers candied, with butter and brown sugar. Either way, they're a frugal addition to the kitchen, from a side dish to stretching out the soup and sauces . . . and feeding unexpected guests.

Preheat oven to 375°. Place carrots in a covered baking dish, dot the tops with coconut oil or butter, and sprinkle with salt (for candied option, add sugar and cinnamon). Bake for 20 minutes or until carrots are tender.

PUMPKIN PUREE

One of my favorite things about autumn is the pumpkins. Oftentimes, the sugar pie pumpkins will hide under the leaves of the vine, and it's not until they ripen that I'll see a bit of orange peeking out at me. They decorate the garden before they come inside to decorate the house.

When you harvest pumpkins, wipe down the outside with a vinegar-moistened towel. This will help remove any bacteria on the outside that would break it down faster. Our pumpkins will last for a couple months on open shelving or front and center on the kitchen table as a centerpiece.

Not only do they make fabulous decorations, but they provide a special treat when they give up their seeds. For baking purposes, a sugar pie pumpkin has the best flavor and is naturally sweeter. These are the smaller pumpkins, not the large ones for carving.

We never buy pumpkin pie filling or pureed pumpkin. It's very simple to do at home and much cheaper. Take your pumpkin and a sharp knife. Pop off the stem (or cut if it's still a bit green) and chop the pumpkin in half. Careful—they tend to roll a bit.

Preheat oven to 375 °. Scoop out the seeds and the stringy flesh parts clinging to the seeds (save the seeds to roast and snack on later), and place each half of the pumpkin cut-side down in a 9 × 13-inch baking pan with an inch of water. Bake for about 30 to 40 minutes (depending upon the size of your pumpkin), or until pumpkin is soft and fully cooked.

Remove pan from oven and allow to cool. Scoop out the soft pumpkin flesh. I use the edge of a large spoon and scrape it off the skin. Place cooked pumpkin into a blender or food processor (you can go old school and use a potato masher too) and puree that baby up. Usually the sugar pie pumpkins have drier flesh, which means more flavor, so you don't need to strain it. You may need to add a teensy bit of water if it's too dry, but just a tablespoon or so.

Look at you—you just made pumpkin puree and it tastes so much better than the tin can stuff at the store. You can use it to bake with immediately, store it in the fridge for up to 5 to 7 days, or pop it in the freezer for later.

Pumpkin puree or pie filling is *not* a candidate for home canning, as it's too thick, even in a pressure canner, for the heat to penetrate through and kill all the botulism spores. Commercial pressure canners can reach higher temperatures than home ones.

When freezing, I like to freeze mine in either 1- or 2-cup portions for ease when baking. You can freeze it in a plastic freezer bag or my favorite, a pint-size Mason jar.

Now let's get our cookie making on!

GRANDMA'S PUMPKIN ROLL

This next dish is one of our favorite ways to serve pumpkin. It comes from my husband's grandmother's kitchen. Grandma gave me a lesson on how to make it, because I don't know about your house, but it seems no matter what, no one makes it as good as Grandma (even if I have her recipe), so I wanted to take notes and have a hands-on lesson.

One of the beautiful things about this recipe is you can bake it ahead of time and freeze it. Then in the mad dash of the holiday, you don't have to worry about preparing dessert. My husband's grandmother is quite renowned for her pumpkin rolls—in fact, I have a hunch she could make these year-round and have a bona fide home business. But lucky for you and me, she shared her recipe.

Cake Mixture:

¾ cup flour
1 tsp. baking powder
½ tsp. salt
½ tsp. ground nutmeg
1½ tsp. ground cinnamon
½ tsp. ground ginger
3 eggs
1 cup sugar
⅔ cup cooked pumpkin

Filling:

1 cup powdered sugar (plus more for sprinkling)
8 oz. cream cheese
½ cup butter, softened
1 tsp. vanilla extract
2 tsp. maple syrup (optional)

Preheat oven to 375°. Grease and flour a 15 × 10-inch jelly roll pan with coconut oil—be generous with your grease.

Mix together flour, baking powder, salt, and spices. In a large mixing bowl, beat eggs for 5 minutes (yes, the whole 5 minutes) until light and foamy; cream in sugar and pumpkin. Then stir in dry ingredients until combined.

Pour into prepared jelly roll pan and spread until even. Pick up and tap the bottom of the pan against the counter a few times; this makes the air bubbles rise up out of the batter. (I jumped when Grandma did this. It makes a bang.)

Bake for 13 to 15 minutes, until cake is done. Place a clean flour sack or tea towel on the counter and sprinkle with a bit of powdered sugar.

As soon as the cake comes out of the oven, run a butter knife around the outside edge of the cake to separate it from the pan. Immediately, using hot pads, turn the pan upside down over the prepared towel.

As soon as cake is out of the pan, place another clean flour sack towel on the short end of the cake and roll up like a sleeping bag. Cool on a wire rack for about 30 minutes.

Prepare your filling by creaming together all the filling ingredients. Unroll cooled cake and spread the filling evenly over the surface. Reroll the cake, cover, and allow to chill in fridge. Before serving, sprinkle with powdered sugar if desired.

PUMPKIN SUGAR COOKIES

It took me about three times to get this recipe just right, as I didn't want a pumpkin cookie that was really a muffin top in disguise. I wanted an honest-to-goodness cookie. Depending upon your palate, you can use either the smaller or larger amounts of spices indicated. Go ahead, make it your own.

- ½ cup melted butter
- ¼ cup coconut oil
- ½ cup brown sugar
- ½ cup white sugar
- 1 T. molasses
- 1 cup cooked pumpkin
- 2 cups all-purpose flour
- 1 tsp. baking powder
- ½ tsp. salt
- 2 tsp. ground cinnamon
- ½ to 1 tsp. ground nutmeg
- ½ to 1 tsp. ground ginger

Melt the butter and then add the coconut oil to the melted butter. The heat from the melted butter will soften up the coconut oil. In a large mixing bowl, cream together the melted butter, coconut oil, brown and white sugars, and molasses. Then add in and combine the pumpkin.

Dump in all your dry ingredients and mix until combined. Cover and allow dough to chill in the fridge for at least an hour or even overnight. Trust me on this part. Chilled dough makes better flavored and textured cookies. Something magical happens upon chilling and all the flavors mingle together.

Preheat oven to 375°.

You have two options after your dough has chilled:

Option 1

For a puffier pumpkin sugar cookie, place some sugar in a bowl and roll a good-size tablespoon of dough (use an ice cream scoop to easily create uniform cookies) into a ball and then roll it around in the sugar until it's fully coated. Place 2 inches apart on a cookie sheet and bake for 8 to 10 minutes, just until cookie has set. Allow cookies to cool for 5 minutes before removing from sheet.

Option 2

For a flatter but still perfectly soft pumpkin sugar cookie, take a heaping tablespoon of dough and plop it on your cookie sheet. With your fingers, flatten it out into the desired size of your cookie, about a quarter-inch thick. The cookies will only slightly spread out as they bake. Sprinkle a light dusting of sugar on top of each cookie. Bake for 8 to 10 minutes, just until the cookies have set. Allow cookies to cool for 5 minutes before removing from sheet.

LEFTOVERS

Is it just me, or do we all need a bit of inspiration for that leftover turkey after Thanksgiving? This past year the smallest turkey I could find (we aren't raising our own turkeys . . . yet) was a twenty-pound bird. We didn't host a big Thanksgiving party, so needless to say, I had mounds of leftover turkey. The dishes below were born of necessity—needing to whip something up for dinner and not wanting any of the leftovers to go to waste.

TURKEY SKILLET SUPPER

- 1 cup wild rice (quinoa would work too)
- 2 T. olive oil
- 1 clove garlic, minced
- 2 T. diced onion
- 1 cup frozen peas (or use canned, drained peas)
- 2 T. water
- Salt and pepper
- 2 cups cubed cooked turkey
- 2 cups brown gravy
- ½ cup milk

Cook the wild rice (or your favorite rice or substitute) according to package directions. Start this first so it will be finished when the rest of the dish is.

Place a large skillet on medium heat and add olive oil. When oil is warm, toss in the garlic and onion and sauté for a minute. Next, add the frozen peas and water. Cook until peas are hot, about 4 to 5 minutes. Season with a dash of salt and pepper.

Add in the turkey and gravy. Stir until gravy begins to melt and coat everything. Thin with the milk to create a sauce, stirring until the milk is incorporated with the gravy. Serve over cooked rice.

WHITE TURKEY CHILI

- 3 cups dried beans, prepared via cold or hot soak method
- 1 cup diced onion
- 8 cloves garlic, minced
- 1 jalapeño, seeded and minced
- 2 cups cooked turkey, diced
- 1 T. chili powder
- 2 tsp. ground cumin
- 2 tsp. sea salt
- 1 tsp. garlic powder
- 1 tsp. onion powder
- Fresh ground black pepper to taste

Now don't get me wrong, I love me some turkey and dumplings, but I needed something a tad bit different on the palate come the sixth night of turning turkey into our supper.

The dried and shelled beans from this year's garden were still sitting in the colander waiting to go in Mason jars for next year's planting and for eating through the winter. That's when my inspiration hit and I popped this chili together.

Normally, I do a cold soak on my dried beans, where I put them in cold water and let them soak for 18 to 24 hours. However, in the busyness of the week, I forgot to soak them the night before.

Thankfully, you can also do a hot soak method when you're running short on time. Put your beans in a large pot and completely cover with water by a couple of inches. Bring to a boil and let boil for 3 minutes. Put the lid on, turn off the heat, and let sit for 1 to 4 hours.

Drain the beans, rinsing thoroughly in cold water. Place them back in your pot, cover with water, and simmer for 1½ to 2 hours, or until tender. Don't add salt until the end, as salt can result in a tough bean.

After soaking your beans via either method, drain and then place them in a large soup pot. Cover with fresh cold water by 2 inches. Bring to a boil. Allow to simmer, stirring occasionally, for 1 hour.

Add the onion, garlic, and jalapeño. Let simmer for another half hour. Add water a half cup at a time if the soup becomes too thick.

When beans are tender and vegetables are cooked, stir in the turkey and seasonings. Continue to cook until turkey is heated, about 5 to 10 minutes, and serve.

This is excellent topped with a bit of grated cheese and a dollop of sour cream or yogurt.

CHRISTMAS

I love lanterns and oil lamps. I have an oil lamp sitting on the counter in our kitchen for both decorative purposes and so it's handy when the power goes out. One of the oldest and simplest light forms that is still in use in many homes today, regardless of electricity or not, is the humble candle.

It doesn't matter how dark a room is, the smallest flame from a candle will push back the night.

I keep a candle in just about every room of the house. When the power goes out, I know I've got a light source until I can get our larger oil lamp lit.

They're also a daily reminder of how the power of Jesus works. It doesn't matter how big and dark our sin is or how much of a mess we've made of our lives, once we allow the flame of His love and salvation to light our soul, it eliminates the dark.

The laws of nature follow the laws of the cross. You can have a candle lit in a sunny room, and as night falls, the shadows will begin to encroach, growing larger as the earth spins. But unless that candle burns out, even at the height of midnight, that darkness can never snuff out that flame. And if you give that candle more fuel, it will burn brighter and brighter, pushing back the dark.

That is the beauty of a life lived with Jesus in our heart and serving Him. As we grow in Him, our light burns brighter, chasing away the dark.

> *"Neither do people light a lamp and put it under a bowl. Instead they put it on its stand, and it gives light to everyone in the house" (Matthew 5:15).*

A pioneer Christmas was much more frugal than our modern ones but every bit as special. Isn't that the key to this old-fashioned life—finding out that spending less doesn't mean actually having less but really having more of what's important?

One of my favorite odes to the people of old is making homemade gifts. Sometimes I'll purchase something from the store to go with it, create a whole basket of homemade items, or even give just one homemade candle or jar of jam.

My kids will often help in the creation, and this is a great bonding time for us. Plus, it teaches them valuable skill sets, not only in the how-to but also in the heart, to create something with someone else in mind.

Below you'll find tutorials and instructions for crafting homemade gifts, but you'll also want to include some of the items from chapter 5. Here are some ideas to get you started:

- For the chef, baker, or foodie in your life, create a basket of all the homemade spice mixes.
- For a spa basket with natural goodness for soul and mind, fill with the Epsom bath salts, Peppermint Chocolate Body Lotion, a Beeswax Candle, and a bar of your homemade soap.
- For natural health–minded folks, how about a bottle of homemade tincture, herbal tea blend, and the Skin-Soothing Salve.

EASY FESTIVE HOLIDAY DECOR

One of my favorite easy ways to decorate is to use fresh cedar or pine boughs. If you have trees on your property, go ahead and snip a few. If not, check with fresh Christmas tree lots. Often they trim the trees to make them more appealing.

Fill a Mason jar or vase with the branches. You can hang small ornaments off them, a string of popcorn, or even a small strand of lights. Their scent fills the air and lends an easy festive feel to any corner of the house.

One of my favorite centerpieces is to take three Mason jars of varying sizes and display them with candles inside—small votives, tea lights, pillar candles, or your homemade beeswax candles. You can also fill one of these jars with small ornaments. I have vintage light blue ornaments that I like to mix with white and silver ornaments, especially with the older blue Mason jars. Scatter some of the ornaments around the base of the jars.

CINNAMON SALT DOUGH ORNAMENTS

Your homemade soaps and candles make great gifts. It's a wonderful thing to be able to give someone gifts made with your own two hands. There's something extra special about a homespun gift during the holiday season.

These ornaments make a lovely gift and a beautiful addition to your tree. Use the cheapest cinnamon you can find—these aren't for eating, just for color and scent.

1¼ cups flour
½ cup salt
¾ cup ground cinnamon
¾ cup warm water

Preheat oven to 275°. In a mixing bowl thoroughly combine flour, salt, and cinnamon. Slowly stir in the warm water until mixture sticks together. Using your hands, knead the dough until it's soft enough to roll out—this also helps the salt to be evenly distributed through the dough to avoid white pockets in the finished ornaments. You may add a bit more water if needed, but you don't want this to be a wet dough.

For easiest rolling, place the dough directly on your cookie sheet and roll out to ⅛-inch thick. If you go thicker, the cookies will puff up and tend to cook unevenly.

Use your favorite cookie cutters to cut out your desired shapes. It's easiest if you leave the cut cookies on the cookie sheet and remove the extra dough from around them—we don't want to smoosh or rip off an arm from our gingerbread man, right?

Remember to use a straw or other item to create a large hole in the top of the ornament for a string or ribbon to hang it by.

You can use whole spices to decorate your ornaments just like regular cookies—think whole cloves or even star anise. If you want to create a pattern in the dough, do so now with a fork, stylist tool, rough weave burlap, or whatever texture you think would look awesome. I use the tines of a fork diagonally across the toe and heel of stocking-shaped ornaments and along the cuff of mittens.

Bake for approximately 1 hour, until ornaments are hard. Your house will smell amazing.

Allow ornaments to cool. For a rustic look, use red, or red and white ribbon to hang on the tree.

Variations:

- If you don't want the cinnamon scent and the rustic brown color, omit the cinnamon and go with a full 2 cups of flour instead.
- Want to let your artistic side flow? Use acrylic paint to create a design and sprinkle the glitter on.
- To create a shiny ornament, paint with a spray-on varnish or clear coat.

Yield: approximately 2 dozen 2½-inch ornaments

CHRISTMAS POTPOURRI

One of the beautiful things about Christmas is the scents. The bright note of fresh-cut pine with the spices of cinnamon, and you can practically see gingerbread dancing in the air.

However, as you might have guessed, I'm not a fan of synthetic fragrances, and neither is your pocketbook or your body. Great news: here's a simple and easy way to have your home smelling like Christmas.

- 1 to 2 sprigs fresh-cut pine branches
- 2 to 4 cinnamon sticks
- Slices of orange
- 1 to 2 tsp. cloves

Place all ingredients in a small to medium saucepan and completely cover with water. Allow to simmer on low to scent your home, adding water as needed to keep it from going dry. This can be done on a woodstove or regular stove, as well as in your slow cooker.

OLD-FASHIONED CHRISTMAS FUDGE

Some foods just say Christmas. Homemade old-fashioned fudge is one of those. Chocolate fudge is a Christmas and New Year's tradition at our home. Let me clarify, the eating of it on those days is tradition. But to save time and stress around the holidays, which can run a tad high, I'm about to let you in on some secrets I've learned.

Many a confectioner has been plagued with grainy fudge. Fudge should be light and creamy, not resembling the texture of sand. When I first set about making cooked fudge, I wanted to find out why some fudge turns out perfect and other batches have the dreaded grainy factor. I should have known my older cookbooks would contain the knowledge.

If you can get your hand on cookbooks published in the 1940s or earlier, they carry a treasure trove of lost advice and tips that are lacking in many modern cookbooks (which is one of the things I hope this book helps remedy for you). Some of the tips below come from a 1944 copy of *The Good Housekeeping Cook Book.*

1. Make sure you're using a heavy-bottomed saucepan. This will help keep your fudge from burning.
2. Take a stick of cold butter and grease the inside of the saucepan, making sure to coat the bottom and up the sides of the pot. This will help keep the fudge from sticking to the pan as much.
3. Follow the instructions exactly to ensure a creamy end product; this isn't the place to "fudge" the directions.
4. Stir the mixture constantly when first heating the fudge (this helps the milk not curdle), but once it reaches a boil, do not stir it. I repeat, DO NOT stir your fudge once it boils, ever. Unless you like grainy, sand-textured fudge.
5. Always take a clean spoon (or rinse off and dry the same one) before allowing it to touch the fudge. Even a few grains of sugar on the spoon entered at the wrong time can cause a chain reaction and create the infamous grit factor to your fudge.
6. After taking the fudge off the heat, do not stir it until it has cooled down to 110°, or lukewarm to the touch. Once it's cooled, make sure you beat in the butter until it's no longer glossy before pouring into your prepared pan.
7. Don't scrape the side of the pan when beating or pouring out the fudge. I know, it will seem wrong to leave some of that delicious chocolate fudge clinging to the sides of the pot, but leave it, or you might cause that fudge to "sugar" and turn grainy.

OLD-FASHIONED CHRISTMAS FUDGE

Many fudge recipes call for the addition of corn syrup. It helps create a creamier texture, but with almost all the corn crops in the United States being genetically modified, I choose not to use it. You can search out an organic or certified GMO-free brand, but I haven't stocked it in our home for years. One less ingredient to purchase, the better in my opinion. I use honey instead.

You'll also find this fudge recipe calls for cocoa powder instead of unsweetened chocolate squares. I use cocoa powder in many different recipes and again, stocking one less ingredient helps keep my budget and supplies down.

- 1½ T. cold butter
- 2 cups sugar (evaporated cane juice works well)
- ⅓ cup cocoa powder
- ½ tsp. salt
- 1 cup milk (or water, though milk is standard)
- 2 T. honey
- 2 T. salted butter
- 1 tsp. vanilla extract

Butter your saucepan by smearing the cold butter all over the bottom and lower parts of the side. Pour in sugar, cocoa powder, and salt; whisk the dry ingredients until mixed. Turn the heat on to low, and add in the milk and honey. Stir until the sugar and cocoa are dissolved into the liquid. Occasionally scrape the bottom and the sides of the pan; once everything is incorporated, increase the heat a smidge, staying in the medium-low range, and stir constantly until the mixture reaches a boil.

As soon as it begins to boil, stop stirring. Allow it to boil gently until the fudge reaches 240° when measured with a candy thermometer, also known as soft-ball stage. (It takes 15 minutes on my stove once the mixture reaches a boil, but generally 12 to 15 minutes is suggested.)

It's normal for the fudge to foam up and climb up the sides of the pan as it boils. Resist the urge to stir it down. If you're close to foaming over, turn the heat down a little bit and don't stir. As it reaches closer to the soft-ball stage temperature, it will begin to recede back down the sides of the pot.

If you don't have a candy thermometer (or even if you do), use the old-fashioned candy-making soft-ball test (see page 211). Because candy thermometers can sometimes be off by a few degrees or more, I prefer to use the thermometer as a guideline to tell me when I'm close to reaching temperature, and then confirm it by the soft-ball stage test.

Once fudge reaches the soft-ball stage, immediately remove it from the heat, but do so gently; try not to knock the pan too much. Place the 2 tablespoons salted butter on the top of the hot fudge; resist the urge to stir. Let it cool about an hour until it reaches 110° or the fudge is lukewarm to the touch.

Once it's cooled, add 1 teaspoon vanilla extract and beat the butter and vanilla into the fudge until it loses its glossiness, for about 4 to 5 minutes.

Either grease or line your pan with parchment paper and pour fudge into it. This will make either an 8 × 8-inch square pan or a 9 × 5 × 3-inch loaf pan. Remember, don't scrape the sides of the pan clean, to avoid crystallizing the sugar in the fudge.

Let fudge cool fully and then cut it into squares. Store in an airtight container or wrap it tightly. It will keep for up to 10 days in the fridge . . . if it lasts that long, which isn't likely due to its fabulousness.

Fudge can be made weeks or even a few months ahead and frozen in the freezer. I learned this tip from a sweet lady in the town where I work. She brought me in a plate, and I thought it was fresh; it was only afterward she told me it had been frozen and thawed. It thaws out beautifully and you can have your candy making done early!

I happen to be a purist when it comes to my chocolate fudge—I don't want any nuts. But I realize not everyone has my finicky taste buds, so if you like nuts in your fudge, finely chop ½ cup of your favorite nuts and add them in with the vanilla.

How to Save Dry, Gritty Fudge

Even with following all the directions, something happened to your fudge. It's either powdery dry, or the dreaded "sand in the mouth" texture has developed. I can't stand the thought of throwing out all those ingredients.

You can salvage it by melting it back down and recooking it to the soft-ball stage. And you do this with a surprising ingredient: water.

It seems contrary, like the water would make the chocolate seize, and the first time I tried it I fully expected it to fail. But it works.

Place your fudge in a saucepan with 1¼ cups of water (for a regular batch of fudge that fills an 8 × 8-inch pan or 9 × 5 × 3-inch loaf pan). Over medium-low heat, stir and melt the fudge until it is dissolved fully into the water. Then gently increase the heat to bring it to a boil. Don't stir once it's reached a boil. Cook until it reaches 240°, or soft-ball candy stage via the cold water test.

Remove from heat, try not to shake or bump it, and let cool to 110° or lukewarm. As directed in the main recipe, beat or stir until no longer glossy (about 5 minutes) and pour into a greased or parchment paper–lined pan.

Enjoy that now-creamy fudge you just saved!

The Soft-Ball Test

Fill a small, shallow glass bowl with cold water. Take a tablespoon of the boiling fudge and drop it into the cold water. If the candy isn't near soft-ball stage, it will simply dissolve into the water.

If it doesn't immediately dissolve, let it sit for a few seconds. The candy will sink to the bottom of the water. Reach your fingers into the water and scoop out the fudge. You should be able to roll it into a ball between your fingers and have it hold its shape, but it should remain malleable and you can still squish it.

If the chocolate dissolves in the water or won't hold the ball shape, it needs to boil for a few more minutes. If you can't squish the ball, you've cooked it too long. It's better to test early rather than too late.

To retest, dump out the water and place clean cold water in the bowl. Make sure you wash your spoon and thoroughly dry it before putting it back into the boiling fudge to test each time.

SOFT MOLASSES SUGAR COOKIES

One of my best tips for Christmas baking, especially when it comes to pie crusts and cookie dough, is to make the dough up ahead of time. With hectic schedules and the busyness of the season, you may feel you can't find enough time to put in a full-on baking schedule. There's a reason those convenience tubes of dough in the store refrigerator and freezer sections sell. But you can make your own convenience for way less money and without the side addition of unsavory ingredients.

But the real reason, my friends, is chilled cookie dough does something magical to the flavors and texture of your cookies. A few hours is better than nothing, but if you can go a full 24 hours or even pop it in the freezer for a few weeks, oh my. The flavors have a chance to really get to know one another, especially in spiced cookies. The fat content, be it butter or coconut oil, becomes firmer (wish the cold did that to me), and the structure and texture of the cookie is always improved.

Usually I can't wait to bake some of the cookies, so I'll bake one pan right when I make the dough and then freeze the other half of the dough for later. The frozen dough always turns out a better cookie.

Along with a small plate of fudge, we like to give a plate of our favorite homemade cookies to neighbors and friends . . . and to keep a small assortment at home to indulge in.

Some of my favorite Christmas cookies involve molasses. If we look back to the farms and homesteads of old, we find many recipes included molasses. One of the reasons is regular white sugar was expensive and hard to come by. For all my Laura Ingalls Wilder fans, you'll remember Ma put out the small amount of white sugar they had only when guests came.

SOFT MOLASSES SUGAR COOKIES

This recipe first came to me via a customer at the pharmacy I worked in years ago. She brought us a plate of Christmas cookies, and the next time she came in I made sure to ask her for the recipe. They melt on your tongue, and you may hear the faint whisper of jingle bells while eating them. If I could make only one Christmas cookie a year, they'd be it. Thank goodness we're not limited to just one.

- ¾ cup softened butter
- ½ cup sugar (evaporated cane juice works fine)
- ½ cup brown sugar
- ¼ cup molasses (blackstrap is what we use)
- 1 egg
- 2 cups flour (all-purpose or a blend of whole wheat pastry and spelt work too)
- 2 tsp. baking soda
- ½ tsp. salt
- 1 tsp. cinnamon
- ½ tsp. ginger
- ½ tsp. nutmeg

In a large bowl, beat together the butter and sugars until creamy. Add molasses and egg, beating until well blended. In medium bowl, blend flour, soda, salt, cinnamon, ginger, and nutmeg; add to molasses mixture and mix well.

Cover and chill at least 20 minutes. Preheat oven to 375°.

Form dough into 1-inch balls. To make uniform balls that bake evenly, use an ice cream scoop. Roll each in sugar and place 2 inches apart on cookie sheet.

Bake 6 to 8 minutes. Let stand 1 minute before removing from pan.

ORANGE-GLAZED CRANBERRY CHRISTMAS COOKIES

This cookie comes from my aunt's kitchen and is one of my favorites. The dried bits of cranberry with the zip of orange make it practically sing on the taste buds.

Cookies:

- 1 cup softened butter
- ½ cup sugar
- 1 cup powdered sugar
- 1 egg
- 2 tsp. vanilla
- 2¼ cups flour
- ½ tsp. baking soda
- 1 cup dried cranberries
- ½ cup mini semisweet chocolate chips
- ½ tsp. zest of fresh orange peel

Glaze:

- 1 cup powdered sugar
- 1 T. melted butter
- 2 T. orange juice
- ¼ tsp. zest of fresh orange peel

In a large bowl, cream together butter, sugars, egg, and vanilla; beat until light and fluffy. Add in the flour and baking soda and stir until combined. Mix in cranberries, chocolate chips, and zest of orange peel. Shape cookie dough into a 12-inch log, cover, and place in refrigerator until firm, at least 2 hours, or up to a couple of days. You may also freeze this dough ahead of time.

When ready to bake, preheat oven to 350°. Using a sharp knife, slice cookies to approximately ⅓-inch thick. Place on an ungreased cookie sheet and bake for 10 to 12 minutes, until cookies are set but not turning brown.

For the glaze: In a medium bowl, mix powdered sugar, melted butter, orange juice, and the orange zest. Pour glaze over cookies and allow to cool.

Variations: You can also substitute currants or dried blueberries in place of the cranberries.

RAISIN COOKIES

This cookie was first introduced to my family by a neighbor. We'd never had anything like them, and they quickly became a favorite.

During the pioneer days, fruit was often dried, as it could be easily carried and did not require the cost of canning, refrigerating, or freezing. If possible, some would be saved especially for Christmas baking. With the raisins and the spices, these are a delicious cookie, served during the holidays and all year.

- 1 cup water
- 2 cups raisins
- 1 cup butter
- 2 eggs
- 1 tsp. vanilla
- 1¾ cups sugar
- 3½ cups flour
- 1 tsp. baking powder
- 1 tsp. baking soda
- 1 tsp. salt
- ½ tsp. cinnamon
- ¼ tsp. nutmeg
- 1 tsp. ground ginger
- ½ cup finely chopped pecans (we don't want large chunks)

Preheat oven to 350°. Combine water and raisins in a medium saucepan and bring to a boil. Simmer for 4 minutes and then let cool.

In a large mixing bowl, cream together the butter, eggs, and vanilla.

In a separate bowl, stir together the dry ingredients. Stir the dry ingredients into the large bowl with the creamed ingredients and blend well.

Add the raisins (do not drain) and the pecans to the cookie dough. Stir until combined.

Drop cookies by tablespoonful onto an ungreased cookie sheet about 2 inches apart. Bake for 12 to 15 minutes, until cookies are set in the middle.

Allow to cool and enjoy!

GREAT-GREAT-GRANDMA'S SUGAR COOKIES

- 3 cups sifted flour, divided
- 1 tsp. baking powder
- 1 cup butter
- 1 cup sugar
- ½ tsp. salt
- 1 egg, beaten
- 1 tsp. vanilla
- 2 T. cream

Mix 2½ cups flour and baking powder together. Cream the butter, add in sugar and salt, and then the egg, mixing until light and fluffy. (A stand mixer does this on high in a few minutes.) Mix in the vanilla and cream. Slowly add in the remaining ½ cup flour to make the dough stiff enough to roll out.

Cover dough and chill for 2 hours. This will keep for up to 3 days in the fridge, or you can pop it in the freezer for several weeks.

When ready to bake, preheat oven to 375°. On a lightly floured surface, roll the dough ⅛-inch thick. Cut into desired shapes with cookie cutters. Place onto a greased cookie sheet and bake for 12 minutes. Remove and allow to cool thoroughly.

HOT CIDER WITH MULLING SPICES

- ½ gallon organic apple juice
- 2 (4-inch) cinnamon sticks
- ½ tsp. whole cloves
- 1 tsp. ginger root, grated works well
- 1 tsp. dried orange peel/zest
- 1 tsp. dried lemon peel/zest

Is there anything better than hot apple cider when there's a chill in the air? I'm having a hard time coming up with anything either. Skip purchasing those bags or bottles in the store and make your own mulling spices.

If you have a large tea infusion ball, you can use that for the spices, minus the cinnamon sticks. Just put the cinnamon sticks whole in your pot.

If you don't have a large infusion ball, you can create a sachet with a piece of cheesecloth. Simply trim a piece large enough to hold the spices and tie it closed with some kitchen twine or thread.

Bring apple juice to a simmer over medium heat. Add mulling spices and allow to steep for up to 20 minutes. Remove spices and serve hot.

HOT COCOA

In a medium saucepan combine the cocoa powder, sugar, water, and salt over medium-low heat. Stir until smooth and then bring to a simmer. Add in the milk, cream, and vanilla and cook until hot but not boiling.

For a truly wonderful cup, use an immersion blender or hand beater and beat until frothy. Serve hot and enjoy.

Variations:

- You can use all milk or all cream, depending upon how decadent you feel for the day.
- Sprinkle with cinnamon for a little bit of spice.
- Use peppermint extract to taste.

⅓ cup cocoa powder
¼ cup sugar (more or less, to taste)
1½ cups water
Pinch of salt
3 cups milk
1 cup cream
½ tsp. vanilla extract

I hope your home and holidays will be filled with love, handmade items, and traditions that will be passed down for generations to come.

I'm honored to have shared this time with you and I hope it doesn't end just because we've reached the last pages of this book.

I'd love to invite you to video tutorials, more handmade goodness, and old-fashioned wisdom in the bonus sections at **https://melissaknorris.com/books/hand-made/**.

END NOTES

Chapter 3

1 Heather B. Patisaul and Wendy Jefferson, "The Pros and Cons of Phytoestrogens," *Frontiers in Neuroendocrinology* 31, no. 4 (October 2010): 400–419, doi: 10.1016/j.yfrne.2010.03.003.

Chapter 5

2 Janmejai K Srivastava, Eswar Shankar, and Sanjay Gupta, "Chamomile: A Herbal Medicine of the Past with Bright Future," *Molecular Medicine Reports* 3, no. 6 (November 1, 2010): 895–901, https://www.ncbi.nlm.nih.gov/pmc/articles/PMC2995283/.

3 "Coumarin," Wikipedia, accessed May 24, 2024, https://en.wikipedia.org/wiki/Coumarin.

4 "Comfrey: Uses, Side Effects, and More," WebMD, accessed May 24, 2024, http://www.webmd.com/vitamins-supplements /ingredientmono-295-comfrey.aspx?activeingredientid=295&activeingredientname=comfrey.

5 Samaneh Hosseinzadeh, Maryam Jamshidian Ghalesefidi, Mehdi Azami, Mohammad Ali Mohaghegh, Seyed Hossein Hejazi, and Mohsen Ghomashlooyan, "In Vitro and In Vivo Anthelmintic Activity of Seed Extract of *Coriandrum sativum* Compared to Niclosamid Against *Hymenolepis nana* Infection," *Journal of Parasitic Diseases* 40, no. 4 (December 2016): 1307–1310, https://www.ncbi .nlm.nih.gov/pubmed/27876936.

6 Prashant Singh Chauhan, Naresh Kumar Satti, Krishan Avtar Suri, Musarat Amina, and Sarang Bani, "Stimulatory Effects of Cuminum cyminum and Flavonoid Glycoside on Cyclosporine-A and Restraint Stress Induced Immune-Suppression in Swiss Albino Mice," *Chemico-Biological Interactions* 185, no. 1 (April 15, 2010): 66–72, https://www.ncbi.nlm.nih.gov/pubmed/20156427.

7 "Dandelion," Mount Sinai, accessed June 20, 2024, https://www.mountsinai.org/health-library/herb/dandelion.

8 "Garlic: Uses, Side Effects, and More," WebMD, accessed May 24, 2024, http://www.webmd.com/vitamins-supplements /ingredientmono-300-garlic.aspx?activeingredientid=300.

9 "Ginger: Uses, Side Effects, and More," WebMD, accessed May 24, 2024, http://www.webmd.com/vitamins-supplements /ingredientmono-961-ginger.aspx?activeingredientid=961.

10 "Marshmallow: Uses, Side Effects, and More," WebMD, accessed May 24, 2024, http://www.webmd.com/vitamins -supplements/ingredientmono-774-marshmallow.aspx?activeIngredientId=774&activeIngredientName=marshmallow.

11 Haifeng Yuan, Minggu Zhu, Wen Guo, Ling Jin, Weihong Chen, Ulf T Brunk, and Ming Zhao, "Mustard Seeds (Sinapis Alba Linn) Attenuate Azoxymethane-Induced Colon Carcinogenesis," *Redox Report* 16, no 1 (2011): 38–44, https://www.ncbi.nlm.nih.gov /pubmed/21605497.

12 "Nutmeg and Mace: Uses, Side Effects, and More," WebMD, accessed May 24, 2024, http://www.webmd.com/vitamins -supplements/ingredientmono-788-nutmeg%20and%20mace.aspx?activeingredientid=788&activeingredientname=nutmeg%20 and%20mace.

13 "Great Plantain: Uses, Side Effects, and More," WebMD, accessed May 24, 2024, http://www.webmd.com/vitamins -supplements/ingredientmono-677-great%20plantain.aspx?activeingredientid=677&activeingredientname=great%20plantain.

14 "Sage: Uses, Side Effects, and More," WebMD, accessed May 24, 2024, http://www.webmd.com/vitamins-supplements /ingredientmono-504-SAGE.aspx?activeIngredientId=504&activeIngredientName=SAGE&source=2.

15 "Stinging Nettle: Uses, Side Effects, and More," WebMD, accessed May 24, 2024, http://www.webmd.com/vitamins -supplements/ingredientmono-664-stinging%20nettle.aspx?activeingredientid=664.

16 Michael Greger, "Turmeric with Black Pepper: What It's Good for and How to Take It," Nutrition Facts, last updated January 23, 2024, http://nutritionfacts.org/2015/02/05/why-pepper-boosts-turmeric-blood-levels/.

17 Richard Nahas and Agneta Balla, "Complementary and Alternative Medicine for Prevention and Treatment of the Common Cold," *Canadian Family Physician* 57, no. 1 (January 2011): 31–36.

18 Behnood Abbasi, Masud Kimiagar, Khosro Sadeghniiat, Minoo M. Shirazi, Mehdi Hedayati, and Bahram Rashidkhan, "The Effect of Magnesium Supplementation on Primary Insomnia in Elderly: A Double-Blind Placebo-Controlled Clinical Trial," *Journal of Research in Medical Sciences* 17, no. 12 (December 2012): 1161–1169, https://www.ncbi.nlm.nih.gov/pmc/articles/PMC3703169/.

19 Anna Serefko, Aleksandra Szopa, and Ewa Poleszak, "Magnesium and Depression," *Magnesium Research* 29, no. 3 (March 1, 2016): 112–119, https://www.ncbi.nlm.nih.gov/pubmed/27910808.

20 Tara Parker-Pope, "The Science of Chicken Soup," Well Blog, *The New York Times*, October 12, 2007, https://well.blogs.nytimes .com/2007/10/12/the-science-of-chicken-soup/.

RECIPE INDEX

Barbecue Sauce 62
Bread
Cheese 37
Cinnamon Raisin 38
Cinnamon Rolls 40
Crescent Rolls 192
French 32
Long Fermented Sourdough Sandwich 95
Master Bread Dough 34
Pizza Dough 43
Pizza Dough, No-Rise 43
Pretzels, Soft 42
Rustic Round Loaf 37
Regular Bread Pan Loaf 38
Traditional Dinner Rolls 194
White, Old-Fashioned 33
White, Sourdough 92
Whole Wheat Sandwich, Sourdough 94
Breadcrumbs 61
Bread Pudding
Custard 27
Chocolate Custard 28
Pumpkin Custard 28
Buttermilk
Biscuits, Flaky 16
Buttermilk (how to make) 104
Pancakes, Overnight 105
Pie 20
Syrup 22
Cake
Birthday 189
Carrot with Buttermilk Syrup 22
Chocolate Depression-Era Crazy 191
Grandma's Pumpkin Roll 199
Peach Pudding 25
Pumpkin Applesauce 23
Carrots
Carrot Cake with Buttermilk Syrup 22
Roasted 197
Chicken
30-Minute Chicken and Dumplings 71
Chicken and Biscuit Bake 71
Dumplings 70
Chili
Chili 53
White Turkey 203
Cider, Hot with Mulling Spices 216
Cocoa, Hot 217
Cookies
Chocolate Chip 17
Great-Great-Grandma's Sugar 216
Orange-Glazed Cranberry Christmas 214
Pumpkin Sugar 200
Raisin 215
Soft Molasses Sugar 213
Crackers 17
Doughnut Holes, Cinnamon Sugar 31
Doughnuts 29
Dumplings
Berry 72
Chicken 70
30-Minute Chicken and 71
Frosting, Buttercream 189
Fry Bread 54
Cornmeal 55
Dessert 55
Fudge, Old-Fashioned Christmas 210
Granola 103
Gravy
Chocolate 190
Turkey 197
Green Beans
Casserole 195
Leather Britches 130
Pressure-Canned
(Raw Pack Method) 123
Jam
Cherry without Pectin (Low-Sugar) 119
No-Sugar Strawberry 117
Kefir, Milk 106
Mayonnaise, Homemade 109
Meatballs 60
Meringue 21
Noodles, Homemade Egg 68
Oatmeal
Pancakes 105
Yogurt Bowl 103
Old-Fashioned 73

Pancakes
Buttermilk, Overnight 105
Oatmeal 105
Sourdough 86
Pesto, Basil 151
Pickles, Fermented 97
Pie Crust
Flaky 18
Sourdough 89
Pie, Chocolate Meringue 21
Pizza
Dutch Oven 76
Fake-It Sausage 45
Tomato Basil Chicken 44
White Sauce Chicken 45
Pizza Dough 43
Pizza Dough, No-Rise 43
Pizza Sauce, Easy 44
Pumpkin
Grandma's Pumpkin Roll 199
Puree 198
Sugar Cookies 200
Pudding, Custard Rice 26
Relish, Mustard Pickle 114
Rolls (see Bread)
Sauerkraut 99
Seasoning Mixes
Chili 150
Italian 150
Popcorn 151
Ranch Dressing 151
Taco 150
Shepherd's Pie 71
Smoothie, Master Recipe 101
Soups and Stews
Bone Broth 52
Black Bean 65
Broth (How to, Canning) 120
Chicken Noodle 67
Crab Bisque 59
Cream of Asparagus 66
Ham and Broccoli Chowder 56
Homemade "Cream of" 195
Meatball Minestrone 63
Son of a Gun Stew 58
Sour Cream 108
Sourdough
Pancakes 86
Pie Crust 89
Long Fermented Sandwich Bread 95
Starter 84
Tortillas 89
Waffles 86
White Bread 92
Whole Wheat Sandwich Bread 94
Spaghetti and Meatballs 60
Sugar, Powdered (how to make) 21
Tomatoes
Canned Tomato Sauce 126
Raw-Packed without Liquid 128
Spaghetti Sauce 60
Turkey
Roasted 196
Skillet Supper 202
Yogurt 100

REMEDIES

Bath Salts 169
Decoctions 154
Elderflower Tea 163
Elderberry Syrup 163
Fire Cider Master Recipe 159
Herbal Tea Infusions 154
Herb-Infused Oil 159
Herb-Infused Oil, Fast 160
Lip Balm 165
Skin-Soothing Salve 166
Stinging Nettle Tea 183
Tinctures 156

HOMESPUN CRAFTS, GIFTS, DECOR

Christmas Potpourri 207
Cold Process Oatmeal Honey Soap 177
Homemade Jar Candle 173
Lemon-Lime Soap 175
Cinnamon Salt Dough Ornaments 206
Peppermint Chocolate Body Lotion 166

MEET MELISSA

Melissa K. Norris inspires people's faith and pioneer roots with her books, podcast, and blog. Melissa lives with her husband and two children in their own little house in the big woods in the foothills of the North Cascade Mountains. When she's not wrangling chickens and cattle, you can find her stuffing Mason jars with homegrown food and playing with flour and sugar in the kitchen.

MORE HOMESTEADING RESOURCES FROM MELISSA

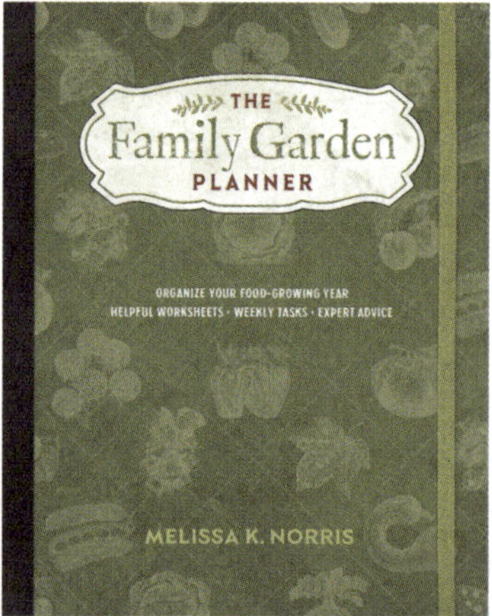